FIRE IN FORESTRY

Volume II

Photo by Bluford Muir

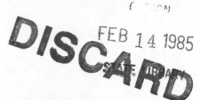
FIRE IN FORESTRY

Volume II
Forest Fire Management and Organization

CRAIG CHANDLER   *Director, Forest Fire and Atmospheric Sciences Research, U.S. Forest Service, Washington, D.C.*

PHILLIP CHENEY   *Chief Fire Scientist, Commonwealth Scientific and Industrial Research Organization, Canberra, Australia*

PHILIP THOMAS   *Head of Special Projects, Fire Research Station, Borehamwood, Herts., England*

LOUIS TRABAUD   *Principal Ecologist, Centre National de la Recherche Scientifique, Montpellier, France*

DAVE WILLIAMS   *Program Manager, Fire and Remote Sensing, Petawawa National Forestry Institute, Chalk River, Ontario, Canada*

A Wiley-Interscience Publication

JOHN WILEY & SONS

New York   Chichester   Brisbane   Toronto   Singapore

Copyright © 1983 by John Wiley & Sons, Inc.

All rights reserved. Published simultaneously in Canada.

Reproduction or translation of any part of this work
beyond that permitted by Section 107 or 108 of the
1976 United States Copyright Act without the permission
of the copyright owner is unlawful. Requests for
permission or further information should be addressed to
the Permissions Department, John Wiley & Sons, Inc.

Library of Congress Cataloging in Publication Data:
Main entry under title:

Fire in forestry.

   "A Wiley-Interscience publication."
   Includes indexes.
   Contents: v. 1. Forest fire behavior and effects—
v. 2. Forest fire management and organization.
   1. Forest fires—Collected works. I. Chandler,
Craig C.
SD420.55.F57 1983   634.9′618   83-5088
ISBN 0-471-87447-7 (v.2)

Printed in the United States of America

10 9 8 7 6 5 4 3 2 1

To Charlie Buck, Alan McArthur and Jim Wright
for reasons that
only they would appreciate

PREFACE

Before the industrial revolution almost 50 percent of the world's land surface was covered with forest. By 1955 this area had been cut in half. In 1980 the forest area of the world was estimated at 2.5 billion hectares, or one-fifth of the land surface. By the year 2000 it is expected to shrink by another half-billion hectares. To supply an expanding world population with adequate fiber, forage, fuel, and oxygen from a steadily shrinking land base will require the utmost of the forester's skill.

Fire has been the primary agent of deforestation. Paradoxically, fire, when properly used, can be a most effective and least expensive tool in maintaining a healthy and productive forest economy. Excepting tropical rainforests, fire has played a natural and important role in the development of virtually all forest, woodland, and grassland ecosystems. If fire is excluded, other processes must be substituted to fill fire's role if the ecosystem is to be maintained. If fire is to be utilized in land management, its role in the dynamics of the ecosystem must be clearly understood and fire applied at the proper time and the proper intensity.

Like fire in the home, fire in the forest can bring comfort and benefit or threat and destruction depending on how wisely it is utilized and controlled. Proper fire management requires an understanding of how a forest fire burns, how it affects the ecosystem through which it burns, and how managers over the years have developed organizations, systems, and equipment to ensure that fire in forestry is a benefit rather than a liability. It is to these ends that we dedicate this book.

CRAIG CHANDLER
PHILLIP CHENEY
PHILIP THOMAS
LOUIS TRABAUD
DAVE WILLIAMS

Arlington, Virginia
Canberra, Australia
Herts, England
Montpellier, France
Ontario, Canada

June 1983

ACKNOWLEDGMENTS

The authors particularly wish to acknowledge the cooperation of Nicolai Andreev, Chief of the Central Air Base, Pushkino, USSR and his Deputy, Evgenii Shchetinskii. Without their wholehearted assistance both in the office and in the field, this book would be much less comprehensive than it is. We only regret that it was not possible to make coauthorship arrangements.

We are also indebted to Fernando Maldonado, Corporacion Nacional Forestal de Chile, for insight into fire problems and practices in South America; P. J. Germishuizen, USUTU Pulp Co., Ltd. of Swaziland, for background information on fire management in southern Africa; Shan Chengyu, Chief of Forest Fire Control, Heilongjiang Province, People's Republic of China, for his frank and candid discussions of forest fire problems and practices in northern China; Captain Bernard of the Service d'Incendié et de Secours du Département de l'Herault for outlining the firefighting organization of France; and Vilhelm Sjolin of the Swedish Fire Research Board for his encouragement as well as for helping us gain access to the Swedish forest fire research literature.

Many colleagues have reviewed this book in whole or in part, but A. A. Brown, C. Bentley Lyon, Steve Pyne, and William T. Sommers provided perceptions and critiques that amounted to substantial contributions to the text.

We are grateful to Jane Conway for translating the French chapters into English and offer our respects to the senior author for his light touch in homogenizing the Canadian, Australian, British, and American versions of that mother tongue.

Special thanks are also due to Bill Hauser, Chief of the U.S. Forest Service Photo Library, who was always helpful in finding the right picture to illustrate a point.

Last, and most, we wish to thank Peggy Casey who was able to decipher the most inscrutable handwriting, spent untold hours over hot and cold typewriters, and added a bit of Irish charm to our commonwealth of firemen. Without her this book could never have been published.

THE AUTHORS

CONTENTS

CONTENTS OF VOLUME I

FIRE IN FORESTRY

Volume II

CHAPTER ONE

Fire Management Policy

Webster defines policy as "a definite course or method of action selected from among alternatives and in the light of given conditions to guide and usually determine present and future decisions" (Gove 1971). Policy formulation requires that there be one or more clear-cut, specific, rational goals against which to test alternatives. Unfortunately, the basic legislation establishing the fire management organization practically never provides unambiguous guidance. For example, the United States Organic Act of 1897 (30 Stat. 34, as amended; 16 U.S.C. 473–478, 479–482, 551) says merely that "The Secretary of Agriculture shall make provisions for the protection against destruction by fire and depredations upon the public forests and national forests. . . ." It is left largely to the fire management organization itself to develop the objectives and policies against which its success will be measured.

POLICY DETERMINANTS

When a fire management organization is in its infancy, it is usually underfinanced to a point where ultimate objectives can be safely ignored and primary emphasis be placed on achieving maximum internal efficiency. Beall (1949) in discussing the evolution of fire protection standards in the Canadian Forest Service points out that

> Viewed in retrospect, it is a remarkable fact that during the first 40 years of organized fire protection in Canada very little thought was devoted to the establishment of ultimate aims or objectives towards which fire control efforts should be directed. "Keep fire losses as small as possible" was a vague but perhaps satisfactory definition during the formative period, when foresters recognized that the means, facilities, and accomplishments of fire control fell far short of any acceptable standard.

1

However, once a fire organization comes of age, which can be defined as that point where higher management authorities begin questioning whether current or projected outlays for fire management will bring commensurate benefits, then a formal set of objectives, standards, and policies becomes an immediate necessity. It is at that point that the organization must prove itself effective as well as internally efficient, and effectiveness requires measures of adequacy external to the organization itself.

The first thing to remember in attempting to formulate fire management objectives and policy is that fire management is not an end in itself, but is only a means to reduce the land manager's risk of loss due to fire damage and increase benefits from the proper use of fire. Consequently, fire management objectives are subordinate to, and controlled by the land manager's objectives. Fire management objectives for a given parcel of forest land will be vastly different, and quite properly so, if the land is to be managed as a tree farm, a multiple-use public forest, or a wilderness park. A fire that results in a net loss in timber production may provide wildlife benefits that exceed the timber losses for the multiple-use forest and result in a totally beneficial example of ecological succession for the park manager.

Fire policy cannot be determined solely on the basis of the interests of the individual owner alone. Fire may affect off-site values as well as those on the area burned. Water quality may be affected over an entire watershed; smoke from even a small fire drifts tens to hundreds of kilometers, public transportation routes may be disrupted and even the threat that a fire may escape to adjoining property may disrupt the plans of adjacent landholders. Fire management policies must consider damages and benefits to the landholder, neighbors, and the public at large.

Since determination of the proper level of fire management depends on an assessment of the costs and benefits associated with forest fires, one might suspect that economic theory would be the proper method of addressing the subject. Theoretically, one would be correct and in Chapter 2 we look in depth at fire economics as it affects fire control policy. However, even though economic theories of fire management are well developed, their practical utility has yet to be demonstrated. Some of the major difficulties facing economic evaluations of fire management are the following.

Nonmarket Values

Most of the products of the forest are difficult to value in economic terms and some are impossible. How much is it worth to a citizen of New York City to preserve a wilderness in Alaska just "so he or she will know that it is there"? How much should be spent to protect the habitat of an endangered species? Sport fish and game are not sold in the marketplace and water is not sold at its source. Even market commodities such as timber are difficult to evaluate when they are harvested by fire rather than by a willing owner cutting trees to sell to a willing buyer. Is the destruction of a 10-year old plantation a greater loss to the owner than the loss of a similar 10-year old stand that regenerated naturally at no expense to the owner? Is the loss of an immature age class valued at the same cost whether or not it disrupts an entire long-term harvesting plan? Is a 12-inch diameter pine on a farmer's wood lot worth the same whether it is intended for use this winter as fuelwood, for sale next year to a pulpwood buyer, or as a legacy for grandchildren? Economists have developed many ingenious answers to these questions, but not all economists have developed the same answers and none of the answers have been universally accepted.

Nonlinearity of Fire Effects

Both the physical and economic effects of a forest fire depend on fire intensity and fire size, and the relationships are often highly nonlinear. A low-intensity litter fire may increase tree growth by releasing nutrients, whereas a crown fire in the same stand may cause 100 percent mortality. Erosion and soil compaction depend on the degree of mineral soil exposure and this is directly related to fire intensity. A fire may be too small to make salvage logging possible, thus resulting in a total loss of the trees that were killed. At the other extreme, a fire may be so large that salvage cannot be completed before the logs are degraded by insects and fungi. Sediment production varies exponentially with fire size. Studies in southern California showed that the downstream damage from runoff and erosion increased from $0.24 per hectare from fires burning less than 10 hectares, to $370 *per hectare* for fires burning 4000 to 6000 hectares in the same watershed (Buck et al. 1948).

Longevity of Fire Effects

Depending on its size and intensity, a forest fire will initiate a chain of ecological succession that may last from a few years to well over a century. At many points along this successional chain, conditions on the burned area will be more or less favorable to the land manager's objectives than would have been the case had the fire not occurred. Accurate prediction of the physical and biological successional changes is difficult. Predicting their economic effects and selecting rational discount factors is even more difficult. To complicate matters even further, land management objectives can be expected to change over the longer time frames as holdings are consolidated or fragmented and markets for timber, water, forage, and various types of recreation change.

FIRE MANAGEMENT GOALS

Because rigorous economic analysis has proven to be unattainable, substitutes have been devised in order to produce quantifiable and measurable goals for fire management programs. These can be grouped into three categories, and each has its own strengths and weaknesses.

Maximum Area Burned

The earliest, and probably still the most widely used standard for forest fire control worldwide is the establishment of a goal to burn less than a fixed percentage of the area protected. The maximum area burned is determined by evaluating the area that can be lost from production over a full rotation period against experience levels of marginal protection costs vs. reduction in burned area (Show and Kotok 1930). This criterion has several advantages: it is simple; it is easily and routinely measured; it is geared to land management objectives (as long as the land management objective is to produce timber on a fixed rotation); it implicitly recognizes cost of the protection organization as a factor in establishing the objective of the organization. It has one overwhelming disadvantage, however, one that has invariably proved fatal as the fire organization increases its complexity and sophistication. Any area burned standard ignores fire size and intensity and assumes that a hectare burned over is a hectare burned up. By assuming the maximum possible damage from every fire in every season in every cover type and geographic area, the fire manager is discouraged from a rational allocation of resources so as to minimize damage rather than simply minimizing area burned.

Economic Efficiency

The economic efficiency policy, also known as the *First Burning Period Policy*, or *10AM Policy*, was officially adopted by the U.S. Forest Service in the spring of 1935 and evaluated, restated, and defended after nine years of experience (Loveridge 1944). The policy states that the fire control organization will organize itself so as to have sufficient strength to control every fire within the first work period (Figure 1.1). Should this not occur, the attack each succeeding day will be planned and executed to obtain control before 10 o'clock the next morning. The policy is really a double one: what to do on initial attack and what to do if initial attack fails. The initial attack policy is based on two premises: it is *always* cheaper to control a small fire than it is to control a large one, and the damages on a large fire are *always* greater than those on a small one. To the extent that these premises are true, adherence to the policy will *always* result in both minimum control cost and minimum damage. Hence, considerations of forest values, or even of land management objectives, are unnecessary since adherence to the policy automatically optimizes net benefits. This logic was so appealing to fire control planners and so convincing to forestry administrators that the policy remained in force virtually unchallenged for 45 years.

The second half of the policy, which really amounts to what to do when

Figure 1.1. Fast and aggressive initial attack is the keystone of the 10AM policy. Photo by Edsel Corpe.

the first half fails, is based on a sound understanding of fire behavior. In general, forest fires achieve maximum intensity and reach their maximum rates of spread during the heat of the day. A force that cannot achieve control before conditions begin to worsen in the forenoon will be ineffective until evening because the fire will be too intense to handle. At evening they will be confronted with a vastly increased perimeter over that of the day before and thus will be even less able to cope with the situation. The only way out of this dilemma is to mass sufficient forces to control the fire during the evening, night, and early morning hours so as to eliminate the *afternoon run*.

The 10AM policy has a great deal to recommend it, as might be expected of a policy that lasted for almost half a century. As opposed to the economic, or *least cost plus damage* policy, it recognizes that fire effects are determined by fire size and intensity and is aimed specifically at minimizing the number and size of large damaging fires. Unlike the *Minimum Area Burned* policy, it treats every fire individually so that the planner cannot reduce the burned area by concentrating forces in places where control is easiest and accepting higher damages on a smaller burned area. By directing the policy to each individual fire it directs responsibility downward from the overall fire management planner to each fire-incident commander.

The 10AM policy was abandoned by the U.S. Forest Service in 1978 as a result of certain weaknesses. First, the policy assumed implicitly that all fires were damaging. As prescribed burning became institutionalized in the southern United States and as park and wilderness managers began to recognize the vital role of fire in ecosystem development, it became more obvious that some forest fires resulted in management benefits rather than damages. In addition, land managers discovered that some firefighting techniques, particularly those utilizing heavy equipment, caused more damage to the site than did the fire itself. Thus the optimum cost benefit ratio is not always realized by putting fires out as small as possible. Second, the policy, or at least the implementers of the policy, refused to recognize the law of diminishing returns. In the period 1911–1920, 5.5 percent of forest fires in California where the 10AM policy was first articulated (Show and Kotok 1923) exceeded class E (120 hectares). In 1970–1979, after 60 years of improved fire protection, only 1.1 percent of California fires were class E or larger. Fires with fireline intensities of 2 to 3 Megawatts per meter are uncontrollable, regardless of their size, by any presently available firefighting technique. Some fires starting in heavy fuels under extreme burning conditions will reach these intensities before they can be reached by any reasonable attack force. Throwing more firefighters, equipment, and money at such fires until weather conditions change for the better simply wastes firefighters, equipment, and money. Lastly, the presumption of the 10AM policy that fires which escape initial attack should be fought principally at night was never institutionalized into tactical doctrine. When the policy was formulated, fires were fought by men with handtools whose off-road transport was by foot, night travel was little more hazardous than travel by day, and night work was less so because of the reduced fire intensity. However, with increasing reliance on bulldozers, smokejumpers, helicopters, and, most particularly, air tankers in the 1950s and 1960s, firefighting became an overwhelmingly daylight operation. When a fireline crew could work all night only to see a bulldozer accomplish the same length of line in two hours the next morning, there seemed to be little reason to staff heavily at night when mechanical equipment, emergency helicopter evacuation, and air tanker support were unavailable for safety reasons. The shift to daytime firefighting repudiated the entire rationale of the 10AM policy for it meant that to secure control by 10AM tomorrow the commander had to have control by dark today. Fire costs escalated accordingly.

Adequate Control

Probably the most widely adopted but least publicized policy for forest fire management is that of providing a level of fire protection sufficient for the needs of the land management organization (Brown and Davis 1973). The concept was first specifically formulated by Flint (1928), who defines it as "that degree of protection which will render the forest property as safe on the average from destruction by fire as are other forms of destructible property in which moderately conservative investors are willing to place their funds." Flint then analyzes National Forest fire costs and losses in relation to the fire costs and losses from several cities and rural farm properties.

Flint's specific methods have not been utilized in practice largely because of the influence of fire insurance rates on urban fire protection budgets and because the prevalence of nonowner occupants in cities complicates the question of liability. However, the idea that the land owner rather than the fire department manager must make the determination of the desirable degree of protection is unexceptionable. This policy also fit well when public lands are involved since the public, acting through its elected officials, sets the forest fire protection budget through the political process. Thus the value of the resource and of the protection organization are set through negotiations between a willing seller (the fire manager) and a willing buyer (the forest manager or the responsible public official). Canadian researchers have developed a theoretical model for this process in the case of the forest manager (Nautiyal and Doan 1974), but their model can be conceptually extended to the public officials' concerns as well.

Each of the four methods of establishing fire management standards (economic analysis, minimum area burned, 10AM policy, and adequate control) have two distinct disadvantages for the fire manager trying to build an optimum fire management organization. None of them consider fire use as a concurrent responsibility with fire control, and none consider the physical–biological–ecological consequences of successful implementation of the policy over the full planning horizon of the organization. This latter difficulty may not only cause problems for the fire manager, but may have serious implications for the parent land management organization. For example, in ecosystems with natural fire-free intervals less than the decay constant, fuels will accumulate whenever fire control is successful in reducing the average annual burned area. After two fire-free intervals, fuel loadings will be twice what the original fire management organization was designed to cope with and continued success merely increases the problem until decay balances accumulation. Then, even if the fire organization is able to keep the area burned constant, the damage per hectare burned is greater because of increased fire intensity due to heavier fuel loadings. Eventually, the ecosystem will be shifted toward a classic climax type rather than a fire community, and in areas of severe lightning fire occurrence no one may know what the climax type may be.

There are, as yet, no established guidelines for integrating fire use and fuels management as well as fire control into a complete fire management system. But the fire manager and the land manager as well need to have long-range vision when they establish goals and policies governing fire management.

POLICY FORMULATION

Utilizing the previous discussion and history, let us look at the considerations that should be given in establishing fire management policy and standards for a number of typical forest situations.

Protection Forest

The term *protection forest* has been used to cover completely different situations. In the first instance the term means a forest in which harvesting or other utilization will be deferred because of inaccessibility, poor production markets, or other management reasons, but which management wants to maintain for later utilization. The first item to consider is whether there is an intent to undertake utilization within the probable lifetime of the existing stands. If not, no protection is justified since natural succession will replace the present stands whether or not they are protected. This reasoning led the Canadian government to withdraw protection forces from several million hectares in their far northern territories. Four Canadian provinces also established northern limits to their *intensive protection* areas. If the existing stands are to be eventually utilized, protection policies should encourage maintenance of the natural fire cycle under which the ecosystem developed. Overprotection will lead to fuel accumulation or ecotype changes, usually undesirable, or both. Heavy emphasis should be placed on keeping human-caused fires within their historic limits. This means that fire prevention should play a major role in fire planning, with presuppression efforts primarily oriented to protection from fires sweeping into the area from outside, and to special protection around settlements and transportation routes. Fire control efforts should be minimal. In many parts of the world, control of shifting agriculture and livestock management practices are all that is needed to maintain existing forest resources, and without such controls adequate fire protection is impossible without vastly increased budgets.

The term protection forest has also been used in an entirely different context: to describe a forest in which the primary purpose is to protect offsite values. In most instances these values are watershed-related such as minimizing the threat of erosion from steep hillsides above residential or high-value agricultural lands, or maintaining water quality in an urban reservoir. In these cases the commodity values on the forest itself are of secondary importance or of no importance. Ecological change may be highly desirable if it is in the direction of a less flammable ecotype or one in which fire control is easier or less costly. One of the objectives of fire protection should be to minimize soil disturbance (Figure 1.2). This requires intensive fire prevention, usually including restricting access to the forest, presuppression readiness adequate to hold all wildfires to a designated maximum size, and the maintenance of a suppression force capable of suppressing fires with a minimum of damage to the site. The use of fire may be quite appropriate under these circumstances; in fact, fire use may be virtually mandatory if fire exclusion will lead to more flammable types or if fuels can be expected to accumulate beyond the capability of the suppression force to meet its as-

Figure 1.2.   (*a*) The objective of fire control in the protection forest is to keep soil on the forest, (*b*) and out of people's homes. Photos by U.S. Forest Service.

(a)

(b)

9

signed maximum fire size objectives. However, fire prescriptions must be such that sufficient duff and litter are left to prevent soil movement or, if this is not possible, that each prescribed fire area be small enough to prevent soil movement off-site. Fire protection should be as intensive as is warranted by the off-site values protected and its long-range goal should be to minimize the possibility of high-intensity large fires. For nearly 20 years the Jarrah forests of western Australia have been burned under prescription on a three to five-year cycle to reduce fuel hazards. The underburning is accomplished from the air with 5,000 to 10,000 hectares being burned per day. The result has been a marked reduction in the number of conflagration fires (McArthur 1966, Packham and Peet 1967, Vines 1968).

Watershed and Grazing Lands

Where the primary management objective for an area is water or forage production, fire management should be aimed at maintaining maximum grass cover with minimum incursions by shrubs or trees. The reasoning in the case of grazing land is obvious, but it is equally true for watersheds. The transpiration requirements of trees and shrubs greatly exceed those of grasses and water yields are greater where the land can be kept in grass. One exception to this axiom is when precipitation occurs primarily as winter snow. In this case alternating strips of grass and conifers may provide maximum snow accumulation with less evaporation and ablation over the winter and a delayed spring run-off, but even here the amount of cover that should be kept in grass greatly exceeds that of a normal forest. Use of fire is a predominant feature of fire management in these situations, but fire control is also important to ensure that the lands are only burned at the proper times of year and at the right frequencies. Although fire alone is rarely capabe of converting brushlands or woodlands to grass, fire, applied at the right frequencies, can maintain established grasslands free of encroaching tree and shrub reproduction. Fire control in grasslands should emphasize speed of attack with lightly equipped, highly mobile forces since the rate of fire spread in grass fuels is very high but the difficulty of control is low.

Park and Recreation Areas

Fire management objectives in park and recreation areas will vary depending on whether the park is primarily intended to provide dispersed recreation opportunities such as hunting, camping, and hiking, to provide an example of a particular ecosystem as part of the national cultural heritage, or to preserve a particular historic or scenic site in as close to its original condition as possible. In the first instance, fire management should be geared to maximizing visitor satisfaction. Efforts should be directed toward obtaining a maximum number and diversity of wildlife and there should be a heavy emphasis on hazard reduction, both to minimize the chance of intense wildfires that might pose a threat to visitor safety and to maintain a clean forest floor for better visibility and easier off-trail travel. Through planned use of prescribed fire there will generally be a higher frequency of low-intensity surface fires than was true in the original forest. Prevention activities should be intensive, and presuppression planning should provide assurance of visitor safety and a maximum size for any individual wildfire.

If the park is established to maintain a particular ecosystem, a natural fire frequency should be maintained insofar as possible consistent with visitor safety. This   to accomplish in ecosystems where the normal fire history   short return periods. It is difficult, a   types such as Pseudotsu   after very long fire-free in   itiate controlled crown fir   rk or wilderness areas it i   file of ecological change.   ot to overprotect the area   dent and ripe for conflag   vel of presuppression sh   y and to ensure that fires d

Par   ral appearance pose the m   is impossible in the long   eriorate regardless of treat   case of Sequoia, for exa   aintaining subclimax stands   ure. In parks intended for preservation, natural   d since the objective is to arrest ecosystem progression, not to   tural measures, including the use of fire where appropriate, should be utilized to suppress overstory competitition. Hazard reduction measures should be taken to the extent that they can be justified by decreased presuppression and suppression costs. Presuppression should be as intensive as possible and suppression of all fires should be immediate. Preservation is an unnatural management objective ecologically and attempts to achieve it through natural fire regimes are counterproductive (Van Wagner and Methven 1980).

Plantations and Intensively Managed Forests

In forests dedicated to intensive wood production fire management can and should be guided by purely economic considerations. Intensive management should not be undertaken unless the forest manager is able to allocate sufficient funds to fire protection to adequately protect the investment in the forestry practices. There is no use planting trees unless there is a reasonable probability that they will survive to rotation age. In planning the total forestry operation the fire manager and the silviculturist must work closely

together. The increasing practice of planting highly flammable pine plantations in parts of the world where experience with such fire types is lacking is
a problem pointed out by Carl Wilson (1975) in a report to the Food and
Agriculture Organization of the United Nations.

Compartmentalization of plantations, orientation of cutting blocks for
ease of slash disposal, and careful consideration of fire hazard reduction in
timber stand improvement operations can save hundreds of dollars per hectare over the course of a rotation. Proper integration and crosstraining of
forestry crews and fire crews will minimize labor costs and consideration of
multipurpose equipment can save capital outlays. In a tightly integrated
forest management organization fire management considerations influence
virtually every operation from the spacing of seedlings in the plantation
(which determines understory composition and time to crown closure) to the
selection of minimum diameter limits for utilization (which determines the
amount of slash left in the woods).

Extensively Managed Multiple-Use Forests

Most public forests and many privately owned ones as well are managed, not
for a single product but for a mixture of wood, forage, watershed, and
recreational outputs. Consequently, fire management policies must also recognize the several, often conflicting, requirements of these desired management outputs. This can be done relatively easily if the protection area is
managed through formal land management plans (Egging and Barney 1979)
but this is often not the case. When there are no formal land management
plans, fire management policies should be developed by negotiation between
the fire manager and the land manager with a clear understanding of the
implications of alternative policies on the production of each desired product. Often the best approach is to divide the forest into compartments or
zones, each with a single "preferred" product such as wildlife or recreation,
set minimum standards for each of the other outputs to be produced on the
compartment, and then optimize fire management for the preferred product
within the constraints of those minimum standards. This method has been
used quite successfully in wildlife management planning (Mealey and Horn
1981).

FIRE MANAGEMENT PLANNING

Once the fire management policies and standards have been established in
concert with the land manager, it is the fire manager's responsibility to
develop the most cost-effective organization to ensure that the policies are
followed and the standards are met. Properly done, fire management planning is a continuing process requiring annual revision as risks and hazards
change and as better data are accumulated.

Intelligent fire planning involves the collection, maintenance, and analysis of vast quantities of data, much of which are best displayed on maps. The following items should be considered as a minimum basis for developing a fire management plan.

Maps

Fire occurrence (past 5 years) coded by month, time of day, cause, and size class.

Fire history coded by area burned, year of fire, and intensity class.

Fuel types—overstory and understory. Special coding for slash areas and plantations.

Land ownership and improvements.

Contour map with watershed delineation with special coding for unstable soils.

Road map coded by width and surface. Overlays of travel times from fixed locations.

Seen area map for selected overlooks (see Chapter 4).

Preplanning map (see Chapter 4).

Environmental Data

Fuels—historic rates of spread and difficulty of control by fuel types.

Weather—daily weather records for the full period of record from all weather stations.

Climate—long-term averages and ninetieth percentiles for all weather elements by weeks or bimonthly periods.

Logistical Data

Fire management personnel—ages, qualifications, training needs.

Cooperator personnel—agency, qualifications, contact point.

Equipment—location, specifications, date of last inspection.

Supplies—amount, location, date of acquisition.

Rental and lease agreements.

Source of emergency supplies.

Economic Data

Cost and productivity of personnel and equipment by slope class, fuel type, and weather severity.

Much of this information and subsequent analysis can be computerized as discussed in the later section on computerized fire planning.

The first decision to be made is what period or periods of the year should be planned for intensive fire protection, that is, to define the *fire season*. Any of several criteria can be used such as the period that will encompass a given percentage of fires (usually 90 percent), the dates within which all fires above a certain size occur, or the period within which fires can be expected to exceed a given intensity or damage level. Establishing a planned fire season is critical to fire management planning since the length of season dictates the kinds and numbers of fire forces that can reasonably be considered in building the fire protection organization. A short fire season precludes the employment of full-time specialists unless they can be utilized in other forest operations during the off-season. Many kinds of fire equipment are uneconomic without a heavy use rate over which to amortize the investment. Others are virtually useless without specially trained and skilled operators. On the other hand, a long fire season, particularly one that coincides with the peak season for other forestry work, may make it imperative to hire specialized fire crews rather than reducing productivity by removing woods workers from the work force to fight fire.

The next fire-planning criterion that must be established is the peak load that the organization will be expected to handle. A great deal of judgment as well as formal analysis is necessary in this step since it is uneconomic and often physically impossible to organize sufficient forces for the worst possible case, but the vast majority of fire damage (usually over 90 percent) is caused by a small minority of the fires (usually less than 10 percent) and an organization that is capable of handling only the average fire situation will have very little effect in reducing forest fire damages. For many years the U.S. Forest Service planned its fire control organization to meet the conditions of the "average worst" year, defined as the year with the third highest number of fires and/or area burned of the preceding 10 years (U.S. Forest Service 1979).

Once the prerequisite data have been assembled and the planning period (fire season) and planning level (peak load) established, the fire manager is ready to prepare the actual fire plan for the year. Fire plans vary widely in length and format depending on the size of the fire management organization and the complexity of the parent forestry organization, but each plan should include, as a minimum:

1. Description of the protection area including management objectives and a brief discussion of relationships with all neighboring ownerships.
2. Statement of fire management goals and policies including organization charts and concept of operation.
3. Fuels management plan including expected abatement of activity

fuels, all hazard reduction work, firebreak and fuelbreak construction and maintenance, and any work such as wildlife habitat burning that will be done by the fire management organization for other divisions of the parent company or agency.

4. Fire prevention plan including all specific activities such as inspections and contacts with a timetable for each.

5. Detection plan encompassing all detection activities including those of cooperators by fire danger classes.

6. Manning plan to govern the placement of personnel and equipment by fire danger classes.

7. Initial attack plan to govern initial dispatching of personnel and equipment, including contractors and cooperators, by fire location and fire danger class.

8. Reinforcement plan listing procedures for obtaining backup forces if initial attack is, or is predicted to be, unsuccessful.

Larger fire management organizations will usually have additions or annexes to the basic plan covering such activities as communication, transportation, training, air operations, fiscal control, reports, and data management.

COMPUTERIZED PLANNING SYSTEMS

Because fire management planning involves repetitive manipulation of large amounts of constantly changing data, it is ideally suited for automation. The use of automated data processing systems in fire management is not new. Fire reports and weather data were stored on punched cards and automatically sorted for statistical evaluations and summaries before World War II. However, it was not until the adoption of operations research techniques such as linear programming in the late 1950s (Jewell 1963) and the development of sophisticated simulation modeling in the middle 1960s (Jarrett 1965) that automation became more than a labor-saving device for handling large quantities of data. Early computers were large, cumbersome, and very expensive. Continued miniaturization and resulting cost reductions have now made it possible to operate computers at fire control centers or even on the fireline. Now computer algorithms are routinely used for evaluating optimum detection coverage by lookouts (Mees 1978), scheduling and routing air patrols (Kourtz 1973), determining the likelihood of occurrence of catastrophic fires for any given location (Friedman 1975), evaluating alternative fire plans (Flatman and Storey 1979), and optimizing the division of forces among multiple fires when there are insufficient forces available to control all of them (Myers 1974).

Probably the most extensive system, which has been conceptualized but not yet implemented, is that of Maloney and Potter (1974) and Simard (1977) in Canada in which all fire management operations are integrated into a single interactive system. The system was designed in the form of a series of building blocks most of which can be developed and put into operation more or less independently of one another but which all contribute toward the realization of the complete system. A number of these building blocks have been developed to the operational state. One of the building blocks of the Canadian system is a fire prediction model that predicts daily the number and locations of both lightning and human-caused fires. Lightning data is provided by a second generation lightning locating system developed in the United States and human-caused data is based on historic records of human-caused fire patterns. Another model uses these predictions to determine the optimum patrol routes and scheduling of detection aircraft, and another indicates the personnel and equipment available to control the predicted fires. Another building block is the provision of up-to-date fuel-type maps from LANDSAT satellite data. The digital nature of the data allows enhancement techniques to emphasize various features of particular interest to fire control officers and, when related to weather, fuel, and topographic data, will allow for the prediction of fire rate of growth. When all the building blocks have been developed they will be integrated into a single interactive fire management system.

The most fully developed system in actual operational use is FIRESCOPE which services several national, state, and local fire agencies in southern California (Chase 1980). In the FIRESCOPE system, fuel, topographic, and transportation data are archived in a computer. The location, availability, and capability of all suppression forces are entered into the computer daily or as often as their status changes. Weather data are telemetered directly to the computer from selected weather stations and weather forecasts are entered in terms of changes expected in the observed values at specific future times. When a fire is reported, the computer automatically calculates the expected rate of fire growth, the number and kind of nearest initial attack forces, and the probability of successful initial attack. If the probability of success is low, the computer also displays the available backup forces, their expected rate of line production by individual units, and the line production rate required for control under the weather changes forecast to occur over the life of the fire. The FIRESCOPE system is as close as wildland fire agencies have come to the automated dispatching systems used by the larger urban fire departments.

It is obvious that the potential for utilizing computerized systems in fire management planning is great and limited only by the imagination of the fire manager, the rate of development of new hardware, and the availability of data. There are several organizational and managerial barriers, however, that must be overcome in order to successfully implement a large-scale computerized system. Martell (1981) provides a good overview of the problems inherent in interfacing computer experts and fire managers.

BIBLIOGRAPHY

Beall, H. W. 1949. An outline of forest fire protection standards. *For. Chron.* **25**(2):82–106.

Brown, A. A. and K. P. Davis. 1973. *Forest fire control and use.* McGraw-Hill, New York, 686 pp.

Buck, C. C., W. L. Fons, and C. M. Countryman. 1948. *Average fire damage from increased run-off and erosion on the southern California National Forests.* Calif. For. and Range Exp. Sta., 22 pp.

Chase, R. A. 1980. *FIRESCOPE: a new concept in multiagency fire suppression coordination.* U.S. For. Serv. Gen. Tech. Report PSW-40, 17 pp.

Egging, L. T. and R. J. Barney. 1979. Fire management: a component of land management planning. *Environ. Manage.* **3**(1):15–20.

Flatman, G. T. and T. G. Storey. 1979. *Decision techniques for evaluating fire plans using FOCUS simulation.* U.S. For. Serv. Res. Note PSW-338, 6 pp.

Flint, H. R. 1928. Adequate fire control. *J. For.* **26**(5):624–638.

Friedman, D. G. 1975. *Computer simulation in natural hazard assessment.* Nat. Sci. Found. Monograph NSF-RA-E-75-002, 193 pp.

Gove, P. B. 1971. *Websters 3rd new international dictionary of the English language unabridged*, Merriam, Springfield, Mass., 2662 pp.

Jarrett, H. F. 1965. *The systems approach to fire problems: an overview.* Systems Dev. Corp. Unnumbered Report, 31 pp.

Jewell, W. S. 1963. Forest fire problems—a progress report. *Oper. Res.* **11**(5):678–692.

Kourtz, P. 1973. *A visual airborne forest fire detection patrol route planning system.* For. Fire Res. Inst. Infor. Report FF-X-45, 29 pp.

Loveridge, E. W. 1944. The fire suppression policy of the U.S. Forest Service. *J. For.* **42**(8):549–554.

Maloney, J. E. and M. O. Potter. 1974. *The fire management system: the fire management centre: preliminary results and design concepts.* For. Fire Res. Inst., 46 pp.

Martell, D. L. 1981. *Implementing computer technology in forest fire management.* Univ. Toronto, Unnumbered Report, 22 pp.

McArthur, A. G. 1966. Prescribed burning in Australian fire control. *Aust. For.* **30**(1):4–11.

Mealey, S. P. and J. R. Horn. 1981. *Integrating wildlife habitat objectives into the forest plan.* Proc. 46th No. Am. Wildl. and Nat. Resour. Conf., pp. 1–43.

Mees, R. M. 1978. *Seen areas and distribution of fires about a lookout.* U.S. For. Serv. Gen. Tech. Report PSW-26, 7 pp.

Myers, J. L. 1974. *Computer-aided decision making for wildland fire control.* McDonnell Douglas Co., MADC Paper WD 2419, 23 pp.

Nautiyal, J. C. and G. E. Doan. 1974. Economics of forest fire control: trading planned cut for protection expenditure. *Can. J. For. Res.* **4**:82–89.

Packham, D. R. and G. B. Peet. 1967. *Developments in controlled burning from aircraft.* C.S.I.R.O. Unnumbered Report, Oct. 1967, 16 pp., illus.

Show, S. B. and E. I. Kotok. 1923. *Forest fires in California 1911–20: an analytical study.* USDA Circ. 243, 80 pp., illus.

Show, S. B. and E. I. Kotok. 1930. *The determination of hour control for adequate fire protection in the major cover types of the California pine region.* U.S.D.A. Tech. Bull. No. 209, 47 pp.

Simard, A. J. 1977. *Wildland fire management: a systems approach.* Dept. of Fisheries and Env. For. Tech. Rpt. No. 17, 25 pp.

U.S. Forest Service. 1979. *Glossary of terms for fire management*, 78 pp. processed.

Van Wagner, C. E. and I. R. Methven. 1980. *Fire in the management of Canada's National Parks: philosophy and strategy*. Parks Canada, Unnumbered Occ. Paper. 18 pp.

Vines, R. G. 1968. The forest fire problem in Australia—a survey of past attitudes and modern practice. *Aust. Sci. Teachers J.,* Nov. 1968, pp. 1–11.

Wilson, C. C. 1975. *Detection and control of forest fires for the protection of the human environment*. FAO, Rome 63 pp.

CHAPTER TWO

Economics of Fire Management

In its relationship to fire management, economics may be perceived as a social science dedicated to optimizing the allocation of limited resources to meet unlimited goals. When used in this sense, economics is devoid of political content, equally applicable to capitalist, socialist, or Marxist societies. For "from each according to his abilities, to each according to his needs" can operate automatically only if the total of societal abilities and needs are exactly in balance. In a dynamic society both abilities and needs are constantly changing; consequently, supply and demand are constantly adapting in an attempt to reach equilibrium. Economic theory, particularly efficiency analysis and marginal analysis, can be used to determine the optimum protection expenditures for a forestry organization, to allocate resources among the various fire management functions such as detection, prevention, and hazard reduction, and to assist in such day-to-day decisions as the size and composition of initial attack forces.

THE LAW OF DIMINISHING RETURNS: LEAST COST PLUS DAMAGE

For the forester, the law of diminishing returns is best illustrated by a silvicultural example. Figure 2.1 shows the superimposed curves of current annual increment and mean annual increment vs. age for a normally stocked hectare of *Pinus taeda* on a good site. The current annual increment peaks at 30 years of age and declines rather sharply for the next 20 years. The mean annual increment (total yield divided by total age) peaks at 42 years, the point at which the two curves cross. To obtain maximum productivity of the site the trees should be harvested at the time of maximum *mean* annual increment, not at the time of maximum *current* annual increment.

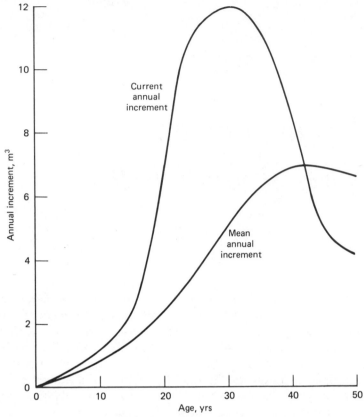

Figure 2.1.   Annual growth.

Another way to look at these same data is to look sequentially at the effect of leaving the stand uncut for one additional year. Clearly, as long as each year's current annual increment is larger than the last, productivity is increasing. However, even after the current annual increment has started diminishing, productivity will increase as long as the next year's increment is larger than the average increment over the life of the stand to date. This method of examining the effect of an additional unit of input on the average output is known as marginal analysis and is as applicable to the growth of fire management organizations as it is to the growth of trees.

Consider a forest area that receives no fire protection but for which the establishment of a fire management organization is being considered. Presumably, the area is sustaining a relatively high level of damage from fire (otherwise management would not consider establishing a fire organization), and the productivity of the organization can be measured in terms of damage averted. Until a force has been assembled sufficient to handle the fire of average size and intensity on the forest, productivity per unit of input can be expected to remain low. As additional units of force, say, for example, firefighters, are added, productivity per unit will increase until the force is sufficient to control the most severe fire to be expected on the forest in any given year. This point is analogous to the maximum current annual increment in our silvicultural example. This force will not be sufficient to cope with concurrent fires, however, and added damages will be experienced whenever concurrent fires occur. Any forces added to cope with simultaneous fires will be less productive than the earlier additions since concurrent fires are a less common event than single fires, but they may increase the average productivity of the fire protection force as a whole depending on the rate of occurrence of concurrent fires. At some point the addition of more firefighters will decrease average productivity since too many will be idle too much of the time.

Another, and simpler, way to calculate the point of maximum average productivity or zero marginal return is to sum the costs and damages associated with varying levels of protection effort and find the point where the sum is minimized, that is, the point of *least cost plus damage*. This method was first explicitly presented by Sparhawk (1925) and his diagram is reproduced here as Figure 2.2. In this figure the line *XY* represents damages and suppression costs. Sparhawk considers suppression costs to be analogous to damage since the cost is an unavoidable consequence of an unplanned fire and because the cost of suppression is inversely proportional to the strength of the presuppression organization. Note that these two assumptions are identical to those underlying the Economic Efficiency or 10AM policy discussed in Chapter 1. Line *AB* represents *primary protection* costs that Sparhawk defines as "the amount that is figured in advance when a definite organization is developed to prevent, detect, and control fires." Sparhawk recognizes that there is a certain ambiguity to his definitions of suppression costs and primary protection costs since the primary protection force will take suppression action when fires occur. For purposes of determining the point of least cost plus damage, the distinction is immaterial as long as double counting is avoided, and fire economists since Sparhawk have used various devices to segregate fire protection costs. Line *ST* represents the sum of the primary protection costs, suppression costs, and damages. Point *P* is the lowest point on the *ST* curve and point *E* is the proper amount of effort to expend on primary protection since any greater or lesser amount would result in a higher total cost plus loss. Sparhawk's classic diagram remained a standard reference for nearly 50 years and served as the basis for extensive analyses of the economics of forest fire protection in both the United States (Arnold 1949) and Canada (Mactavish 1965).

Despite the almost universal acceptance of the Sparhawk least cost plus damage model, there are some disturbing discrepancies between Sparhawk's diagram and our scenario for the establishment of a fire management organization for a previously unprotected forest. Sparhawk's damage curve *XY* is exponential, implying that the maximum marginal productivity

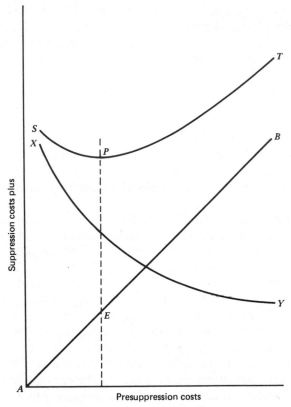

Figure 2.2.   Least cost plus damage.

of the protection force is reached when the first unit of force, say, the first firefighter, is employed. However, this is belied by all firefighting experience which teaches that unless sufficient force is dispatched to control the head of the fire, the effect on area burned and fire damage will be minimal. The minimum force required to control the head of the fire will vary with the rate of spread, intensity, and size of the fire at time of arrival, but only very rarely will it be equal to or less than the smallest unit that could be sent as curve *XY* requires. Simard (1976) recognizes this shortcoming and introduces a separate curve for productivity vs. fire management effort. He also recognizes, however, that the curve shape varies by fuel type and climatic severity, and that the precise form for any particular situation is largely conjectural. Later studies (Gale 1977) of highly intensive fire management organizations have questioned whether there is any functional relationship whatever between damage as estimated by area burned and fire control force as estimated by dollar expenditures.

One reason for the lack of correlation between fire control expenditures and area burned lies in the assumed linear shape of Sparhawk's line *AB* which equates fire control costs with fire control force. To begin with, the relationship between cost and force is a step function, not a straight line, and for sophisticated equipment such as airtankers or specialized engines the steps can be quite high. Secondly, the relationship is not likely to be linear unless perfect judgment is used to match the type of force dispatched to that required by the particular fuel type and fire intensity involved. A bulldozer may represent a fire control force equivalent to 100 workers on a fire in heavy fallen timber yet be no more effective than a single worker for a small fire in a light layer of litter. Even the simplest unit of force, the firefighter with a hand tool, has a differing effective force depending on how he or she is utilized and combined with other force units.

Despite these difficulties and the problem of how to measure and evaluate fire damage, discussed later, the least cost plus damage approach has been used successfully to guide the development of fire control organizations, particularly in their formative stages. Craig et al. (1945, 1946) were able to establish satisfactory production functions by carefully screening data from areas where fuel types and fire control activities had remained relatively static over a number of years. The most thorough study utilizing the classic least cost plus damage approach was undertaken for the Tennessee Valley area of North Carolina by the North Carolina Department of Conservation and Development and the Tennessee Valley Authority (Vogenberger et al. 1957). Data on costs, area burned, and timber damages were obtained from 15 counties for a 13-year period. When the data for four "blowup" years were discarded, the variable operating costs (equivalent of presuppression costs) vs. area burned fitted the equation

$$Y = 1.75 \times 10^{-5} X^{-1.16}$$

where Y = Decimal fraction of protected area burned
        X = Dollars of variable operating cost per acre protected

The coefficient of correlation was 0.96. Damages were determined by stand type, age, and degree of stocking and present worth determined by discounting from a predetermined harvest age using a three percent discount rate. Damages were apportioned to counties by assuming that damage is directly proportional to area burned and that area burned by stand classes is directly proportional to the distribution of stand classes within each county. The available data did not permit testing either of these assumptions.

The point of least cost plus damage, county by county, was determined by calculating the derivative $dB/dx = 0$ where B = variable operating costs plus average damage per acre times annual area burned. The results were utilized to allocate state protection funds among counties.

Probably the most significant finding of the Tennessee Valley study is the total lack of correlation between expenditures and area burned when the protection load exceeds the design criteria of the protection system, as

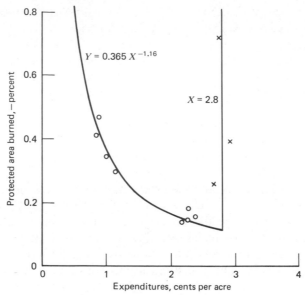

Figure 2.3.   Area burned vs. protection expenditure for 15 North Carolina counties.

occurred nearly one-third of the time during the period of study. Figure 2.3 shows the data and calculated regression line for the 15 counties. Circles represent the "normal" years and Xs the "blowup" years. Once operating expenditures reach the maximum that the base protection organization can accommodate, area burned becomes purely dependent on the weather and the number of additional fire starts. It is logical to assume that increasing expenditures on the base fire organization beyond its existing design limit will result in a decrease in area burned, but there is no basis whatever for determining what the increase should be or how much might be saved.

The Tennessee Valley study resolved this dilemma by the following reasoning. The average burned area during blowup years is three and one-half times larger than during the average year. This "excess" area burned times the average dollar damage gives the "excess" dollar damage due to blowups. Since blowup years can be expected one year out of three and since money expended for fire protection should at least pay its own way, the authors divide the total "excess" damage by three and propose that that amount be used as a reserve fund to finance extra protection during drought years. They admit that this procedure is purely speculative, but show that the only feasible alternative—increasing funding sufficiently to lower area burned during average years enough to compensate for the excess lost during blowup years—would cost nearly twice as much as the reserve fund they propose.

The need to isolate years where fire load exceeds the design capabilities of the protection system is vital to any successful analysis of least cost plus damage. In an analysis of U.S. Forest Service statistics for the 11-year period 1965–1975, the average annual area burned either increased 24 percent or decreased 34 percent between the early and late periods depending on where one places the disaster year of 1970 (Gale 1977) when fire activity on the Pacific Coast was twice the 11-year average and damages in southern California alone exceeded $700 million.

FIRE DAMAGE ASSESSMENT

Evaluation of least cost plus damage, or indeed any economic analysis whatever of forest fire protection, requires that the consequences of fire be known and expressible in common terms. The unit of commonality is usually monetary, although some analysts have proposed working with units of "satisfaction" and "dissatisfaction" to avoid the difficulties inherent in placing money values on some forest outputs (Nautiyal and Doan 1974).

The economic, as opposed to the physical, biological, and ecological consequences of fire depend almost entirely on the management intent of the landholder. In some parts of Asia and Africa, as in early colonial America, forests are considered as an impediment to agriculture and thus valueless in and of themselves. Fire protection is economically unnecessary. In much of Australia, the southwestern United States, and Mediterranean Europe shrublands are considered valuable only as a protective cover for watersheds. Fire protection, often extremely intensive fire protection, is justified to reduce the risk of fire escaping from the forest and damaging agricultural and residential lands outside the forest boundaries. Off-site values and risks are the overriding economic determinants; on-site values and fire effects are negligible (Luke and McArthur 1978). In the USSR, forests are considered to be a capital inventory reserve that determines the degree of industrial development permitted within each forest zone (Tsymek 1966). In this instance fire protection must be justified on the basis of opportunity costs incurred when areas are removed from potential production consideration because of fire. In Canada and Scandinavia where timber products represent a large share of the national export income and the majority of forest land is state-owned or controlled, the economic effects of fire can best be considered in relation to even-aged, sustained-yield management for timber values alone (Mactavish 1966). The value of land for growing timber on a fixed rotation is determined by the formula

$$SE = \left[\frac{Y}{(1 + P)^n - 1} \right] - \left[\frac{e}{P} \right]$$

where Se = Net present worth
Y = Net expected stumpage revenue
e = Annual management costs
P = Discount rate
n = Length of rotation period

If a stand consists of timber ready for immediate harvest, the total net worth of the property is $Se + Y$; that is, the value of the land alone plus the net value of the stumpage on it. Should a fire burn through the stand, the damage would be $Y - S$ (where S = net return from salvage) plus or minus any effects on the land itself that will affect its future ability to grow timber. There may be many such effects depending on circumstances.

If natural regeneration is relied upon to establish a new stand following fire, it may take longer to establish a new stand than would have been the case had the area been logged rather than burned. If so, the interest on the land value during the idle period represents a real damage chargeable to the fire. This can be calculated as:

$$DR = Se \left[\frac{(1 + P)^X - 1}{(1 + P)^X} \right]$$

where X = Number of additional years to regenerate stand

It should be noted that X may be zero or even negative in the case of fire-dependent species such as *Pinus banksiana*. In the latter case fire results in a benefit to reproduction and should be subtracted from stumpage loss in the same manner as returns from salvage.

If the area is planted rather than regenerated naturally, the cost of planting is chargeable to the fire, whereas the additional yield derived from a planted as opposed to a natural stand represents a benefit from the fire. The regeneration damage is then calculated as:

$$DR = C - \left[\frac{(Ya - Yb)}{(1 + P)^n} \right]$$

where C = Cost of planting
        Ya = Expected net return from a planted stand
        Yb = Expected net return from a natural stand

Similarly, if succession following fire can be expected to differ from that following logging in species composition, stocking, growth rate, or any other factor that will affect yield, the formula $(Y1 - Y2)/(1 + P)^n$ should be used to determine the damage or benefit.

Young stands require more intensive fire protection than mature stands, and snags and debris from fire and subsequent salvage operations often add appreciably to the natural hazard. If added fire protection costs are required to safeguard the young stand, they are chargeable as fire damage by the formula:

$$DF = F \left[\frac{(1 + P)^y - 1)}{P (1 + P)^y} \right]$$

where F = Annual added fire protection cost
        y = Number of years added protection will be required

The foregoing discussion was based on burning a stand of timber of harvestable age. For immature stands the basic formula for damage is:

$$D = \frac{Y[(1 + P)^a - 1]}{[(1 + P)^n - 1]}$$

where a = Present age of the stand
n = Rotation age

This represents the compound interest on the gross land value of the stand $(Se + Y)$.

In another approach to the question of how forest fire influences forest productivity, Van Wagner (1979, 1982), develops a model that deals with the substitution problem by spreading the economic impact of a fire across the present value of the whole forest rather than on just the burned stand. The model's principal output is the equilibrium annual harvest (AH) at any combined levels of fire and cutting. The model also demonstrates the effects of varying rates of growth and interest rates and is capable of indicating net benefits of fire as readily as net loss.

Up to now we have discussed the primary economic effects of fire on an organization dedicated to timber production. These are the effects on society as a whole that result from the physical interruption of tree growth due to fire. For a very large organization such as the crown lands of Canada, the societal effects and the organizational effects are virtually identical except for instances of conflagrations involving hundreds of thousands of hectares. For firms or agencies with smaller landholdings, however, the secondary effects may be more serious than the primary damage. The volume of timber requiring salvage may exceed the capacity of the organization or the local demand for stumpage, thus reducing the return to the landowner. Fires in the more accessible stands may force increased capital costs for roadbuilding as well as higher log transportation costs. Fires will usually affect different age classes unequally, requiring a modification of harvest schedules. In the most severe case fire may make sustained yield forestry impossible for a smaller landowner, thus forcing a liquidation operation with serious effects on the local economy. Since these secondary damages are essentially transfer payments where the loss to one locality or organization is balanced by a profit by another, they are not direct losses to society as a whole. However, they are very real to the individual landholder and pose a barrier to successful establishment of a system of forest fire insurance.

When a forest property is being managed for multiple benefits rather than purely for timber production, fire damage assessment becomes vastly more complicated (Figure 2.4). There is little agreement, even among specialists, on how some forest resources such as wildlife and recreation should be valued, and there is even less agreement on how these resources are affected by fire in an economic sense. Noste and Davis (1975), for example, show that a fire in Minnesota caused $1,731,687 damage as assessed by the

Figure 2.4. On multiple-use properties, fire damage lies largely in the eye of the beholder. Burned over redwoods in Klamath, California. Photo by W. I. Hutchinson.

methods of the U.S. Bureau of Land Management but only $335,557 damage using U.S. Forest Service damage assessment procedures. Similarly, after carefully investigating the net cash flows before and after a series of fires that burned nearly 50,000 hectares in Washington State, Bakker (1975) reports damages 2.7 times as great as those projected in the official government report of the fires.

There are four general types of price indicators that can be used to place a value on a good or service. These, in order of preference, are market price, conversion return, replacement cost or opportunity cost, and user cost.

Market price is the preferred measure of value provided that a free and competitive market exists. In some cases, clean air or aesthetic vistas, for example, markets may not exist. In others, usually monopoly or government-restricted situations, markets may exist but be controlled at artificially low or artificially high levels. Public campground fees are a good example of the former instance and world petroleum prices of the latter.

In valuation by conversion return, a resource that serves as an input for some derived product is valued at the price of the derived product minus all intermediate costs of production. A classic example is the tree on the stump which is converted into logs which are converted into boards which are converted into furniture which may undergo several wholesale and retail steps before winding up in the hands of the consumer. The value of the tree can be determined from the market price of any of the products in this chain, but obviously the task of determining the intermediate costs will be least if one chooses the first product for which a competitive market price exists.

Both the market price and the conversion return can be calculated for future products, assuming that future prices can be accurately calculated and discounted to the present. This, as we have just seen, is the standard method of appraising immature timber stands, but it is equally valid for evaluating any land that is planned for future development. For example, if a landholder expects to develop a particular area as a commercial campground, fire damage can be calculated from its effect on future costs and returns exactly as is done for immature timber.

Opportunity cost is the value foregone by investing in one resource instead of another. Replacement cost is one example of opportunity cost since it represents benefits foregone by replacing the resource. Opportunity cost is a very powerful tool since it makes it possible to determine monetary values for nonmarket products. A wilderness preserve, for example, must be worth at least as much as the value of the timber within it. Opportunity cost is subject to misuse, however. The value of the second best choice or use (the foregone opportunity) is always less than the actual use and may be very much less. Consequently, opportunity cost always undervalues the resource to a greater or lesser extent. Secondly, and of more importance to fire managers, the economic effect of fire on the resource depends entirely on the use or proposed use of the land, not on any other use. If a fire burns a portion of the wilderness reserve in our example, the effect of its value as a wilderness is totally unrelated to its effects on the timber values.

User costs are even more liable to misuse than are opportunity costs. User costs are the costs incurred by the user of a good or service that must at least equal the value of the resource or the user would not have incurred the costs. In our wilderness example the value of the wilderness would be the capitalized sum total of annual visitor expenditures for travel, camping equipment, food, and so on directly related to their wilderness experience. Despite the fact that it is virtually impossible to sort out the costs associated solely with a wilderness trip—people will eat wherever they are, and perhaps eat more expensive food away from the wilderness—user costs have been used rather effectively to develop curves of economic demand for National Parks in the United States (Clawson 1959).

At least two authors have tried to segregate all potential fire related effects for multiple-use lands and develop standardized methods for evaluating them (Crosby 1977, Streeby 1970). These are, in roughly descending order of ease in quantification; timber, physical improvement, forage, recreation, wildlife, watershed, life safety, air quality, scenery, habitability, and indirect costs.

Fire damage appraisal methods for standing timber have already been discussed but it is well to reemphasize that they are only appropriate if the trees were intended for processing into lumber, fiber, or fuel. If the land was not intended for commercial logging, the prefire value of trees should be determined by other methods even if they were salvage-logged after the fire.

Damage to physical improvements such as buildings, fences, and roads can be assessed from insurance payments, depreciated original costs, or depreciated replacement cost. Insurance payments are used by most urban fire departments because they represent actual cash flows and because most urban improvements are insured at the owner's estimate of value. The same is seldom true in rural areas where insurance rates are more capricious. Depreciated original cost tends to underrate damage due to the worldwide increase in the real cost of energy and construction materials. Discounted replacement cost is suggested as the most rational method. This is analogous to the method for appraising immature timber. Presume that an improvement has a normal replacement schedule of n years but is destroyed by fire after m years and replaced at cost Y. The loss is the difference in present value between replacing the improvement in $n - m$ years and every n years thereafter, and replacing the improvement now and every n years thereafter.

$$D = Y\left[\frac{(1 = P)^{n-m} - 1}{(1 + P)^{n-m}}\right]\left[\frac{(1 + Po)^n}{(1 + P)^n - 1}\right]$$

where P = Discount rate

Damage to forage values depends entirely on the time of the fire in relation to the timing of grazing use. In many instances the damage may be negative (indicating a net benefit). Damage consists of the net loss of forage, which can be measured by replacement cost of hay or alternative grazing land, plus the net effect of the fire on successive crops of forage. This net effect is more often beneficial than not. It can be estimated directly in areas where research studies have established the relationship between fire and forage production or it can be equated with the cost of prescribed burning in areas where range burning is common practice. This might be considered as a negative opportunity cost.

Appraisal of fire damages to recreation resources is difficult. Forest recreation takes many forms, occurs seasonally and, except for campgrounds and ski lifts (Figure 2.5), is seldom priced with any regard for supply and demand. If fire merely degrades the quality of a recreation area, damages can be determined from rehabilitation costs and estimated user costs foregone until rehabilitation is complete. If the attraction of the area is destroyed or rendered unusable for decades as can occur following a large crown fire, damage assessment is more complicated. Many authors advocate using the replacement costs associated with establishing a comparable recreation site plus the opportunity cost of withdrawing the new site from its former management objective plus the depreciated costs of any capital improvements on the old site (Clawson and Knetsch 1967). However, recreation areas are practically never identical on a substitution basis and opening a new area

Figure 2.5. Fire can damage recreation sites. Fire overrunning ski lift in Colorado. Photo by U.S. Forest Service.

may attract a totally different clientele than that which utilized the destroyed site.

Since every fire will modify the vegetative habitat it follows that every fire will prove relatively beneficial to some species of organisms and detrimental to others. Economics, however, is concerned solely with human satisfactions, so assessment of the economic effect of fire on wildlife rests solely on which species of wildlife are desired by management. Wherever particular wildlife species are sufficiently important to be considered in management planning, sufficient biological expertise should be available to assess the immediate and long-range effects of a particular fire on the habitat of that species. When the effects are beneficial they can be valued as the cost of a prescribed burn on the same area. When the effects are detrimental they can be evaluated as the sum of rehabilitation costs and user costs foregone during rehabilitation.

A watershed does not produce water, but it does serve to modify the amount, timing, rate, and quality of water falling upon it and released from it. The economic effects of fire on a watershed depend in large measure on how the water is stored, handled, and used off-site. Removal of vegetation will normally result in an increase in total annual runoff because of decreased transpiration. In arid country where movement is largely underground or in intermittent streams fire provides a benefit. Where water moves in year-long water courses, the value of the additional water is often offset by a reduction in water quality. When reservoirs are used for storage to even out seasonal flows, the value of the increased amount of water following fire is usually outbalanced by the cost of increased siltation. Hydrologists can predict the flood and erosion damages that can be expected to follow fire during a normal hydrologic year (Buck et al. 1948). However, these damages depend almost entirely on the extent and frequency of storm systems in the first few years following the fire and it is greatly preferable to wait and calculate these effects as they occur. Rehabilitation, added maintenance, and discounted replacement costs for destroyed or damaged improvements are usually readily obtainable. In evaluating the effects of fire on watersheds, rehabilitation measures such as grass seeding and removing debris from stream channels only serve to reduce subsequent flood and erosion damages. Watershed rehabilitation is not watershed replacement and adding rehabilitation costs plus subsequent or expected damages is not double counting as claimed by some economists (Gorte and Gorte 1979). The cost of new construction such as water filtration plants or debris dams is only chargeable to the fire to the extent that it ameliorates fire-caused changes.

Loss of life in forest fires is not an everyday occurrence, but neither is it so rare as to be negligible. In both Spain and the United States forest fires are the direct cause of nearly five deaths per year (NWCG 1980, Velez 1981). There is no single accepted method for establishing the value of a human life. In a survey of life valuation methods in the United States, the Coast Guard found a range of mean values from $97,000 to $5,000,000 (Cornell et al. 1976) with an average of about $200,000 which is comparable to the 50,000 pound sterling average for United Kingdom subjects advocated by Melinek (1972). In view of the wide discrepancies between various methodologies, average values would appear adequate and case-by-case analysis unjustified.

Smoke from forest fires can range from a nuisance to a very significant cause of economic loss depending on the lifting, dilution rate, and trajectory of the plume. Effects should be considered individually and may include costs of highway accidents due to decreased visibility, closures of airports and costs of rerouting air traffic, closures or slowdown of manufacturing operations by air quality regulations, and costs plus damage of other fires undetected because of reduced visibility.

Streeby (op. cit.) distinguishes scenic from recreation values and hypothesizes that the scenic values can be related to the intrinsic aesthetic quality of the view, the number of people who will see it, and the conditions under which it will be seen. With respect to fire damage the important factors are proportion of vista burned (fire size), the distance between the burn and all logical observation points, whether observations will be made while stationary (summer homes, campgrounds, parking turnouts, etc.) or moving in automobiles or railroads. The only method of damage assessment suggested is the residual depreciation in property values, if any, after proper accounting for losses in real property, recreation, and watershed value. This damage measure is the same as that proposed by Crosby (op. cit.) to measure "habitability" damage, though Crosby includes other criteria besides scenic values in his definition of habitability.

Indirect costs, defined as the total monetary costs to society other than damage to property, can be quite high in residential fires. Examples of indirect costs are costs of obtaining temporary shelter, costs due to work missed, legal fees associated with fire and recovery, and extra transportation costs. In a study for the U.S. Fire Administration, Munson and Ohls (1980) find that the average indirect costs were $3275 for fires causing injury or death, $1185 for fires with no injuries but with damage to improvements exceeding $1000, and $80 for fires where damage to improvements was less than $1000. There was no simple relationship between direct and indirect loss since indirect losses were step functions depending on whether the residence had to be evacuated and for how long. No comparable studies have been conducted on indirect costs of forest fires but the figures should be directly applicable when forest residences are involved.

VALUES PROTECTED: VALUES AT RISK

Because forest fire effects depend so heavily on fire size, fire intensity, and subsequent weather events, fire damage cannot be assessed accurately until after the event—in some instances not until several years after the event. Since budget formulation and other planning activities must take place before the fire season, some means must be available to predict fire damages before they occur. Historically, most forest fire protection agencies have used predictions of the area that would be expected to burn under various alternatives as a direct equivalent of damage. For reasons already explained, hectarage burned is a very imprecise substitute for economic benefit or damage. Another method of rating the intensity of protection is common in the urban fire services and has potential applicability to forest fire agencies as well. This method consists of appraising the values being protected from fire or other hazard, the degree of risk involved, and the cost of protection. The cost per unit of value protected is then compared with the costs or returns for other investments of equal risk to determine whether additional protection is desirable.

Logically, the values being protected from fire should include only those values that are, in fact, at risk should a fire occur. For urban fire departments, gross fire insurance coverage is an acceptable measure since insurance is readily available and accurately represents the sum that property owners themselves believe to be at risk. In forests, determining values at risk is not so simple since fire insurance is less readily available and many of the resources are publicly rather than privately managed. For each resource, a determination must be made of what proportion of the total value is at risk. In practical terms this means what would be the maximum damage a resource could sustain from the largest, most intense fire that could occur on the area. As always, the assessment must be done very carefully bearing in mind the present and projected use of the area. For example, one might presume that mineral values are clearly not values at risk since the minerals are unaffected by fire. However, this presumption is belied by the nearly universal practice of removing vegetative cover, by fire whenever practical, before beginning mining operations. Immediately prior to mining, fire has a beneficial effect on mineral values.

Because proper valuation is a prerequisite to any valid assessment of damages, all the references previously cited in the damage assessment section are equally applicable to determination of values at risk. In addition, general procedures for determining forest values in relation to fire protection have been developed for national (U.S. Forest Service 1973) and state (Ala. For. Comm. n.d.) use. Both references follow the general discounting and capitalization methods outlined earlier but contain tables of timber volumes, average selling prices, and activity indices that serve to simplify computation and put all users on a common database.

Once the protected values have been determined, the risk can be assessed by analyzing past trends on number of fires and area burned, and projecting the probable effect of various management alternatives. Ideally, the data should be stratified by fire size and intensity (Gibson et al. 1976) but an assumption that the majority of fires are small and of low intensity, whereas the majority of the hectarage is burned by large, high-intensity fires will not invalidate the analysis since in almost all countries that have sufficient fire protection forces to warrant an economic analysis fewer than 10 percent of the fires burn more than 90 percent of the hectares, and these fires are almost invariably of higher than average intensity for the area concerned (Figure 2.6). Present and projected fire costs, risks, and values protected can then be compared with the costs, risks, and values of other forestry operations such as planting or disease control, or with other social undertakings such as police protection or flood prevention.

EFFICIENT FIRE MANAGEMENT: OPTIMIZING THE FIXED BUDGET

Only rarely is the average fire manager called upon to develop an optimum budget for the total organization, but nearly every day all managers face decisions on how to spend the budgets they have. Whether to build a new fire station or expand the existing one; deciding on the ratio of full-time to seasonal personnel; choosing between buying a bulldozer or contracting an air tanker—these are the kinds of economic decisions that face the fire manager, and the quality of those decisions determines the economic efficiency of the fire management organization.

One principal that the fire manager must never forget is that the purpose of the fire organization and the fire budget is to minimize the damage from fire to the parent organization. All other goals are subsidiary to minimizing

Figure 2.6. More than 20 years after the fire, this Oregon forest is still nonproductive. Photo by U.S. Forest Service.

damage once the budget has been fixed, and minimum damage is the anvil on which all fire resource allocation decisions can be tested. It is all too easy to succumb to pressures to reduce the number of fires, reduce travel costs, hold down overtime, or undertake similar measures that are unrelated or only weakly related to damage reduction.

To illustrate: in the United States in 1977, 158,850 wildfires burned over 1,173,000 hectares. The average (mean) fire size was 7.4 hectares. If we array these fires by size, from smallest to largest, the average (median) fire was a 1.5 hectare spring burn in a 50-year-old Georgia pine stand with a total estimated damage of $750. The average (median) hectare burned over was near the middle of a 246 hectare fall crown fire in an 25-year-old Alabama plantation of *Pinus taeda* that caused $272,000 in direct damage plus an estimated $91,000 cost to replant. Only 126 fires that year were larger than the one on which the median hectare burned. Clearly, management decisions that treat all fires alike or are based merely on gross statistical data will be economically inefficient.

Allocation systems that operate within a given fire management function such as detection, prevention, or fuels management are discussed in context with those subjects. Allocation between functions is equally important but, until very recently, decisions on proportional allocations among functions have been largely intuitive. With the advent of high-speed computers it has become possible to test the effects of several different mixes through simulation modeling (Bratten et al. 1981). Programs can be tested against historical weather and fire occurrence data for easy and bad fire years and a "best" mix selected from among those tested. It should be noted that simulation gaming is not an optimizing process—it merely allows selecting the best of the alternatives presented. The results of simulation models are also critically dependent on the assumptions selected when designing the rules of the game.

BIBLIOGRAPHY

Alabama For. Comm. n.d. *Assessment of values at risk relating to fire protection in Alabama.* Unnumbered, 45 pp.

Arnold, R. K. 1949. *Economic and social determinants of an adequate level of forest fire control.* Ph.D. diss., Univ. Mich., Ann Arbor, 205 pp.

Bakker, Pieter. 1975. *Economic aspects of forest fires: The Entiat case.* M.S. thesis, Univ. of Wash., Seattle, 113 pp.

Bratten, F. W. and others. 1981. *FOCUS—a fire management planning system—final report.* U.S. For. Serv. Gen. Tech. Report PSW-49, 34 pp.

Buck, C. C., W. L. Fons, and C. M. Countryman. 1948. *Fire damage from increased run off and erosion: Cleveland National Forest.* U.S. For. Serv. Unnumbered Report 63 pp.

Clawson, M. 1959. *Methods of measuring the demand for and value of outdoor recreation.* Resources for the Future, Reprint No. 10, 37 pp.

Clawson, M. and J. Knetsch. 1967. *Economics of outdoor recreation,* Johns Hopkins Press, 327 pp.

Cornell, M., P. Daniels, J. Kirkland, and A. Wolff. 1976. *A survey of methods of estimating the costs of human life.* U.S. Coast Guard Report. No. CG-D-66-76, 63 pp.

Craig, R. B., B. Frank, G. L. Hayes, and G. M. Jemison. 1945. *Fire losses and justifiable protection costs in the southern Piedmont of Virginia.* U.S. For. Serv. Appalachian For. Exp. Sta., 27 pp., processed.

Craig, R. B., B. Frank, G. L. Hayes, and T. F. Marburg. 1946a. *Fire losses and justifiable protection costs in the southwestern coal section of Virginia.* U.S. For. Serv., SE For. Exp. Sta., 45 pp., processed.

Craig, R. B., T. F. Marburg, and G. L. Hayes. 1946b. *Fire losses and justifiable protection costs in the coastal region of South Carolina.* U.S. For. Serv., SE For. Exp. Sta., 46 pp., processed.

Crosby, J. S. 1977. *A guide to the appraisal of wildfire damages, benefits, and resource values protected.* U.S. For. Serv. Res. Paper NC-142, 43 pp.

Gale, R. D. 1977. *Evaluation of fire management activities on the National Forests.* U.S. For. Service Policy Anal. Staff Report, 127 pp.

Gibson, H. P., L. F. Hodgin, and J. L. Rich. 1976. *Evaluating National Forest planning methods and measuring effectiveness of presuppression expenditures.* U.S. For. Serv., 57 pp., processed.

Gorte, J. K. and R. W. Gorte. 1979. *Application of economic techniques to fire management—a status review and evaluation.* U.S. For. Serv. Gen. Tech. Report INT-53, 26 pp.

Luke, R. H. and A. G. McArthur. 1979. *Bushfires in Australia.* Aust. Gvt. Pub. Svc., 359 pp., illus.

Mactavish, J. S. 1965. *Economics and forest fire control.* Dept. For. Can. Pub. 1114, 24 pp.

Mactavish, J. S. 1966. *Appraising fire damage to mature forest stands*. Can. Dept. of For. Rural Dev., For. Branch Dept. Pub. No. 1162, 31 pp.

Melinek, S. J. 1972. *A method of evaluating human life for economic purposes*. J. F. R. O. Fire Res. Note No. 950, 16 pp.

Munson, M. J. and J. C. Ohls. 1980. *Indirect costs of residential fires*. U.S. Fire Adm. Pub. FA-6, 30 pp.

NWCG. 1980. *Study of fatal/near fatal wildland fire accidents*. National Wildfire Coordinating Group, Washington, D.C. Unnumbered Report, 76 pp.

Nautiyal, J. C. and G. E. Doan. 1974. Economics of forest fire control: trading planned cut for protection expenditure. *Can. J. For. Res.* 4:82–89.

Noste, N. V. and J. B. Davis. 1975. A critical look at fire damage appraisal. *J. For.* 73(11):715–719.

Simard, A. J. 1976. *Wildland fire management: The economics of policy alternatives*. Can. For. Ser. Tech. Report 15, 52 pp.

Sparhawk, W. N. 1925. The use of liability ratings in planning forest fire protection. *J. Agric. Res.* 30(8):693–762.

Streeby, L. L. 1970. *Foundations of an improved fire damage appraisal system*. Univ. Wisc., Dept. For. Unnumbered Report, 118 pp.

Tsymek, A. A. 1966. Main principles of forest economic zoning. In: *Forestry and Industrial Utilization of Wood in the USSR*. Lesnaya Promyshlennost Publishing House, Moscow, 611 pp.

U.S. Forest Service. 1973. *A model for the determination of wildland resource values*. USGPO:1973–728–553/691, 39 pp., illus.

Van Wagner, C. E. 1979. The economic impact of individual fires on the whole forest. *For. Chron.* 55(4):137–139.

Van Wagner, C. E. 1982. *Forest fire and the annual allowable cut*. Dept. Environ. Can. For. Serv., Chalk River, Ont. Unnumbered Report.

Velez, R. 1981. *Forest fires in the Mediterranean area*. FAO Report GE 81–40240, 15 pp.

Vogenberger, R. A., E. F. Olson, and B. H. Carpening. 1957. *A method for determining public fire control expenditures for private lands*. N.C. Dept. of Cons. and Dev., TVA, Unnumbered Report, 22 pp.

CHAPTER THREE

Fire Prevention

The only fire which never disrupts the community, never incurs any costs, and never causes any damages is the fire that never starts. This truism of the fire services is perfectly valid, but difficult to accomplish. Successful fire prevention depends on utilizing "the three E's"—Education, Enforcement, and Engineering—in logical, well-planned combinations designed to counteract those fires that cause the most damage within the protection area, and not merely those that result from the most obvious or prevalent causes.

EDUCATION

In order for a protection agency to obtain the funds to conduct a fire prevention campaign, to have laws enacted prohibiting indiscriminate forest burning, or to gain the assistance of forest residents and visitors in maintaining fire safety, the general public must be conditioned to view forest fires as a serious threat to the national welfare. With populations throughout the world becoming increasingly urbanized, forest fires seldom pose an immediate danger to the life or property of the average citizen. Yet a strongly favorable public opinion is a vital necessity in any effort to reduce the number of human-caused fires. This can best be achieved by utilizing the talents of advertising experts through the mass media outlets of radio, television, newspapers, and magazines.

Undoubtedly, the most successful attempt to influence public opinion regarding forest fires has been the creation and manipulation of the Smokey Bear forest fire prevention symbol in the United States (Morrison 1976). Smokey was "born" in 1945 as a poster character produced by the Wartime Advertising Council in an effort to reduce the number of forest fires at a time when most experienced firefighters and other able-bodied men were serving in the armed forces. At the end of the war the Advertising Council was retained as a volunteer agency to sponsor public service advertising campaigns. The forest fire prevention campaign maintained a prominent position in this effort and Smokey Bear with his trooper's hat and cowboy jeans became a prominent figure on the billboards and buses of postwar America. It was a chance event in the spring of 1950 that catapulted Smokey Bear onto the front pages and indelibly into the public memory. Following a fire in the Lincoln National Forest, a warden from the New Mexico Department of Game and Fish found a black bear cub with burned paws clinging to a tree in the burned area. After seeing the results of a bandaging session at the local veterinary hospital, New Mexico state officials decided that the cub's story and picture would make good copy for a fire prevention message. They succeeded beyond their expectations. The story was picked up by the national wire services and people all over the United States began sending cards and messages. The identification of the live bear with the poster bear was a natural one and before long the new living Smokey was flown to Washington, D.C. and presented with suitable ceremony by the senior Senator from New Mexico to the Director of the National Zoo as a gift to the school children of America. This symbiotic relationship between the live animal and the cartoon character is unique in American history (there has never been a living Mickey Mouse or Donald Duck). Within two years the number of Smokey Bear promotional materials had grown to such proportions that the United States Congress enacted Public Law 359-82nd Congress "an act prohibiting the manufacture or use of the character 'Smokey Bear' by unauthorized person." Under this act, the Chief of the Forest Service, through the Secretary of Agriculture was given the sole authority to license the use of the Smokey Bear name or image and stipulated that any use of Smokey Bear must be for the primary purpose of preventing forest fires. This prerogative has been guarded very zealously ever since, and is the principal reason why Smokey Bear's message has remained simple, direct, and essentially unchanged for nearly 40 years. As a result, the slogans "carelessness causes 9 out of 10 forest fires" and "only *you* can prevent forest fires," though not strictly factual, are universally known and widely remembered by all segments of the U.S. population. In 1968, over 90 percent of all persons shown a picture of Smokey Bear could correctly name him and associate him with forest fire prevention (Haugh Associates 1968). Ten years later the Advertising Council could claim that "The number of forest fire has been cut in half since the Smokey campaign started and $17\frac{1}{2}$ billion dollars of natural resources have been saved even though ten times more people are visiting the forests now than did when the campaign began" (The Advetising Council 1979).

The success of Smokey Bear launched a veritable explosion of fire prevention animals (Figure 3.1). Australia has a koala, Spain a rabbit, France a hedgehog, Chile a coypu, Russia a moose, Alberta a beaver, Quebec a chipmunk (Garofeu), Mozambique an antelope, Turkey a stag, and Mexico its own bear named Simone. Even the forest fire research community has

Figure 3.1. In most countries of the world, forest fire prevention is represented by an animal. Fidel the rabbit protects the forests of Spain. Photo by ICONA.

adopted its own symbol "Smokye Mouse, Living Symbol of Forest Fire Research" whose slogan has been translated in 17 languages (Chandler 1977).

One of the major activities of the Fire Management Study Group of the North American Forestry Commission, FAO, is the exchange of information between Mexico, the United States, and Canada on wildfire prevention activities and the promotion of joint fire prevention projects. One such project involved the design, testing, and acceptance of eight international fire prevention sign symbols with wording in English, Spanish, and French (Figure 3.2). The intention is that, after a period of familiarization, the signs will be used without words and thus will become truly international. The Group also promotes fire prevention posters and film festivals at meetings of the North American Forestry Commission as well as assigning one committee at each

Figure 3.2.   Eight international fire prevention sign symbols.

of the Group's meetings to study, discuss, and recommend action on wildfire prevention problems of the three member countries.

Although favorable public opinion is an absolute prerequisite for a successful forest fire prevention program, an enlightened public alone is not enough. The prevention planner needs to know who is starting fires within his or her area of protection responsibility, where they are starting, when they are starting, and to the extent possible, why they are starting. Only then can one hope to prepare a course of action that can be expected to significantly reduce the number of fires at a reasonable expenditure of prevention effort. In order to obtain the statistical base needed for a comprehensive fire prevention analysis, certain activities must receive continuous attention. First, there must be a conscientious effort to determine the exact cause of every fire on which the agency takes action. It is not possible to do a reasonable job of analysis if an appreciable percentage of fires are listed as being of "unknown" origin. The proper techniques of fire cause investigation are discussed in a later section. Secondly, a standard fire reporting system must be developed and used without modifications for a sufficiently long period (at least three to five years) to obtain statistically reliable data. It is preferable to work with a less than perfect system than to attempt to change definitions of terms, or revise classifications at frequent intervals. In the United States, most fire agencies insist that fire reporting systems be modified only once a decade.

For the 1980s, fire agencies in the United States have agreed to adopt a reporting system similar to that of the National Fire Protection Association (1981). This system requires that 24 mandatory items be reported for each forest fire incident. In addition, 18 additional items are listed as desirable and recommended for inclusion by all forest fire protection agencies.

The mandatory items are as follows:

Identification of Fire:

1. *Agency Name.*
2. *Fire Number.*

Location of Fire:

3. *State.*
4. *County.*
5. *Latitude and longitude to nearest $\frac{1}{10}$ minutes.* (If this is not feasible, then delineation by township, range, and section to nearest $\frac{1}{16}$ of a section.)
6. *Class of Ownership at Point of Origin.*
   a. Private.
   b. Federal.
   c. Other public (additional breakdown of this category can be made according to agency needs).

Causal Factors:

7. *Equipment Involved in Ignition.* The equipment that provided the heat that started the fire, for example, vehicle, incinerator, transformer.
8. *Form of Heat of Ignition.* The form of the heat energy igniting the fire, e.g., flame, spark, hot surface.
9. *Type of Material First Ignited.* The type of material that was first ignited, e.g., wood, paper, hay.
10. *Ignition Factor.* The factor that allowed the heat of ignition and material first ignited to combine, e.g., misuse, mechanical failure, natural conditions.

Demographic Factors:

11. *Age of Person Responsible for Fire Start.*
12. *Sex of Person Responsible for Fire Start.*
13. *Category of Person Responsible for Fire Start.*
    a. Visitor.
    b. Seasonal.
    c. Permanent resident.
14. *Activity Involved.*
    a. Occupation related, e.g., farming, logging, trucking, etc.
    b. Recreational related, e.g., hunting, hiking, camping, etc.
    c. Residential related, e.g., debris burning.
    d. Incendiary.
    e. Other activities.
15. *Date/Time of Ignition.* Estimated or known.
16. *Date/Time Fire Reported.* That time when fire is reported to the fire agency responsible for suppression action.
17. *Date/Time of First Attack.* That time when suppression action begins by an individual or agency.
18. *Acres Burned by Land Classification.*
    a. *Nonforest Land.* Land that has never supported forest, or lands not now supporting forests and that are not being managed for commercial forest crops, or land that has been developed for nonforest use.
    b. *Forest Land, Commercial.* Land producing, or capable of producing, wood products such as saw timber, posts, poles, etc., and not withdrawn from timber use.
    c. *Forest Land, Noncommercial.* Land not capable of yielding wood products or not valued for commercial forest products or commercial forest land which has been withdrawn from timber use.
19. *Acres Burned by Class of Ownership.*
    a. Private.
    b. Federal.
    c. Other public (Additional breakdown of this category can be made according to agency needs.)
20. *Fuel Type of General Fire Area.* Appropriate fuel model from the 1978 National Fire Danger Rating System.
21. *Suppression Costs.* The total direct cost of all suppression action, including mutual aid and cooperator assistance, attributed to the fire.

22. *Damage*. The best tangible damage figures available, within the limits of current technology to quantify actual damage and the ability of the agency to utilize such technology.
23. *Agency with Statistical Fire Reporting Responsibility.*
24. *Name of Person Preparing Report.*

The desirable items are:

1. *Landowner's Name.*
2. *Day of Week of Ignition.* For agencies not having computer capability for conversion from date.
3. *Method of Detection.*
   Air Patrol
   Ground Patrol
   Tower
   Local Resident
   Transient
   Other Aircraft
   Other
4. *Size Class*
   A—0.1 hectares or less (0.25 acres)
   B—0.1 to 3.5 hectares (0.26 to 9 acres)
   C—3.6 to 40 hectares (10 to 99 acres)
   D—41 to 120 hectares (100 to 200 acres)
   E—121 to 400 hectares (300 to 999 acres)
   F—401 to 2000 hectares (1,000 to 4999 acres)
   G—over 2000 hectares (5000 acres and over)
5. *Size of Fire at First Attack.* Hectares (acres).
6. *Slope Class at Point of Origin.*
   0–25%
   26–40%
   41–55%
   56–75%
   76+
7. *Aspect at Point of Origin.* Eight cardinal directions.
8. *Elevation at Point of Origin.* In 150m (500 ft) increments.
9. *Topographic Features at Point of Origin.*
   Ridge Top
   Upper $\frac{1}{3}$ of Slope

Mid ⅓ of Slope
Lower ⅓ of Slope
Valley Bottom
Rolling or Flat

10. *Method of Initial Attack.*
    Ground Crew with Handtools
    Ground Tanker or Pumper
    Plows or Trenchers
    Dozers
    Smokejumpers
    Helicopter with Handtool Crew
    Helicopter Tanker
    Airplane Tanker
    Other (specify). Use "other" category if initial attack was by pass-
    ersby or people other than regular suppression personnel.

11. *Fire Behavior at Initial Attack.*
    a. *Smoldering.* A fire burning slowly through direct oxidation, in
       leaf mold, duff, peat, etc., in which there is little or no visible
       flame and little or no visible smoke, but some spread and
       definite heat output.
    b. *Creeping/Spreading.* A fire burning in fuel, such as leaf mold,
       litter, or light grass, with both visible flame and smoke.
    c. *Running.* A fire with significant output of heat such that direct
       attack might be impossible. Flame length could be expected to
       be in excess of 1.5 meters (5 ft).
    d. *Running and Spotting.* Fire behavior similar to running but
       burning embers and firebrands are carried aloft and new igni-
       tions started.
    e. *Torching.* A fire in which the crowns or canopies of individual or
       groups of trees ignite; however, the fire does not continue into
       the canopy of surrounding vegetation.
    f. *Crowning.* The fire tends to move through the overstory or
       canopy generally keeping pace with or perhaps even preceding
       the surface fire.
    g. *Crowning and Spotting.* The same as crowning with firebrands
       carried aloft starting fires some distance ahead.
    h. *Erratic Behavior.* Involves fire whirls, fire storms, blowup con-
       ditions, or other fire behavior in which the fire's rate and direc-
       tion of spread is largely unpredictable.

12. *Rate of Spread at Initial Attack.* Measured or estimated in meters
    per minute (feet per minute).

13. *Date/Time Fire Controlled.* That point in time that comprises completion of control lines around a fire, any spot fire therefrom, and any interior islands to be saved; burning out any unburned area adjacent to the fire side of the control lines; and cooling down all hot spots that constitute immediate threats to the control lines until these can reasonably be expected to hold under foreseeable conditions.

14. *Map of Fire Area.*

15. *Degree of Certainty of Form of Heat of Ignition.*
    a. *Certain.* Form of heat of ignition is established by admission, statement of reliable witness, or physical evidence. This category is intended to cover cases where form of heat of ignition is established beyond doubt.
    b. *Reasonably Certain.* Form of heat of ignition is established by strong circumstantial evidence. This category covers cases where form of heat of ignition is reasonably certain, but witness statements or physical evidence present may not be conclusive.
    c. *Most Probable.* Form of heat of ignition is established by weak circumstantial evidence, by process of elimination between two or more possible forms of heat ignition, or by fire history of the area and experienced judgment of the investigator.
    d. *Undetermined.* No definite clues, or could have started from any one of several probable forms of heat of ignition, or fire not investigated.

16. *Restrictions in Effect for the Activity Involved.* Requires a yes or no answer.

17. *Name of Person Approving Report.*

18. *Nearest Fire-Danger Rating Station.*

Armed with a few years of factual data, the analyst can pinpoint the major sources of damaging fires, their times and patterns of occurrence, and their trends over time (Nickey 1980). Special prevention programs can then be designed to reduce particular risks. Several such programs have been reported and all have been markedly successful.

One of the earliest fire prevention efforts aimed at a particular group of forest users was undertaken between 1925 and 1928 in six townships in Massachusetts (Massachusetts Forestry Association 1928). Previous analyses had shown that the forest fire problem in the area was primarily caused by two groups: tourists and summer residents who flocked to the area for summer vacations increasing the 15,000 permanent population to more than 100,000, and non-English speaking residents who burned the forest to increase the blueberry crop. A forester and two special wardens from the local area were hired to undertake special educational campaigns in the winter and forest patrols contacting forest visitors during the fire season. At the end of the three years the results were impressive. Average hectarage burned was reduced from 11,500 hectares to 2,400 hectares and the total costs for prevention and suppression were 20 percent less than the costs for suppression alone in the three years prior to the experiment. However, the number of fires *increased* from 219 to 249.

The Cape Cod experiment is a particularly interesting example because it incorporated virtually all of the techniques that have proven to be successful in later fire prevention campaigns, and because its results were similar to most of its successors. The positive aspects of the Cape Cod experiment included: (1) a careful analysis to identify the "problem publics"; (2) heavy reliance on local citizens recognized as peers by the "problem publics" to conduct the educational efforts; (3) insistence on personal face-to-face contact as the cornerstone of the educational program; (4) an emphasis on propagandizing children through schools, scouts, summer camps, and other organized activities.

The results also typified those of later campaigns: (1) a significant reduction in protection costs and hectarage burned, (2) an increase in the number of human-caused fires, and (3) an end to the effort after a relatively short period despite a convincing record of success. The second result, an increase in the number of fires in the face of an increased prevention effort, is less paradoxical than it seems. During an intensive fire prevention campaign, the number of fires reported, both by the newly aroused public and by the added prevention patrolmen, increases. Small fires that would previously have been extinguished without fanfare become statistics. As a result, the number of fires goes up, the hectarage burned goes down and the average fire size drops dramatically. What is more difficult to understand is the third result, the speedy demise of a demonstrably successful program. William Folkman, in a little-referenced but remarkably perceptive article draws an analogy between forest fires and accidents and advances two theories to explain why fire prevention receives less attention than it seemingly deserves (Folkman 1965).

Folkman's first point is that forest fires, other than those caused by incendiarism or lightning, *are* accidents. That is, they are the result of inadvertent or negligent human acts. Accident research has shown that accidents are perceived by the general public as unpredictable acts of God that "just happen." To most people accidents, including forest fires, are the result of mysterious runs of luck that defy systematic study and are immune to human intervention. Without constant reinforcement, people will lapse from good fire safety habits because the connection between cause and effect is simply not perceived.

Folkman's second proposition is more disturbing to the fire management community. He postulates that firefighters enter the profession to foster or enhance a masculine image of courage and daring where firefighting provides the "moral equivalent of war" and where the experience of "trial by fire" fulfills a deep psychological need. To this type of personality, prevention activities rate on a par with the noncombatant work undertaken by conscientious objectors in time of war. Although this thesis is denied vigorously by many fire management professionals, at least two studies have shown that success in fire prevention is considered unimportant as a basis for advancement in the organization both by fire management administrators and by fire prevention personnel themselves (Anonymous 1975, Christiansen, et al. 1976).

Even though specialized fire prevention campaigns tend to be ephemeral, they are of proven value and much has been learned about tailoring a campaign toward specific groups.

Children playing with fire represent a serious risk in most forested countries of the world. Juvenile firesetters are virtually always (over 90 percent) boys, and their ages are younger than is popularly assumed (Block and Block 1975). Young adolescents (11 to 15 years old) set between 25 and 35 percent of the children-caused fires studied by psychologists in the United States; 12 percent were set by preschoolers (under 5 years old), while over half were started by young school children with the peak ages for fire starting being around 8 or 9 years (Vreeland and Waller 1978). The adolescents tend to set their fires away from home, chiefly for excitement, and usually while playing in pairs or groups. Nearly two-thirds of the adolescents interviewed admitted to setting more than one fire, and most had started playing with fire at an early age. In contrast, the younger children usually set their fires out of curiosity while playing alone near home.

On the basis of these and similar findings, the State of California reoriented its public school fire safety program, which had been geared to grade five (11–12 year olds), and introduced special fire safety courses in kindergarten and grades one and two (Ryan et al. 1978). In addition, prevention materials were designed for use in nursery school or other preschool group situations (Folkman and Taylor 1972). The results were almost immediately evident in a reduced number of fires set by younger children, and within 10 years the entire "children with matches" category had been reduced significantly indicating that the fire safety attitude had persisted through the school years.

In Spain the problem of children-caused fires is addressed indirectly but apparently very effectively by developing an appreciation for the value of forests (Rico Rico 1977). Forestry clubs are encouraged and each pupil is given an opportunity to plant trees personally so that by assisting in the birth of his or her tree, giving it initial care, and observing its development, the child grows attached to this new living thing and, consequently, to the forest. Similar campaigns to link forest conservation and fire prevention are common in southern France and elsewhere in Mediterranean Europe.

Hunters, like children, pose an unusually high fire risk for forests. Successful hunters must spend much of their time in the woods alone, far from traffic, and often in remote inaccessible places (Figure 3.3). By necessity,

Figure 3.3. Hunters pose an unusually high fire risk because they are often in the forest alone and in locations difficult of access. Photo by U.S. Forest Service.

hunters rarely camp in the larger improved campgrounds and the degree of fire safety of their camps depends entirely on what they themselves supply. The hunter who smokes is often distracted by game or visions of game and proper disposal of smoking materials can be overlooked while the chase is hot. Consequently, hunter fires tend to be slow to be discovered, difficult to access, and often large and damaging. Surveys of hunter knowledge and attitudes towards forest fires have found them to be highly knowledgeable and positively motivated towards camp and smoker fire practices, although a much higher proportion of hunters perceive fire as benefiting wildlife habitat than is true for the general population (Folkman 1963). Successful prevention campaigns designed to reach hunters avoid oversimplified "ABC" approaches and attempt to present detailed "how to do it" information geared to the local area. Written materials are best distributed at the point of sale such as sporting goods stores and hunting license distributors. Well-trained prevention patrolmen who can talk intelligently about hunting as well as fire can also be markedly effectively in reducing hunter-caused fires.

To a greater extent than most fire managers care to admit, forest fires, like charity, begin at home—from the ignorance, carelessness, or malice of the local population. One study by the State of Maine, which prides itself on being "America's Vacationland" entertaining several million out-of-state visitors each year, showed that state residents caused 97 percent of Maine's forest fires and 85 percent were caused by residents of the same township as the fire (Banks and Holt 1966). Most of the "in-depth" studies of the attitudes and practices of local residents toward forest fire protection have been conducted in the southern United States and have been psychologically or sociologically oriented, beginning with the pioneer work of psychologist John Shea in the 1930s (Shea 1939) and culminating with the studies of various sociologists in the 1970s (Bertrand and Baird 1975). Some of the conclusions from this work which spans a 40-year period are probably applicable only to the particular culture of the rural southern United States. Some of their conclusions, however, appear to have widespread, if not universal, applicability.

1.   No forest fire prevention campaign can be successful without general support from the local community. This is the basic theme of the Smokey Bear campaign on the national level, but it holds true on the local level as well. If a community is complacent about fire setting, forest fires will be set. Instilling a general concern about fire within a rural community requires the cooperation of local press and radio managers and the active support of community leaders.

2.   Face-to-face communication is the most effective way to change attitudes toward forest fire safety. Favorable attitudes can be reinforced by mass media and advertising displays, but these techniques do little to influence people with initially unfavorable attitudes. Direct contact with a respected person can change attitudes (Burns and Doolittle 1973).

3.   The best prevention communicators are local residents. The key to changing attitudes by face-to-face communication is that the communicator be respected by the recipient of the message. Unlike sophisticated city audiences where an expert is defined as anyone more than 500 kilometers from home, rural people often have an innate distrust of outsiders. The most respected members of the community are usually older men with an educational and socio-economic background approximately average for the community involved (Doolittle and Welch 1974).

Another serious source of forest fires, and one even closer to the forest manager than local residents, is the forestry operation itself. Woods workers have the highest motivation to prevent forest fires—their very livelihood is at stake—but they can be just as careless as the rest of the human population. Clear rules and training programs to ensure their understanding and acceptance are necessary in order to minimize the common causes of fires during forestry operations.

Smoking should be forbidden or confined to cleared locations under continuous surveillance.

Warming and cooking fires should be built according to prescribed standards and never left unattended.

Chain saws and other portable equipment should be maintained to specified standards. Refueling should be performed at a central location or fire extinguishing equipment should be carried by the operator.

Landings and loading points should be kept free of debris.

Debris from road construction should be disposed of as the road is built and not allowed to accumulate on roadsides.

Off-road vehicles should be strictly maintained and inspected daily before beginning operation.

Operations should be curtailed or halted during periods of extreme fire danger.

FIRE LAW ENFORCEMENT

Law enforcement is a potentially valuable technique for forest fire prevention since an adequate body of fire laws, properly publicized and impartially administered can serve to educate the public on specific fire safety measures as well as deter the negligent or malicious from destructive behavior. Forest officials in state or federal service usually have some specific law enforcement responsibilities, but even private forest managers must be familiar with the principles of fire investigation and legal procedures in order to properly protect the property in their charge.

Originally, the protection of life and property was considered to be an individual rather than a governmental responsibility. As people began to cluster together in towns and cities, local ordinances were enacted to ensure community survival. Not until the midnineteenth century did national governments begin to assume a responsibility for and authority over fire safety legislation. Even today, fire regulations are primarily left to the most local jurisdiction feasible. In the United States, laws affecting fire safety represent an exercise of the powers reserved to the states under the Tenth Amendment to the United States Constitution. Federal regulations governing fire safety are confined to matters affecting federal land or property and do not apply outside of the federal jurisdiction. State laws governing such forest fire prevention measures as woods closures, slash disposal, and outdoor smoking vary widely from state to state and are usually reinforced by individual county or municipal ordinances (U.S. Forest Service 1968).

In contrast to the late arrival and local nature of proscriptive fire safety legislation, individual responsibility for liability for fire-caused damages in English common law dates back to the fifteenth century where "every man is obliged by custom of the realm to keep his fire safe so it shall not injure his neighbor; and to be liable to an action at law, if a fire, lighted in his own house or upon his lands, should burn the house or property of another.'' The hardship of this law was so great that an Act of Parliament in 1648 decreed that no action should be maintained against any person in whose house, stable, barn, or any other building any fire should accidentally begin, and no recompense be made by him for any damage occasioned thereby, unless the spreading of such fire was due to negligence (National Fire Protection Association 1976). This provision that remedy for fire loss requires proof of negligence has been the despair of fire investigators and enriched generations of lawyers over the past 300 years.

In law negligence is the opposite of diligence and signifies the absence of care. It implies a failure of duty but excludes the idea of intentional wrong. Negligence is not absolute or intrinsic but always relative to some circumstance of time, place, or person. The test of negligence is what should be expected of a reasonable person acting with proper regard for others under the same circumstance. If a property owner allows his or her land to become in such a condition as to constitute a danger to other property in case of an accidental fire, the owner may be considered negligent. If an owner is using fire, or equipment that might cause fire on his or her own lands, reasonable care commensurate with this danger and risk that could rationally be anticipated must be used.

The theory of negligence was summed up by the Supreme Court of the United States in 59C197:

> The obligation or duty is devolved by law on all men to use their unimpeached legal rights so as not to injure others. It is beyond the power of the judiciary, or any other tribunal or officer known to our laws, to compel the special performance of this duty, but the courts may indirectly compel it by condemning in damages the erring party and redress the injury done in a particular case by a judgment for damages in money, which can be enforced against the property of the delinquent. No one is responsible for that which is merely the act of God, or inevitable accident. But when human agency is combined with it and neglect occurs in the employment of such agency, a liability for damages results from such neglect.

If a fire loss results from willfulness or intent rather than carelessness, then the concept of negligence does not apply and the case is subject to state or local criminal law. Although intent exists only in the mind of the person committing the act, it can be reasonably deduced from physical evidence and need not be restricted to a confession. For example, if a fire was known to be started by a cigarette, it probably would be judged intentional if it could be proved that the cigarette was tied to a packet of matches in such a way as to ignite the matches after a time delay. If, on the other hand, a discarded cigarette alone was responsible for the fire, the fire probably would be judged accidental, and the only criminal action would be illegal smoking or disposal of smoking materials if state or local laws covered such offenses.

A thorough and competent investigation of every fire is essential to establish liability and preserve evidence that might indicate criminal intent. The ultimate objective of a forest fire investigation is to present to a court of law both the physical evidence and the suspect. The success or failure of this effort often depends on the action taken by the forest manager at the time an offense is brought to the manager's attention. The facts that are obtained and the evidence that is discovered and protected are instrumental in assisting law enforcement authorities to a successful conclusion to the case.

Since it is easiest to establish the cause early in the course of the fire, initial attack crews should be trained in fire-cause investigation even if they have no law enforcement responsibilities. One firefighter should be designated as fire-cause investigator and provided with proper materials and supplies. Most handbooks (National Wildfire Coordinating Group 1978) recommended that an investigation kit include at least:

Flagging to mark and protect the area of wildfire origin.

Straight edge to serve as background to scale photographs of evidence.

Magnet with a pull of at least 25 kilograms.

Camera with black and white film.

Notebook, pencils, and pens for notes.

Graph paper for sketches.

Steel tape for measuring accurate distances.

Compass to ensure proper orientation of sketches.

The investigator should take complete notes beginning at the time the first alarm is received. Because the notes may be used as evidence in court, all words should be spelled out and not abbreviated. Before reaching the fire scene, the investigator should have recorded the date and time of alarm, the name and address of the person reporting the fire, descriptions and locations of all vehicles coming from the direction of the fire, weather and fire behavior, and any fresh vehicle tracks or footprints in the vicinity of the fire.

On arrival at the fire the investigator should immediately attempt to locate and secure the point of origin. Early determination of the fire's origin is vital to preserve any evidence that may be present, to prevent disturbance from firefighters or their equipment, and to be able to swear in court that any evidence discovered originated before firefighters arrived. Usually, the point of origin can be fairly easily located from the fire shape in relation to the prevailing wind and slope. But when the origin is not obvious there are several indications that can be used to point the way. In low winds burned grass stalks will fall with their tops facing the point of origin. Less intense fires will burn more deeply on the side of the fuel that faces the approaching fire. Consequently, the burned area will look lighter when looking away from the point of origin and darker when looking toward the origin. Leaves and small twigs will tend to "freeze" pointing in the direction toward which the fire was spreading. Fence wires will have soot on the side nearest the origin but not on the other.

Once the general area of the fire's origin has been located, it should be flagged and protected from further disturbance. When the area of origin is secure, the investigator should look quickly for clues such as vehicle tracks in the general fire area. This should be done as early as possible before firefighting activities obliterate or confuse potential evidence. After all evidence has been photographed the investigator should return to the area of origin and proceed to make a detailed search for the fire's cause.

Lightning fires are usually easy to determine because of the physical evidence of a recent strike in the area of origin combined with the knowledge of electrical storm activity in the vicinity. Remoteness and improbability of human activity are also indications of lightning as a possible cause.

Many other causes of accidental fires such as broken powerlines, crashed aircraft, and burning buildings or vehicles are readily apparent, but others leave more subtle traces and require careful investigation. Metal fragments collected with a magnet may indicate unsafe cutting or welding operations, or mechanical failure of equipment, clutch parts, or brakeshoes. Vehicle tracks and the position of the fragments relative to road or railroad rights of way will narrow down the possibilities. Vehicle tracks on steep, grass-covered slopes where no metal fragments can be found raise the possibility of an overheated exhaust system. Fireworks, fusees, and flares all leave a characteristic residue.

Distinguishing between accidental smoker-caused fires and incendiary fires can be difficult since both often involve cigarettes and the evidence is often destroyed by the fire. A cigarette by itself will rarely start a fire if the humidity is above 25 percent. Most incendiary devices require binding matches and cigarettes with wire, string, tape, or rubber bands. Careful search can often turn up fragments of these bindings. Candle wax soaked into the soil is a nearly certain indicator of incendiarism.

In addition to securing physical evidence, the investigator should attempt to interview any potential witnesses. Persons who were in the vicinity can often supply important clues or aids to the investigator. Eyewitnesses may have seen the offense committed. They may be able to identify the culprit; they may have observed likely suspects in the area, or have other important information pertinent to the case. Although the investigator may be convinced of the reliability of an eyewitness, every effort must be made to obtain all other evidence available to corroborate or substantiate oral testimony. If a witness states that he or she talked with some other person at about the time of the trespass, the other person should be interviewed to check the accuracy of the statement. In some instances, the witness is also the offender and has fabricated an imaginary conversation for an alibi. Investigators have learned through experience to check on all statements. They are particularly alert to check the accuracy of statements made by (1) the person who discovered the fire, (2) the overly helpful person who takes a leading part at the scene, (3) the person who gives more details than would normally be expected to be noticed or known, and (4) the person who rarely permits his or her eyes to meet those of the investigator.

The most effective place to interview a witness is at the scene of the trespass. The most effective time is as soon as possible after the trespass has been committed. People will more readily and more accurately describe what they have seen, heard, or otherwise know immediately after the act has occurred. Their actions and expressions can be more accurately depended on at this time, before other considerations and influences affect their reasoning. In most all cases, it is desirable that the witness be alone. The interview should be conducted in quiet and comfort.

The degree of success to be gained from an interview depends on the investigator's attitude. The investigator should be short, snappy, and commanding with the bold, patient and considerate with the timid. Unnecessary officiousness, insolence, or contempt will cause most people to be uncommunicative. Courteous and considerate treatment will bring the most success. Never treat a witness like a criminal.

The same investigator should ordinarily handle all main issues of a given case.

In most instances it is advisable to have another officer present to witness the interview, but it should be thoroughly understood that only one officer will conduct it.

There are certain main considerations: (1) to get as complete a statement from the witness as possible—be sure nothing essential is omitted, but do not let the witness ramble aimlessly; (2) to be sure the witness is telling the truth. Statements may be written on an affidavit form or on any paper available at the time. The statement should show where and when it was written. Exact words or expressions used by the witness should be included whenever possible to reflect in his or her own words the thought the witness wishes to convey.

If a witness refuses to make or sign a written statement but will talk, have the witness tell the story in the presence of reliable witnesses. The essential substance of the witness' statements, as nearly verbatim as possible, should be written down afterward.

In addition to the record of what was said, put down in the notebook the circumstances of the conversation, persons involved, witnesses, time, and the conclusions drawn from the facts learned.

All signed statements should be carefully preserved where they will be available for future use in court.

Careful fire-cause investigation may not seem glamorous in the heat of battle when the fire is burning, but it pays off in successful prosecution in court months after the fire is out. The fire-cause investigator is a key participant in fire prevention through law enforcement. For unless the cause can be proven by a preponderance of the evidence or beyond reasonable doubt, neither civil nor criminal liability can be sustained.

Beyond the fire-cause determination stage, fire law enforcement is ordinarily out of the hands of forestry officials and becomes the responsibility of local or state law enforcement and judicial officers. It is important for forest managers to maintain close personal contact with local police, prosecutors, and judges and to impress them with the potential seriousness of fire law violations. Law enforcement can be an effective fire prevention technique only if violators can reasonably expect to be apprehended, prosecuted, and appropriately punished.

FIRE PREVENTION ENGINEERING

Education and enforcement are valuable fire prevention measures when forest fires are caused through ignorance, carelessness, or malice. Often, however, well-intentioned prudent people cause fires through sheer inadvertence or accident. These causes can be reduced only through modifications of the ignition sources or the fuels that act as ignition receptors.

Pottharst and Mar (1981) develop an engineering system model by which a decision can be made as to whether an engineering approach to a specific fire-cause problem is likely to be cost-effective. Their model requires data inputs on the level of activity associated with wildfire ignitions, a measure of fire hazard by time period for each geographic area under consideration, and a time series of fire statistics sufficient to identify the probable impacts of implementing various engineering alternatives. They use the model to show the relative effectiveness of improved brakeshoes and installation of exhaust spark arresters in reducing the number of railroad fires in several states, some of which had mandatory spark arrester laws and some of which did not. They also use the model to predict the effectiveness of several engineering approaches to reducing vehicle-caused fires in California—exhaust system heat shields, for example. However, for many if not most fire causes, the lack of sufficient accurate input data severely limits the model's applicability.

Some engineering solutions to fire problems have proven extremely simple, such as moving the striking surface from the front to the rear of paper match covers. Others are quite complex; decades of research were required to develop effective spark arresters for power saws and other portable gasoline-powered equipment (U.S. Forest Service 1976). Some approaches are, so far, intractable—the search for a means of producing a marketable self-extinguishing cigarette has been underway for more than half a century. However, foresters working in concert with equipment manufacturers have been able to increase the fire safety characterstics of a wide variety of equipment ranging from railroad locomotives to gasoline camp stoves.

Because many forest fires start in easily identifiable, relatively restricted areas such as roadside, railroad and powerline rights of way, and campground margins, it is often possible to undertake fuel modification procedures that would be too costly to carry out on a broad scale forestwide. Most of the commonly used techniques for fuel modification are covered in Chapter 4, but those specialized hazard reduction measures that are used exclusively for fire prevention are covered here.

In high fire hazard country, the use of cleared lanes or firebreaks to protect valuable property is as old as human settlement. In order to be effective, however, firebreaks must be kept clear of flammable annual vegetation and litter. As long as labor is cheap, firebreaks can be cleared by hand once or twice a year. In areas where labor is scarce or expensive, other methods must be employed. Grazing can maintain clean firebreaks if there is sufficient summer rainfall to maintain a perennial grass cover (Halls et al. 1960). Chemicals, both soil sterilants and hormone-type herbicides, have been used since World War II but their use has declined in recent years because of environmental concerns (Brown 1966, Crafts, et al. 1941). One alternative to annual clearance or soil sterilization is to permit a low ground cover to develop on the firebreak but to maintain the fire resistance of the cover through irrigation. Unfortunately, irrigation is almost invariably too expensive to be practical except in the immediate vicinity of homes or highly developed campsites where it can be justified as an aesthetic landscaping practice. Several experiments to utilize sewage effluent for firebreak irrigation and shift the cost burden from the fire service to the sanitation service have been unsuccessful because of the threat of heavy metal build-up in the irrigated soils (Youngner et al. 1976). Another practice that has been tried with little long-lasting success is to plant firebreaks with exotic plants that are naturally fire resistant or of low flammability. Several succulents as well as species with high salt contents such as *Tamarix* and *Atriplex* have been tested (Nord and Green 1977). In all cases the exotics were eventually crowded out by native species. This may be fortunate since introduced plants that do compete successfully with native species almost invariably result in causing more problems than they solve.

Because of the high cost of maintenance, the firebreak system in the United States has been virtually abandoned and replaced by the fuelbreak concept discussed in Chapter 4.

One intriguing way of modifying fuel flammability, and one that has been tested operationally by several countries around the world, is to increase fuel moisture content by increasing spring and summer precipitation through weather modification. Cloud seeding of winter storm systems to increase snow pack is accepted operational practice in many parts of the Northern Hemisphere, but cloud seeding for fire prevention involves increasing the precipitation from individual cumulus clouds. For this purpose, ground-based generators have proven ineffective and aircraft and rocket-applied systems too expensive. Although the Russians utilize cloud seeding as a suppression strategy on large wildfires, it is no longer considered cost-effective for fire prevention.

BIBLIOGRAPHY

Advertising Council, The. 1979. *Forest fire prevention: 1942–1979.* Annual Report. 1978–1979, 10 pp.

Anonymous. 1975. *Wildfire prevention analysis: problems and programs.* U.S. For. Serv., U.S.D.I. Bur. Land Manage., Nat. Assoc. of State For. Unnumbered Report, 28 pp.

Banks, W. G. and F. E. Holt. 1966. *Who starts forest fires in Maine, and how?* U.S. For. Serv. Res. Note NE-51, 4 pp.

Bertrand, A. L. and A. W. Baird. 1975. *Incendiarism in southern forests: a decade of sociological research.* Misc. Ag. Exp. Sta. Bull. 838, 40 pp.

Block, J. H. and J. Block. 1975. *Fire and young children.* Univ. of Calif., Berkeley, Unnumbered Report, 168 pp.

Brown, J. K. 1966. *Firebreak maintenance with soil sterilants.* U.S. For. Serv. Res. Note NC-8, 4 pp.

Burns, D. P. and M. L. Doolittle. 1973. Man to man: the key to fire prevention. *So. Lumberman* 227(2824):136–137.

Chandler, C. C. 1977. *Smokye Mouse—living symbol of forest fire research.* U.S. For. Serv. Unnumbered Report, 12 pp., illus.

Christiansen, J. R., W. S. Folkman, W. K. Warner, and M. L. Woolcott. 1976. *Organizational factors in fire prevention: roles, obstacles and recommendations.* U.S. For. Serv. Res. Paper PSW-116, 13 pp.

Crafts, A. S., H. D. Bruce, and R. N. Raynor. 1941. *Plot test with chemical soil sterilants in California.* Univ. Calif. Bull. 648, 25 pp., illus.

Doolittle, M. L. and G. D. Welch. 1974. Personal contact pays off. *J. For* 72(8):488–90.

Folkman, W. S. 1963. *Levels and sources of forest fire prevention knowledge of California hunters.* U.S. For. Serv. Res. Paper PSW-11, 22 pp.

Folkman, W. S. 1965. *Forest fires as accidents.* Proc. 56th Western For. Conf., Western Forestry and Cons. Assoc., pp. 136–142.

Folkman, W. S. and J. Taylor. 1972. *Fire prevention in California's Riverside County headstart project . . . an evaluation.* U.S. For. Serv. Res. Paper PSW-79, 29 pp.

Halls, L. K., R. H. Hughes, and F. A. Peevy. 1960. *Grazed firebreaks in southern forests.* U.S.D.A. Ag. Info. Bull. No. 226, 8 pp., illus.

Haugh Associates. 1968. *Public image of and attitudes toward Smokey the Bear and forest fires.* U.S. For. Serv. Unnumbered Report, 191 pp.

Massachusetts Forestry Association. 1928. *The Cape Cod fire prevention experiment.* Mass. For. Assoc. Unnumbered Report, 8 pp., illus.

Morrison, E. E. 1976. *Guardian of the forest: a history of the Smokey Bear program.* Vantage, New York, 129 pp., illus.

National Fire Protection Association. 1976. *Fire protection handbook,* 14th ed. National Fire Protection Association, Boston, 1263 pp.

National Fire Protection Association, 1981. *Uniform coding for fire protection—1981.* NFPA Standard No. 901-1981, 210 pp.

National Wildfire Coordinating Group. 1978. *Fire cause determination handbook. Handbook No. 1,* National Wildfire Coordinating Group, Washington, D.C., 41 pp., illus.

Nickey, B. B. 1980. *Fire occurrence analysis by "c" control charts.* U.S. For. Serv. Unnumbered Report, 91 pp., processed.

Nord, E. C. and L. R. Green. 1977. *Low volume and slow-burning vegetation for planting on clearings in California chaparral.* U.S. For. Serv. Res. Paper PSW-124, 41 pp., illus.

Pottharst, E. and B. W. Mar. 1981. Wildfire prevention engineering systems. *Can. J. For. Res.* **11**:324–333.

Rico Rico, F. 1977. *Prevention policy regarding forest fires.* FAO/UNESCO Technical Consultation on Forest Fires in the Mediterranean Region, FO:FFM/77/2-0, pp. 87–99.

Ryan, F. L., F. H. Gladen, and W. S. Folkman. 1978. *Team teaching fire prevention program: evaluation of an education technique.* U.S. For. Serv. Res. Paper PSW-129, 6 pp.

Shea, J. P. 1939. *The psychologist makes a diagnosis.* U.S. For. Serv. Unnumbered Report, 151 pp., processed.

U.S. Forest Service, 1976. *Spark arrester guide.* 350 pp., illus.

U.S. Forest Service. 1968. *Analysis of state fire control laws.* Div. of Coop. For. Fire Control, 6 pp.

Vreeland, R. G. and M. B. Waller. 1978. *The psychology of firesetting: a review and appraisal.* U.S.D.C. Nat. Bur. Standards Report NBS-GCR-79-157, 51 pp.

Youngner, V. B., T. E. Williams, and L. R. Green. 1976. *Ecological and physiological implications of greenbelt irrigation.* Calif. Water Resources Center Contribution No. 157, 104 pp.

CHAPTER FOUR

Presuppression Activities

Fire presuppression includes all activities undertaken before a fire occurs that are directed at ensuring safe and effective fire suppression.

RECRUITMENT AND TRAINING

Forest firefighting is physically demanding, dangerous work requiring strength, stamina, and the ability to remain alert despite fatigue and stress. Firefighters who are not physically or emotionally fit for the work are an impediment rather than a help on the fireline and represent a potential danger to others as well as to themselves. Proper screening of new personnel and continuous training and monitoring of the fire force is a necessity whether the crews are full-time professional firefighters, forestry personnel who only fight fire during emergencies, or volunteers from outside the land management organization.

Physical fitness for forest fire work can be adequately predicted from measurements of aerobic capacity (Sharkey 1976). Aerobic capacity is the extent to which the body can absorb oxygen, transport it, and use it to metabolize fats and carbohydrates in the active muscles. Aerobic capacity is measured in units of milliliters of oxygen per kilogram of body weight per minute. Ideally, aerobic capacity is determined by measuring a subject's oxygen consumption while exercising on a laboratory treadmill or stationary bicycle. This procedure is too expensive for routine testing and several indirect tests have been developed that have a high degree of correlation with measured aerobic capacity. The simplest test is the 12-minute run. The subject runs on a flat course for 12 minutes. Aerobic capacity is equal to the distance covered (km) times 20.5 minus seven. The *step test*, which takes less time and area, is to have the subject step up and down to a 40-centimeter bench at a rate of 90 steps per minute. After 5 minutes, the subject's pulse rate is measured for 15 seconds beginning 15 seconds after the 5-minute test has ended. Aerobic capacity is a nonlinear function of pulse rate and age:

$$C = (118 \times 10^{-.0125R}) - \frac{(A - 25)}{5}$$

where C = Aerobic capacity (ml/kg/min)
        R = Pulse count/15 sec
        A = Age (yrs)

This latter test is used by forest fire agencies in the United States to screen workers for fireline duty. Required aerobic capacity scores range from 35 for camp workers and other light duty positions to 45 for fireline crew members.

In addition to the basic physical capabilities to undertake sustained hard work which is evaluated through aerobic capacity, each fireline job has associated physical skills needed for successful performance. Digging trench with hand tools requires extensor muscle endurance and lower back strength. Carrying hose requires leg endurance and strength in the trunk and abdominal muscles. Tests such as sit-ups, chin-ups, and back lifts can be designed to fit each individual crew position. The *fitness trail* is an installation that is useful for training and development as well as for screening potential firefighters (Sharkey et al. 1977).

Once a firefighting force of physically fit individuals has been selected, they must be trained for the jobs they will be expected to perform (Figure 4.1). Since there may be as many as 50 different job classifications working on a large fire, establishing and maintaining an effective training program is an important aspect of presuppression activity.

The first step in developing a training program is to undertake a task analysis for each position in the suppression organization. All tasks required for adequate performance are listed in sequence to provide a basis for establishing performance requirements. Next, all the specific skills and knowledge required for each task are identified and separated into those that will be expected of the trainee before admission to the course (prerequisites) and those to be taught in the course.

All performance requirements not included as prerequisites must be met in the course content. Each identified task is then redescribed in behavioral terms as an instructional objective. Each instructional objective should precisely state what the trainee must know or be able to do upon completion of that phase of training. Tests are then developed to measure proficiency for each instructional objective.

Only after the tasks, performance objectives, and test instruments are developed is the technical content of the course considered. This ensures that the course meets true training needs and does not include material that is of interest to the instructor but extraneous to the student.

Figure 4.1. Forest firefighting requires physically fit individuals trained to function as a unit. Photo by U.S. Forest Service.

Although course content varies from position to position and from country to country, most fire management organizations require approximately 40 hours of formal training as a basic prerequisite to any position on the fireline. This usually includes fundamentals of fire behavior, fire organization, fire control methods, tool and equipment use, and fireline safety. All leadership positions require additional training in fire strategy and tactics, time and record keeping, and first aid.

Training in individual skills is readily accomplished in a standard classroom setting. However, success on the fireline depends as much on close and effective teamwork as it does on the skills of the individuals involved. Teamwork training can best be accomplished through on-the-job instruction or by participation in well-planned simulation exercises.

On-the-job training consists of assigning a student trainee to observe a particular job assignment throughout the course of a large fire operation. In this way the student becomes familiar, not only with the requirements of the particular position, but also with the interactions of that position with the other fire overhead and with the time pressures and stress relationships that accompany a large fire. On-the-job training is only as successful as the trainer, however, and overhead positions on large fires are selected for their firefighting expertise rather than their training ability. Unless the trainee's role model makes a conscientious effort to explain his or her actions and decisions, the experience may leave the trainee with little more than a sense of frustration.

Simulation exercises lack the sense of urgency that is ever present during a real fire, but if carefully planned they can be quite effective. Exercises offer two advantages over on-the-job training; instructors can be selected on the basis of teaching ability, and the exercises can be conducted at convenient times and locations. In a simulation exercise, trainees are assigned to certain overhead positions and instructors to the others. The exercise is conducted according to a script that is known to the instructors but unknown to the trainees. At successive stages in the proceedings, the exercise is stopped and the trainee's performances critiqued with particular reference to those principles emphasized in the previous segment of the exercise.

Simulation exercises can be conducted in the classroom, in special fire simulator facilities, and in the field—often at the site of old wildfires. Field exercises offer the most realism but have two inherent disadvantages; the fire and its progress must be imagined, and time constriction, which is necessary for optimum course content, is difficult to achieve. Simulation exercises for fire management trainees are seldom held in the field unless line crews and equipment operators are to be trained at the same time. Planning for simultaneous training of line and overhead is as complex as military war gaming—or as fighting a large fire.

Classroom exercises lack the immediacy of field simulations but they are easier to structure and control. Time can easily be constricted to cover the events of an entire shift in an hour, and such time compression can serve to instill the feeling of pressure and urgency that accompanies the real fire situation. But maps are poor substitutes for real topography and fuels, and visualizing fire behavior during classroom exercises requires more fire experience than many trainees possess.

The fire simulator facility attempts to overcome the defects in both field and classroom simulations. The simulator consists of a large projection screen, several image-reversing overhead projectors, two rotating partly opaque discs, communications equipment (specific to each training exercise), and sound effects equipment. The screen is placed between the trainees and the instructors, and all communications between trainees and instructors are by telephone or radio. A forest scene is projected on the screen. Fire is simulated by superscribing smoke onto the scene on a second projector and superscribing burned-over area (black ash) onto the scene from a third projector. The rotating discs in front of the second projector give a realistic "rolling" motion to the smoke. Sound effects are used to enhance realism. The training staff, sitting on one side of the screen play various roles such as dispatcher, lead plane pilot, or resource manager and present various fire situations to trainees sitting on the opposite side of the screen. Time cannot be compressed as tightly as in classroom simulation because of the necessity for the projected fire behavior to proceed in quasireal time. However, rates of spread can be increased by a factor of two without seriously distorting the exercise, and scenes can be changed while the role players are stopped for a critique. The fire simulator has proven to be a most successful training device as shown by its use in such divergent countries as the United States, Canada, Spain, Portugal, Chile, and Korea. Simplified versions of the simulator, often referred to as fire games, have evolved. They are much more portable than the simulator and are designed mainly to train, test, and upgrade firefighters at small remote centers. An example is the Wildland Fire Game developed by Maloney (1974).

PRESUPPRESSION PLANNING

The secret to success for any emergency management organization lies in careful and detailed planning in advance of the event. Forest fire management is no exception. Presuppression plans must be flexible enough to cover every contingency from a single fire in the off-season to the most severe likely combination of large fires occurring at one time. As a minimum, specific written plans should be prepared to cover the following:

1. Fire organization and finance.
2. Fire equipment and supply.
3. Fire detection.
4. Dispatching procedures.
5. Manning guidance.
6. Special hazard areas.

The Fire Organization and Financial Plan includes a listing and budget by position and location of all employees paid directly, either full-time or part-time, by the fire management function and the annual capitalized costs of equipment and supplies. This allows the fire manager and higher officials in the land management organization to analyze the amount spent for basic fire protection vs. past and projected fire risk, compare fire costs by subunits, evaluate trade-offs among various mixes of personnel and equipment, and perform the many administrative and management analyses common to the efficient direction of any organization.

The Fire Equipment and Supply Plan should be developed to quickly provide the necessary amounts and proper distribution of firefighting apparatus sufficient for the most serious situation that could reasonably be expected. In addition to lists of equipment and supplies owned by the fire management organization, the plan should catalogue the location of equipment available from potential cooperators as well as identify commercial suppliers where equipment can be obtained on short notice.

Detection Plans and Dispatching Guides are discussed under their respective sections later in this chapter.

The Manning Guide fulfills a dual purpose. It is first a list of all personnel not included in the fire organization who are available for duty under specified conditions. These may include employees of the parent organization who have nonfire assignments such as timber fellers or road maintenance crews, personnel from cooperating organizations with whom specific preseason agreements have been reached, and other local sources of trained labor such as large ranches or sawmills. Secondly, the Manning Guide provides instructions on how to increase readiness as the fire season advances and fire danger increases. The plan should provide for the following actions:

1. Placing cooperator crews on alert.
2. Arranging special communications with work crews in the forest.
3. Initiating special fire prevention programs.
4. Increasing fire detection coverage.
5. Closing high hazard areas to public use.
6. Issuing special radio, television, or newspaper bulletins.

The Manning Guide is usually organized by classes of fire danger rating and the presence or absence of uncontrolled fires. Thus with a weather prediction for the following day, the fire manager can tell at a glance what actions should be taken and what outside forces are available.

Plans for special hazard areas such as active logging areas, residential sites, and zones of insect epidemic should be prepared to ensure adequate protection above that provided in the general Manning Guide. Each plan should specify the suppression action to be undertaken when fires start within or near the area and designate the unit responsible for initiating suppression action. The plan should be thoroughly reviewed by the responsible unit prior to the fire season.

Maps and Records

The adage that those who do not understand the past are condemned to repeat it is perfectly applicable to presuppression planning. Proper planning requires a plethora of information on past fire occurrence, fuel types, weather, improvements, and financial data. Many of these are best summarized on maps or transparent overlays. The minimum requirements for maps and records have already been discussed in Chapter 1 under Fire Management Planning. For presuppression planning the following additional items are highly desirable.

Soil Erosion Potential Overlay showing all areas where erosion is expected to be serious enough to require emergency mitigation efforts.

Machine-Line Construction Overlay showing areas where mechanized equipment can be used for fire suppression; consider performance characteristics of each type of equipment as affected by slope, ground cover, and soil type.

Water Supply overlay distinguishing potable water, water accessible by road for ground tankers, and water accessible only by portable pumps.

Air Operations overlay including landing fields, helispots and hazards such as powerlines and communications towers.

Special Areas Overlay showing areas of archaeological significance, endangered species habitats, and similar sites where special fire protection and/or line construction measures may be necessary.

Another approach to utilizing past data is through the application of computer technology. Computerized inventory programs have been developed for both equipment and fire control personnel (Middleton 1977). Used in conjunction with efficient data retrieval systems, these programs are capable of storing large quantities of information and making it available to the dispatcher or other fire officer in whatever format required. Similar programs are being developed for the storage and retrieval of data on forest fuels, past weather, lightning activity, and fire behavior (Latter 1980).

Preattack Fire Planning

The ultimate in presuppression planning is individual preattack fire planning where the tactics to be used are decided upon in advance, the necessary logistical data are calculated, and all pertinent information is not only mapped but permanently signed on the ground (Grace 1951).

The purpose of a preattack fire plan is first to inventory all possible control lines, water sources, camp sites, helispots, tractor loading areas, and the like, and calculate the needed firefighters and equipment to construct fire control lines within the time limits required to make a successful attack on any large fire occurring within the area. The logical beginning and ending point for each stretch of fireline is marked on the map and permanently signed on the ground with a metal marker visible from the nearest road or trail, and whenever possible also visible from the air (Figure 4.2). Signing enables the user to refer quickly from map to field notes and also provides positive ground identification to field crews.

Field notes which accompany the maps display equipment and manpower requirements together with transportation directions as illustrated.

FIRE LINE DATA

East ½ of Block A

A-14 to A-15 HAND LINE: 665 m, 96%, med. brush, steep knife ridge, 3 m line required, 160 man-hr.

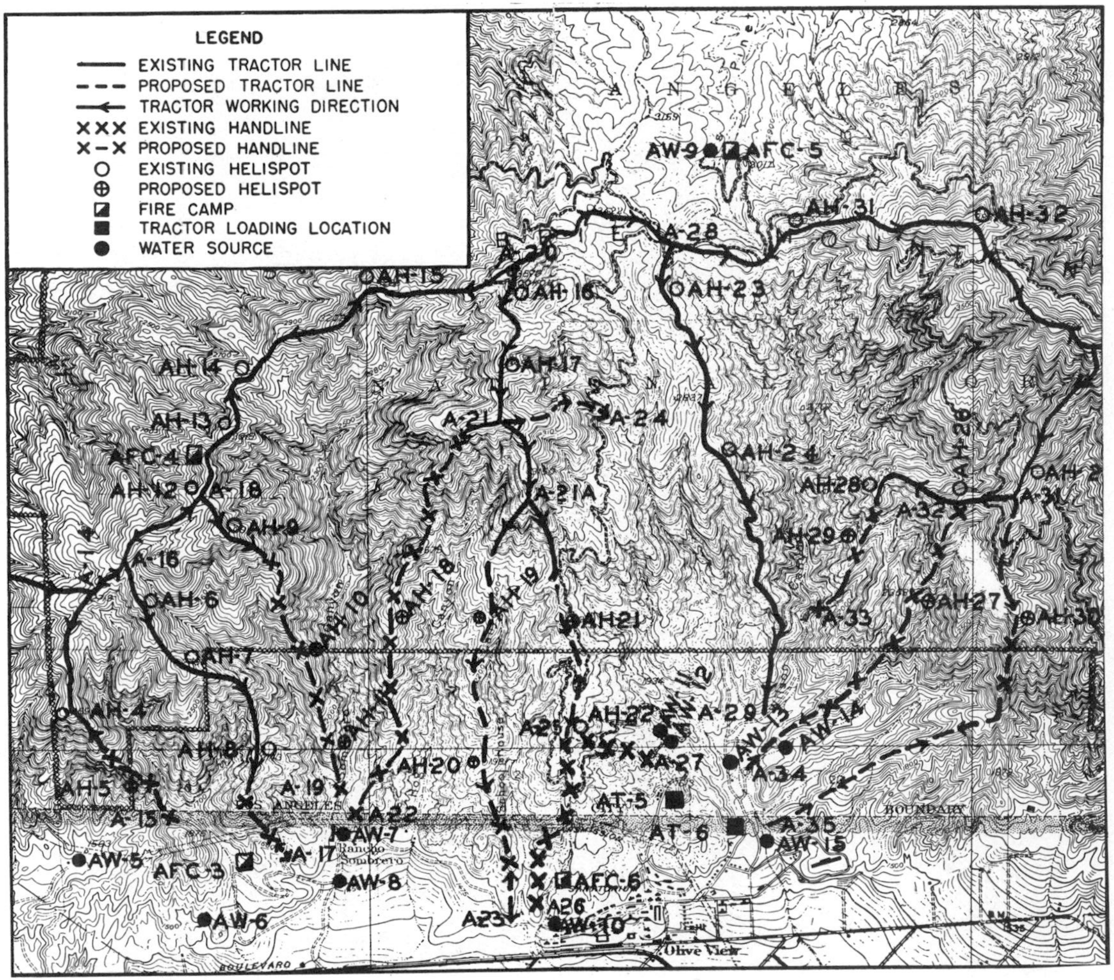

LEGEND
EXISTING TRACTOR LINE
PROPOSED TRACTOR LINE
TRACTOR WORKING DIRECTION
EXISTING HANDLINE
PROPOSED HANDLINE
EXISTING HELISPOT
PROPOSED HELISPOT
FIRE CAMP
TRACTOR LOADING LOCATION
WATER SOURCE
AW-9
AFC-5
AH-31
AH-32
A-28
A-20
AH-15
AH-16
AH-23
AH-14
AH-17
AH-13
A-21
A-24
AFC-4
AH-24
AH-12
A-18
A-21A
AH-28
AH-26
A-31
A-32
AH-9
AH-29
A-16
AH-6
AH-10
AH-18
AH-19
AH-21
A-33
AH-27
AH-7
AH-4
AH-22
A-29
AW-13
AW-14
A-25
AH-8
AH-20
A-27
A-34
AH-5
A-19
AT-5
A-15
A-22
AT-6
A-35
AW-7
AW-15
AW-5
AFC-3
A-17
AFC-6
AW-8
A-26
AW-6
A23
AW-10
Olive View
BOUNDARY

Scale: 1 cm = 250m

Figure 4.3 Sample preattack fire plan

TRACTOR LINE: 665 m, 37%, heavy brush, 12 m line required, 1 cat 6 hr, 2 cats 3 hr.

TRAVEL: Tractor from AT-4 via Grapevine T.T., A-13, A-12 to A-14, $1\frac{1}{4}$ hrs.

HELISPOTS: AH-4, $\frac{1}{4}$ hr tractor, 4 man-hr; AH-5, 2 man-hr.

WATER: AW-4, 12,000 1, Circle M Ranch draft; AW-5, 20,000 1, Symonds Reservoir draft.

FIRE CAMP DATA

East $\frac{1}{2}$ of Block A—AFC-2 to AFC-6

AFC-6 Located at Olive View Park. From Foothill Blvd. at east end of Olive View Sanatorium, turn north on Colbalt Ave. to Olive View Ave. Turn right (east) on Olive View Ave. to Sycamore Ave. Turn left (north) on Sycamore Ave. to AFC-6 at Olive View Park. Water from Olive View water system available at campsite. Telephone available at Olive View on Calif. Water & Tel. Line. Radio communication switch A-50 at Newhall Ranger Station.

TRACTOR LOADING AND ROUTE OF TRAVEL

Block A

AT-6 Transport tractor via Foothill Blvd. to east end of Olive Sanatorium. Turn right (north) on Colbalt Ave. to Olive View Ave. Turn right (east) on Olive View Ave. to Sycamore Ave. Turn left (north) on Sycamore Ave. to AT-6 at Olive View Park near gate on the Armstrong Rang. $1\frac{1}{2}$ hours transport travel from Arcadia.

Although preattack fire planning is expensive, it can save even more expensive mistakes when large fires occur. Dispatching instructions send equipment by way of predetermined routes, time-consuming scouting is eliminated, and firefighting requirements have been determined dispassionately rather than in the heat of battle.

DETECTION

In the management of forest fire, a relatively ancient truism is that the best way of reducing forest losses is to detect fires early and attack them quickly and thoroughly. Following this philosophy, one of the earliest activities in forest fire control was the organization of patrols through forested areas to discover any fires that might have occurred since the last patrol. Early patrolmen or rangers traveled the forest on foot, by canoe, or horseback and were usually equipped to take action on small fires they might find. Those on foot and horseback generally followed established trails and favored high ground and ridges where the altitude would give them an advantage in searching the forest for telltale smoke columns.

The fact that these rangers found that certain points would give them a good vista of a part of the forest they were patrolling led to the next stage in the evolution of detection—the erection of lookout cabins and towers from which the ranger or observer could survey the surrounding forest without moving about.

Many towers of varying sophistication were built ranging from crude platforms attached to the tops of the tallest trees to highly engineered metal towers with specialized cupolas, measuring devices, and radio communications (Figure 4.3).

Shortly after World War I, aircraft were recognized as having a high potential as fire detection platforms. The first use of aircraft in forestry was in the 1920s for fire detection and other forms of forest observation. As aircraft became faster and more dependable, they were combined with fixed lookout systems and have, in recent years, tended to replace lookouts for various reasons discussed later. Up until this time, whether from patrolling, lookout, or aircraft, the instrument of detection has been the human eye. More recently, electronic instruments have been designed, if not to eliminate the need for the human eye, to extend its capability of detecting incipient wildfires. Significant studies have been made in the application of new technology and the potential for improved effectiveness is very good. In

Figure 4.3. Fixed lookouts are being replaced by aerial detection but many are still in use. Anderson Butte Lookout, Washington. Photo by U.S. Forest Service.

many parts of the world, however, at least a part of the fire detection chore still falls to the patrolman or ranger, and to observers in fixed lookout positions. It should also be stressed here that throughout forested areas and, particularly, in those having a high human population, a good proportion of fires are detected by the public.

Visibility and Detection

Since most forest fires are detected by the human eye, it is of interest to discuss the attributes and limitation of that remarkable organ. In most instances the detectable evidence of an incipient fire is a column of smoke, usually of light color, that the eye is able to discern against the dark background of the forest. It is almost impossible to describe to a potential observer what a genuine smoke will look like but once familiarized with genuine or simulated smokes, the eye can be trained to search out and identify the real thing.

To be effective, the lookout should be able to recognize a smoke up to distances of approximately 15 kilometers. There are a number of factors that have a definite influence on the *visibility distance*. The time of day, apart from the obvious difference between night and day, determines the way in which the light is reflected from the smoke. A number of studies of this influence have been made, one of the most thorough being reported by Byram and Jemison (1948). In general, it was found that a smoke viewed into the sun is less likely to be seen when the background is the forest but more likely to be seen if viewed against the sky. Conversely, when the sun is at the observer's back a smoke contrasts against a forest background but not against the sky.

Other factors influencing the visibility of a small smoke are the clarity of the atmosphere and, obviously, the size of the smoke. Fog, smoke, and haze in the atmosphere between the observer and the smoke can greatly reduce or eliminate entirely the value of a lookout. One of the disadvantages of fixed lookouts is their ineffectiveness when the smoke from large fires in the area *smoke in* their viewing area. Finally, all people do not have the same ability to detect small or indistinct objects. Obviously, if a person is to be hired as a lookout, he or she should be tested for visual perception. Special tests have been developed for this purpose, again by Byram and Jemison (op. cit.). This, of course, applies whether the observer is in a fixed lookout or in a patrol aircraft.

Organization for Detection

It is obvious that any detection system adopted by a fire management agency must be planned as an integral part of the organization. There is little point in having a highly organized detection system that is able to locate a large proportion of fires minutes after ignition if there is not a correspondingly

Figure 4.4. Turbo Otter aircraft on detection patrol. Photo by Ontario Department of Lands and Forests.

efficient initial attack capability. Similarly, the method of detection should be closely correlated with the type of detection problem, fuel types to be contended with, and topography.

The most prevalent detection systems may be designated (1) ground detection and (2) aerial detection. In recent years, particularly in North America, there has been a move away from ground detection and favoring aerial detection (Figure 4.4). Two of the major reasons for this are the increasing cost of maintaining and operating a fixed lookout tower or cabin and the flexibility of an aerial system. The high costs of ground detection include the salary of the observer which has increased with unionization and requirements for overtime. The flexibility of the air patrol refers to their ability to change area covered and frequency with daily changes in fire danger and risk. The advantages of an air detection system are the following:

1. Its ability to concentrate surveillance over areas of particular high risk such as recreation areas on weekends or on paths followed by recent lightning storms.

2. The reduction of detection costs when detection is not required; air patrols can be eliminated or greatly reduced on days of low fire danger.

3. Once a fire has been located, an observer in an aircraft is able to take a close look at the fire and surroundings and provide headquarters with more information than can someone in a tower who may be many kilometers away from the fire.

The offsetting disadvantage of air patrols is that they provide intermittent detection coverage of any particular point as compared to the theoretic full daylight coverage provided by a fixed lookout.

As air detection began to gain in use over ground detection, a number of studies were made in attempts to compare the results of one system vs. the other but, in general, no definite conclusions could be reached and in time it became generally accepted that each had its own place and, for many fire management areas, the best results could be obtained by use of a combination of the two, whereas for other areas a full aerial system is most effective.

Much has been written since the 1920s about fixed lookout facilities and the factors to be considered in their planning, construction, and operation. An excellent description of these factors is given in *Forest Fire Control and Use* (Brown and Davis 1973) in the chapter on detection.

Advances in remote sensing technology have opened up new possibilities for the early detection of incipient forest fires.

Television

Shortly after television became a widespread form of family entertainment, foresters began to speculate on its potential to replace human presence in lookout towers. The subsequent development of television cameras designed for industrial surveillance created further interest in the proposal, and in the mid1950s the Louisiana State Forestry Commission in cooperation with the California Division of Forestry began a series of tests in the United States. In the tests an industrial television camera was used with vertical and horizontal movements remotely controlled by an observer. The tests did demonstrate that smoke columns could be detected by television cameras at distances of up to 20 kilometers. Various lenses were tested and it was recommended that a multiple lens installation be used so that, once a smoke was detected, a larger focal length lens could be brought into use for a closer scrutiny of the smoke column and surrounding area.

Similar tests were carried out in southern France and elsewhere but, generally, results were inconclusive and the television camera has not received widespread use in forest fire detection. Reports in the late 1960s and early 1970s from the USSR make mention of the use of television for forest fire detection and a report (Karlikowski 1981) presented at the Seminar on Forest Fire Prevention and Control in Warsaw, in May 1981 describes the use of television in Poland. Tests were made during the period 1967 to 1970 that led to the development of the system now in use in that country. It has been found to be highly efficient in forests having areas greater than 50,000 hectares, and at present there are 90 instruments in use in Poland. The camera, enclosed in a dustproof and waterproof housing, has a telephoto lens having a focal length of 500 mm and is mounted on a rotatable table on the top of a mast. A remote control is used to rotate the camera a full 360° and to change its vertical angle through an arc of $+30°$ to $-30°$ from the horizon. The observer can set the machine at an automatic rotation speed of from 50 seconds to 8 minutes per full rotation, or can stop the camera at a suspicious point and take a closer look by manipulating the telephoto lens. The author of the report claims good results with this system within a radius of 20 km.

There does appear to be a place for television in wildfire detection in those areas of high population density such as Poland. In the more remote forests of the world such as in parts of the USSR, Canada, Australia, and wilderness areas in the United States, the use of television is impractical and aircraft are the main instrument of detection.

Infrared Detection (IR)

Electronic instruments for detecting infrared radiation were developed for the military during and following World War II. In the 1950s a number of scientists began exploring the potential of infrared detection for purposes other than military including its application in the medical and fire detection fields. All bodies or objects whose temperature is above absolute zero emit energy derived from the motion of their atoms in the form of waves. These waves, known as electromagnetic waves, also include visible light and, hence, the infrared waves exhibit many of the characteristics of visible light. There is, in fact, a broad spectrum of electromagnetic waves including gamma rays, x-rays, visible light, infrared, microwaves, and radio waves. The only physical difference is the length of the wave as shown in Table 4.1.

Since there is a direct relationship between the temperature of an object and the wavelength at which it radiates electromagnetic waves, it was reasoned that an electronic device sensitive to those infrared waves radiated by an incipient wildfire could be used to detect this source of radiation against the much cooler background of the forest or other terrain. This proved to be true and formed the basis for the development of infrared fire detection devices.

The infrared band encompasses that portion of the electromagnetic spectrum from approximately 1 to 1000 microns, but the most detectable infrared wavelengths from a wildfire are in the 1 to 5 micron range. There is another consideration, however. The energy given off by the fire in the form of electromagnetic waves travels through the atmosphere to reach the detecting instrument and there are only certain rather narrow bands of infrared

Table 4.1. Electromagnetic Waves. Wavelength in Microns[a]

Gamma Rays	X-rays	Visible		Infrared	Microwave and Radio	
1	1	1	1		1	1
10^{-14}	10^{-6}	1			1000	10^{10}

[a] 1 micron equals 1   10,000 cm.

waves that readily penetrate the atmosphere. These narrow bands are known as *windows*, and in designing infrared detectors scientists have selected one or more of these windows as the specific infrared wavelength to which the instrument will be sensitive. An effective detector, then, must be responsive to wavelengths in the range of maximum energy output of the fire but also to wavelengths that coincide with a window as well. Fortunately, this is possible to achieve and it has been found that the most suitable window for an infrared detector is that occurring at about the 5-micron wavelength.

Electronic infrared detectors should not be confused with infrared photographic film which is widely used in cameras for purposes other than detecting fires. Infrared film is sensitive to only a very small fraction of the near-visible end of the infrared spectrum. It is not specifically sensitive to those wavelengths given out by a fire nor does its sensitivity coincide with an atmospheric window.

An electronic infrared detection system for forest fire use consists of (1) an optic lens or system of reflectors and lenses through which the infrared energy emitted by the viewed terrain may be focused on (2) the infrared detection cell. This cell, which is the heart of the system, is able to convert the infrared energy into minute electrical impulses. These are amplified electronically to the point where they constitute usable signals (3); these signals may then be used to produce a *thermal picture* on a film or screen or both, of the terrain being viewed. The physics of electronic infrared detection are such that the system is capable of discerning differences in terrain radiation sufficient to produce a thermal picture of the terrain detail in the vicinity of a fire. Detail such as roads, rivers, and lakes can be seen and used to help establish the exact locations of a fire.

One of the major advantages of infrared detection lies in the ability of infrared waves to penetrate smoke. This allows the scanner to detect small fires through the smoke of other fires in the area and, more importantly, to delineate the perimeter of a fire where it is otherwise obscured by smoke. This allows the production of a thermal picture of the fire that provides valuable information to the fire boss. This so-called fire mapping capability was developed as an offshoot of equipment originally designed for infrared detection and has been given considerable emphasis in the United States where several airborne fire mapping units have been developed. These special units provide valuable fire information on large fires or multiple fires where heavy smoke obscuration makes it difficult to determine where individual fire fronts and hot spots are located.

One of the major disadvantages of infrared detection arises from the inability of infrared waves to penetrate air having a high water vapor content. This means that fire detection is severely restricted by fog, mist, or cloud cover, the most important of which is cloud cover. Data on cloud cover show that the probability of obtaining a view of the ground from an aircraft clear of cloud decreases with increasing altitude and varies considerably with time of day. There is a greater likelihood of cloud in midafternoon than in the morning or evening, and the least at night. Thus if an infrared detector is used in a light patrol aircraft or helicopter, its most efficient mode of operation is in the morning or evening at relatively low altitudes. However, because of the narrow strip covered by the detector at altitudes dictated by small aircraft and cloud cover limitations, it is not practical to use such a system for blanket patrol of a large fire management unit. Under these conditions, the system is best used to patrol particularly high-risk areas during high fire danger periods, to follow reported lightning storm paths, and in local fire mapping and patrolling burned areas after mop-up to detect incipient rekindles along the fireline.

To partially avoid the cloud cover problem and allow for a wider strip scanned, the U.S. Forest Service has developed a high altitude airborne system that is able to operate at night using electronic navigational aids to maintain the aircraft on a prearranged course and to assist in the location of fires detected. An additional advantage of the system is that there are fewer *false signals* at night. Most such false signals are the result of sunlight reflecting from an object on the ground. To further eliminate false signals and enhance the signal received from a fire, the system is designed to receive IR signals from two different segments of the IR spectrum coinciding with two atmospheric windows.

With the earlier IR airborne detectors, photographs of the video screen produced electronically by the scanner were dropped to fire officials on the ground using streamered capsules. More effective methods of transmitting the information are continually being developed. At the same time, improved electronics and optics are evolving, largely from military sources, that hold promise of improving the overall system. Infrared detectors mounted in satellites are also continually being improved and made more precise in their resolution indicating that the time may not be far off when satellites will be able to play an important role in forest fire detection.

It was noted earlier that IR detectors have the disadvantage of not being able to "see" through cloud or fog. There has been some speculation that similar detectors operating in the microwave band may be able to detect and locate fires through cloud and fog. Although little field research has been done in this area, it is known that small fires emit microwave radiation and that these electromagnetic waves are able to penetrate cloud and fog.

Another potential detection system is based on the electronic detection of a selected gas given off by a small fire or a smoldering fire. An instrument known as an interferometer is capable of identifying the selected gas in very small quantities in the atmosphere. In theory, the ideal fire detection interferometer should be able to detect the smoke plume above an incipient fire even before it can be seen by identifying the area of higher than normal concentration of the gas selected as being characteristic of such a fire. Some research is being done in this area but a major problem with such instruments is that of selecting a *signature* gas that does not appear from time to time in the atmosphere from sources other than potential forest fires or is not in the atmosphere as the result of numerous or large forest fires burning in the area.

Computerized Aerial Detection System

In many parts of the world, as was discussed earlier, an increasing proportion of the detection task is being carried out by aircraft rather than by observers in fixed lookouts.

This move to aerial detection has usually been done to achieve a savings in detection costs. These savings, in turn, result from the greater flexibility offered by an aerial detection system. A good air detection system can provide whatever level of detection intensity is required for the current level of visibility and fire danger. However, to date, the real significance of this daily flexibility is just beginning to be recognized and its advantages realized. Computer programs are being developed for a series of fire management objectives as decisionmaking aids. Those programs developed to assist in forest detection are designed to predict probable fire occurrence and potential fire behavior and to help the manager in planning aerial detection flight routes and patrol frequencies.

The fire prediction program attempts to predict the number and approximate location of visually detectable fires started by people or by lightning. It does this by referring to data located in fire, lightning, and weather databases. Using past data resident in these databases, it is possible to test the prediction system by asking the program to predict how many fires would have occurred on a past date and comparing this with actual history. In actual operation, a fire management organization would normally apply the prediction program toward the end of the day to obtain the probable number and location of fires expected the following day, and again in the morning in light of changing weather parameters, lightning patterns, and so on.

The human-caused fire prediction program considers local historical occurrence patterns, current year changes in traditional occurrence patterns, fire start record over the past several days, and a relative value figure for each forest cell. The predicted number of human-caused fires for the fire management area is then the sum of the fires predicted for each cell. This predicted figure is used with the Poisson distribution to indicate the chance of obtaining one or more fires as well as the maximum number to be expected (Martell 1975).

The lightning fire prediction program uses the lightning database which contains the date, time, and location by cell of every cloud-to-ground lightning strike that occurred over the area. This data is obtained from an electronic lightning location system that may automatically feed the data to the database. The predicted number of fires is a function of the number of strikes in a cell modified by consideration of ignition, smoldering, and arrival processes that are linked to fuel moisture. In arriving at the final prediction of lightning-caused fires, lightning activity for the past several days is taken into consideration and predicted fires are totaled to all cells, and, when combined with the predicted human-caused fire figure, provides the total number of fires predicted for the region.

To utilize this data in fire detection, a detection program has been developed (Kourtz 1973) that utilizes the fire prediction program to route air patrols over the fire management region in a pattern most likely to detect predicted fires. The major objective of the program is to ensure that detection patrol flights pass within detection distance of each cell at intervals frequent enough to detect fires while they are still small enough to be controlled by an initial attack crew and to do this in the most efficient manner. It is designed to advise managers not only where the patrols should go but also how frequently they should cover the area.

COMMUNICATIONS

The need for reliable communications has been recognized as vital ever since the beginning of organized fire protection. To exemplify this, the most common worldwide insignia for a fire department officer is a badge of crossed trumpets commemorating the megaphones with which the chief issues commands to the firefighters. This is particularly true in forest fire control where distances are great and forces often widely scattered. More than any other support activity, successful control of forest, brush and grass fires depends on communications (Office of Emergency Planning 1967).

A fire protection organization needs to consider its communications system from four different standpoints.

1. Communications between the public and the fire organization.
2. Communications within the fire organization under both emergency and normal conditions.
3. Communications among other fire organizations.
4. Communications with nonfire agencies and organizations.

Communications between the public and the fire organization should be designed to permit rapid reporting of fires or other serious emergencies. From a practical standpoint, this usually requires a telephone system with different telephone numbers for administrative and emergency traffic. The emergency number should terminate at the dispatcher's office.

Communications within the fire organization are normally accomplished by radio. There are three general communication links required for intraorganization use: reporting of fires by agency personnel to the fire dispatcher, assignments and coordinating information from the dispatcher to agency employees, and communications among agency personnel assigned to a fire or other emergency. In order to ensure a clear channel for fire reports to the dispatcher it is normal practice to have at least two, and sometimes several, separate frequencies assigned for intraorganization radio use.

Communication among adjacent fire organizations is always useful in order to be aware of the total fire load within a region and to receive early notice of fires reported to other agencies. Interagency communication is a necessity when organizations are linked by formal mutual assistance agreements. Although interagency communications can be handled by telephone, it is normally preferable to use radio. This can be accomplished by sharing a common frequency with one or more adjacent fire agencies, by monitoring (receiving only) the frequencies of other agencies, or by dedicating a radio frequency to interagency fire communications. This last option is commonly used in the United States for communications between forest fire organizations and urban fire departments.

Emergency communication needs between fire organizations and nonfire agencies are common during large fire situations. Examples are public works departments, road maintenance crews, utility companies, law enforcement agencies, newspapers, radio and television stations, and fire weather forecasters. The greatest demand for communications with outside organizations occurs during major fires when the internal communications load is also greatest. Plans must be made in advance to handle the volume of message traffic without overloading the entire communications system.

Communications Equipment

Many types of equipment comprise a fire telecommunications system.

Public telephone is the basic element of any system since it is the only link between the fire organization and many cooperators as well as the general public.

Private telephone systems ranging from sophisticated central switchboards to military field telephones are a valuable adjunct to the system. Much of the message traffic on a large fire consists of lengthy equipment and supply orders. When these can be handled by land line the airways are free for more interesting, if not more important, messages.

Because fire operations are highly mobile, radio is, of necessity, the primary method of communication. The first choice faced by a fire organization is which frequency to select. Radio frequencies are divided into the high band (HF:3 to 30 MHz), the very high (VHF:30 to 300 MHz), and the ultra high: (UHF:300 to 3000 MHz). High band gives the longest signal range per unit of power, but is extremely susceptible to long-range interference, especially at night. VHF provides a stronger signal with a shorter range and less interference than high band, whereas UHF is practically interference-free but has the shortest range and, in addition, UHF transmission is limited to line of sight which reduces its utility in broken terrain unless radio repeaters are located on adjacent mountain peaks or the signal is relayed through a geostationary communications satellite. In general, high-band radios are preferred by agencies that have a large territory to protect and in countries where competing radio traffic is minimal, while UHF use is confined to urban–suburban organizations where only short distance communications are necessary and frequency competition is intense.

Fire radios are almost universally frequency modulated (FM) rather than amplitude modulated (AM) because FM is less subject to static from vehicular electrical systems and from lightning.

Radio equipment for fire organization use can range from a dispatcher's base station of a size and complexity equivalent to a commercial broadcast station to a simple one-channel personal receiver the size of a cigarette packet to be carried by a line scout.

In addition to telephone and radio, data transmission systems such as a teletypewriter or facsimile duplicator are often used to transmit maps and data between base units or from a base unit to fire camp.

Communications Systems Design

Every fire communications system is an attempt to reconcile two mutually exclusive functions: to provide a common communications link for safety purposes between all parties in urgent need of such a link, and to provide separate communication links for use in support of specific tasks. On the fireline some personnel need to hear everyone but speak to only one other person, while others need to speak to everyone but hear from only one other person. Thus every fire communication system represents a compromise.

A radio network (net) is defined as a number of radio stations within a given geographical area, jointly administered, or communicating with each other by sharing the same channel or channels. Normally, a net consists of a base station which may be at organization headquarters, a dispatcher's office or fire camp, and a number of mobile stations which may be in aircraft, vehicles, or hand-carried. A net may be single or multiple frequency and simplex or duplex. Simplex means that signals can be transmitted in only one direction at a time between two users, and duplex means that both users can transmit simultaneously.

A single frequency simplex net represents the least complicated, least expensive, and most widely used fire communications system. With this net both base and mobile units share the same frequency. This means that only one user of the system can transmit at any one time. Multiple transmissions usually interfere with each other to the point where neither is intelligible. All receiving units hear the same message just as many people listen to the same station on their home radios. Single frequency operations have an advantage to fire control agencies in that all units converging on a fire location are kept informed of all messages that affect the firefighting operation.

The multifrequency simplex net is used when there is more than one base station. Each base station broadcasts on a different frequency but receives messages from mobile units on a common frequency. This prevents broadcasts from one base from interfering with the broadcasts of mobile units to another base. The disadvantage of this mode of operation is that mobile units cannot hear each other's transmissions since their receivers are tuned to the frequency of their base station transmitter.

A base station serving many mobile units will usually opt for a two-frequency half-duplex mode. Here the base station can receive and transmit simultaneously. For an air net where immediate contact from the aircraft to the base station may be vital, a full duplex net may be warranted.

A large forest fire suppression operation usually requires the establishment of more than one communications net, such as the following:

1.   *Command Net* to link the senior fireline officers, both ground and air and to serve as an emergency communications device. The command channel must remain uncongested. The total number of stations assigned to the command net should not exceed 20.

2.   *Tactical Net* to link all ground units working on the fire. At least three frequencies are usually required for a tactical net. Frequencies may be assigned by sectors or by type of equipment (one for tractors, one for line crews, etc.; Figure 4.5).

3.   *Air–Ground Net* to provide positive control of aircraft by line personnel at the fire scene. Separate frequencies are needed for fixed wing and helicopters. If air attack is anticipated on several sectors of the fire simultaneously, several channels may be needed to avoid confusion of instructions.

Figure 4.5.   A tactical radio net is needed on all large fires. Here a line scout reports fire behavior to his division supervisor. Photo by Montana Division of Forestry.

4.   *Air Net* to link individual aircraft with their airbase and with any airborne supervisory personnel.

5.   *Service Net* to link supply orders from fire camp to the home dispatcher's office. A service radio net is only required if telephone service cannot be provided.

6.   *Fire Camp Net* to link service subunits such as the motor pool, supply officer, and supply dumps. Here too, telephone is preferable to radio if such service can be provided.

Radio Codes

Because radio transmission at the fire scene occurs under less than ideal conditions and is often plagued by weak signals and interference, most countries have devised shortcut verbal codes to enhance audibility and/or to

Table 4.2.   Radio Alphabets

Letter	Morse Code	ICAO Alphabet	APCO Alphabet
A	·—	ALFA	Adam
B	—···	BRAVO	Boy
C	—·—·	CHARLIE	Charles
D	—··	DELTA	David
E	·	ECHO	Edward
F	··—·	FOXTROT	Frank
G	——·	GOLF	George
H	····	HOTEL	Henry
I	··	INDIA	Ida
J	·———	JULIETT	John
K	—·—	KILO	King
L	·—··	LIMA	Lincoln
M	——	MIKE	Mary
N	—·	NOVEMBER	Nora
O	———	OSCAR	Ocean
P	·——·	PAPA	Paul
Q	——·—	QUEBEC	Queen
R	·—·	ROVEO	Robert
S	···	SIERRA	Sam
T	—	TANGO	Tom
U	··—	UNIFORM	Union
V	···—	VICTOR	Victor
W	·——	WHISKEY	William
X	—··—	X-RAY	X-Ray
Y	—·——	YANKEE	Young
Z	——··	ZULU	Zebra

Table 4.3. **APCO "TEN" Code**[a]

10–0	Caution
*10–1	Unable to copy—change location
*10–2	Signals good
*10–3	Stop transmitting. To be used when other vehicles or stations are interfering with emergency traffic. (i.e., 10–3, 10–33 in progress)
*10–4	Acknowledgement
*10–5	Relay. Can be used to indicate the relay of a person, property, or a message. If for the relay of a message, indicate destination. "10–5 to _____"
*10–6	Busy—stand by unless urgent
*10–7	Out of service (give location and/or telephone number)
*10–8	In service
*10–9	Repeat
10–10	Fight in progress
10–11	Dog case
*10–12	Stand by (Stop). Physical stand by, remain alert. Not a stand by (10–6) on the radio
*10–13	Weather and road report
10–14	Report of prowler
10–15	Civil disturbance
10–16	Domestic trouble
10–17	Meet complainant
*10–18	Complete assignment quickly
*10–19	Return to _____
*10–20	Location
*10–21	Call _____ by telephone
*10–22	Disregard
*10–23	Arrived at scene
*10–24	Assignment completed. Indicates personnel is back in service and available for assignment
*10–25	Report in person to (meet) _____
10–26	Detaining subject, expedite
10–27	Driver's license information
*10–28	Vehicle registration information
10–29	Check records for wanted
*10–30	Illegal use of radio
10–31	Crime in progress
10–32	Man with gun
*10–33	EMERGENCY. Maximum priority. Should be used on the initial call to indicate traffic pertaining to danger to life or property. All stations or vehicles not involved in the emergency should maintain radio silence until the emergency is over or under control
10–34	Riot
10–35	Major crime alert
*10–36	Correct time
10–37	Investigate suspicious vehicle

Table 4.3. (Continued)

10–38	Stopping suspicious vehicle (Give station complete description before stopping)
10–39	Urgent—use light and siren
10–40	Silent run—no light or siren
*10–41	Beginning tour of duty
*10–42	Ending tour of duty
*10–43	Information. Use when asking if any, or supplying information
10–44	Request permission to leave patrol ____ ____ for _____
10–45	Animal carcass in ____ lane at ____
10–46	Assist motorist
10–47	Emergency road repairs needed
10–48	Traffic standard needs repairs
10–49	Traffic light out
*10–50	Accident
10–51	Wrecker needed
*10–52	Ambulance needed
10–53	Road blocked
10–54	Livestock on highway
10–55	Intoxicated driver
10–56	Intoxicated pedestrian
10–57	Hit and run
10–58	Direct traffic
*10–59	Convoy or escort
10–60	Squad in vicinity
10–61	Personnel in area
*10–62	Reply to message. Use when inquiring for, or furnishing, reply to a previous message. Refer to previous number, if any
*10–63	Prepare to make written copy. Used to inform a vehicle to park and write down the forthcoming radio message—the officer will not advise the station to "go-ahead" until ready to copy
*10–64	Message for local delivery. Used when the message is not to be relayed by radio but must be delivered to someone in person or by telephone—may require a message in duplicate
*10–65	Not message assignment. Used by nets to obtain the next message number to be assigned
*10–66	Message cancellation
*10–67	Clear to read net message. Used to capture the circuit and to indicate all units and stations are to copy
*10–68	Dispatch information. Used for "attempt-to-locate" messages, etc.
*10–69	Message received
*10–70	Fire alarm
10–71	Advise nature of fire (size, type, and contents of building)
10–72	Report progress on fire
10–73	Smoke report. Used in Forestry Service when smoke has been observed. Give location or coordinates
*10–74	Negative

Table 4.3. *(Continued)*

*10–75	In contact with. "10–75, 11?" "10–4, 10–75, No. 11"
*10–76	En route
*10–77	ETA (Estimated Time of Arrival)
10–78	Need assistance
10–79	Notify coroner
10–80	Chase in progress
10–81	Breatherlizer report
10–82	Reserve lodging
10–83	Work-school Xing at _____
10–84	If meeting _____ advise ETA
10–85	Delayed due to _____
10–86	Officer/operator on duty
10–87	Pick up checks for distribution
*10–88	Advise present telephone number of ___
10–89	Bomb threat
10–90	Bank alarm at _____
10–91	Pick up prisoner/subject
10–92	Improperly parked vehicle
10–93	Blockade
10–94	Drag racing
10–95	Prisoner/subject in custody
10–96	Mental subject
10–97	Check (test) signal
10–98	Prison or jail break
10–99	Records indicate wanted or stolen

a An asterisk (*) is used in this table to indicate codes most often used in forest fire communication.

decrease transmission time. The International Civil Aviation Organization sponsors a spelling alphabet that has been adopted by all North Atlantic Treaty Organization members for international use. In the United States, all public safety agencies use the Associated Public Safety Communications Officers (APCO) phonetic alphabet for spelling names of persons and locations. The terms in the phonetic alphabet (Table 4.2) have been found to be the most understandable over the air. APCO standards also govern the "ten signals" (Table 4.3) which codify information and directions most often used by the safety services.

DISPATCHING

Dispatching comprises those activities that affect the speedy control of fires: checking to ensure that firefighting forces are available, keeping advised on fire weather conditions and forecasts, obtaining reports on all fires detected or under attack, determining the location of every fire reported, calculating fire behavior and probable manpower requirements on all new fires, and sending personnel and equipment sufficient to control each fire within policy standards at minimum cost.

The dispatcher is one of the key personnel in the fire organization. A good dispatcher must have the following qualifications:

1. Know the protection area well enough to visualize the conditions and problems that may be encountered when a fire occurs.
2. Know local fuel types including their rates of spread and resistance to control under given weather conditions.
3. Know the location and current condition of all roads and trails sufficiently to estimate travel time between any two points.
4. Know topography and ground cover sufficiently to estimate cross-country travel times.
5. Know all activities within the protection area that may pose an unusual risk of fire starts.
6. Know the detection coverage and blind areas from all lookout points and ensure adequate alternative coverage during high danger periods.
7. Know the fire plans for the protection area and assist in their preparation and revision.
8. Know the availability of initial attack and reinforcement forces of all adjacent protection agencies and cooperators.
9. Know the capabilities of all protection forces under the control of the fire management organization, including strengths and weaknesses of individuals as well as equipment.
10. Know the fire communication system and arrange for immediate replacement in the event of component failure.
11. Know local weather peculiarities sufficiently to assess the probable specific weather elements at a particular site given a general meteorological forecast.

Dispatching Procedures

Immediately on receiving a report of a fire the dispatcher should record the location, identify the source of the report, give the fire an identification number, and log the date and time of the report.

If the fire is located in an area under the jurisdiction of another fire organization, the dispatcher should promptly notify a responsible representative of that agency and supply complete details. The time and name of the person contacted should be recorded in the dispatcher's log.

If the fire is located within the dispatcher's area of responsibility he or she should immediately send to the fire the firefighter or crew whose travel time will be the shortest. If the organization is operating under a *closest forces* agreement with adjacent cooperators, the nearest force is dispatched regardless of organizational affiliation. As soon as this unit has been sent, the dispatcher should attempt to determine the probable size and rate of spread of the fire and estimate the reinforcements that will be required to control it within established standards.

The dispatcher should promptly fill weak spots caused by the initial dispatch by moving up crews and equipment from other locations.

The dispatcher should anticipate potential needs well in advance of actual needs. This may require alerting additional crews or equipment and checking outlets of firefighting supplies.

Once a fire has been manned and contact with the dispatcher's office established, the dispatcher's job is to give the fire team all possible assistance and to supply requested needs promptly and effectively.

Dispatching Records

The capacity of a dispatcher to handle a heavy fire load and correlate a great many details relating to several fires and crews without making numerous mistakes depends largely on the orderliness with which the job is organized and the maintenance of systematic records. Each order must be tracked until it is received and the location of each crew and piece of equipment must be known until they return to their home stations.

These kinds of transactions are ideally suited for computerization, and with the advent of low-cost minicomputers many local systems for automated dispaptching, resource status monitoring, and record-keeping have been developed (U.S. Forest Service 1977). However, a surprising amount of information can be maintained, manipulated, and managed with the traditional tools of maps, colored pins, card files, and filing baskets.

HAZARD REDUCTION

In forest fire terminology, hazard is defined as that part of the fire danger contributed by the fuels available for burning. It follows then that hazard reduction is synonymous with fuel treatment. Fuels can be modified in many ways to reduce their hazard. They may be isolated by barriers such as firebreaks or fuelbreaks. They may be reduced in volume by burning or physical removal. Their compactness may be increased by lopping or chipping. Their vertical continuity may be disrupted by pruning or selective shrub removal. Their moisture content may be increased by irrigation or by removal of dead material. Their chemistry may be altered by species manipulation. Each of these methods of treatment has its advantages and disadvantages and each should be considered in developing a balanced fuel management program.

Fuel Isolation—Firebreaks, Fuelbreaks, Greenbelts

The idea of building a strip or track down to mineral soil to keep fire from spreading from wildlands into crops is as old as agriculture itself. As forests came to be considered valuable, the process came to be extended to building firebreaks between roads or trails to compartmentalize the forest and reduce the risk of fires sweeping through the entire stand.

Firebreaks have an advantage over other means of hazard reduction in that the labor of fuel removal is concentrated on a relatively small area so that many hectares can be protected for a minimum expenditure of money and effort. There are several disadvantages to firebreaks, however. The primary one is maintenance. Firebreaks must be recleared at least annually—twice a year in areas with a spring and fall fire season. Firebreak annual maintenance costs average about 10 percent as much as the original construction cost, and maintaining an extensive firebreak system can quickly absorb all the labor and funds that a fire organization can afford to spend on hazard reduction. Various methods such as asphalting or applying chemical soil sterilants have been tried to reduce maintenance costs, but except where the firebreak also serves as a permanent road or trail, none of these have proven economic. The second major difficulty with firebreaks is that they can be relied upon to stop only the least intense fires. As a general rule, a firebreak will be breached at one or more points whenever fireline intensity exceeds 500 kilowatts per meter. Studies of a very intensive series of firebreaks in California early in the century showed that the breaks were successful in stopping fires 46 percent of the time, but were unsuccessful in 54 percent of the encounters (Cecil 1934).

In the 1950s, the fuelbreak concept was introduced in the United States as an attempt to overcome the disadvantages of the traditional firebreak (Green 1977). A fuelbreak differs from a firebreak in that the vegetation type on the break is permanently converted to a cover of low fuel volume and/or low flammability. In practice the preferred cover is almost always a perennial grass or some type of prostrate shrub. No attempt is made to maintain a mineral soil line unless the break is also intended to serve as a roadway. Fuelbreaks are, by necessity, much wider than firebreaks since permanent type conversion requires sufficient separation to avoid edge effects (Figure 4.6). An absolute minimum width of break is established as that necessary to prevent incapacitating burns to fire personnel on the break from radiant heat by a fire reaching the break as a line front during the worst probable fire danger (Bentley et al. 1962). The purpose of a fuelbreak is not to stop a fire, but to provide a line that can be occupied under any burning conditions and a place where fireline can be built and backfired easily, rapidly, and safely. Fuelbreaks represent a distinct improvement over firebreaks, but they have

Figure 4.6. A fuelbreak is of variable width, with the minimum wide enough to prevent incapacitating burns to personnel working on the break. This fuelbreak in California separates timber from chaparral. Photo by Carl Smith.

not been without their problems. The initial cost of fuelbreaks are much higher per kilometer of break, or per hectare protected, than those of firebreaks both because fuelbreaks are wider and thus contain more treated area per kilometer of break, and because permanent-type conversion requires intensive treatment such as seeding and herbicide spraying. Whether fuelbreaks can be cost-effective unless they are protecting high-value improvements has been questioned (Davis 1965). Also, experience has shown that fuelbreaks are not totally maintenance free. Ground fuels will accumulate sufficiently to jeopardize the break within 5 to 10 years unless the break is periodically cleared by prescribed fire, livestock, or mechanical treatment.

The next logical progression beyond the fuelbreak is the greenbelt. A greenbelt is a strip that has been converted to a nonflammable cover type and is maintained in that state by irrigation and mechanical treatment. A golf course is a perfect example of a greenbelt (however, a golf course would be a better fire hazard barrier if all 18 holes were laid end to end in the same direction). There have been some experiments on establishing greenbelts by irrigation with sewage effluent, but concerns over public acceptance and the possibility of heavy metal concentration in the soil have kept the technique from being widely adopted (Youngner et al. 1976). Although greenbelts are prohibitively expensive for a forestry organization, land-use planners and suburban developers should be encouraged to site park and landscaped recreational developments where they can serve to alleviate wildfire hazards. Unfortunately, however, population growth and urbanization pressures soon push the houses over the belts and the greenbelt then resembles the middle ring of an archery target rather than a buffer between forest and town.

Fuel Removal—Prescribed Burning and Intensive Utilization

Although the old fire triangle (fuel, oxygen and heat—take away any one and the fire goes out) is overly simplistic, it is perfectly true that a clean forest floor does not produce problem fires. In areas where decay is not sufficiently rapid to cope with the annual accumulation of forest debris, fire will eventually do the job. It is argued by some that forest fires should be tolerated or even encouraged since they are "Nature's way." The authors firmly reject that argument, remembering that nature is also fond of tsunamis, tornadoes, bubonic plague, and syphilis. However, fire is a tool that, when properly used, can be effective and relatively inexpensive for reducing fuel loads in most forest types without undue damage to the residual stand.

Underburning, the use of prescribed fire for fuel reduction beneath a canopy of desired species, is affected by antecedent and current weather and by the method of ignition. Underburning is easiest and most successful when the overstory is mature. In pole-sized stands or areas with heavy advanced reproduction, fuel loading may actually be increased following burning due to the addition of material killed but not consumed in the fire. A second burn the following year or the year after that is usually necessary to achieve a net reduction in ground fuels in young stands. Unless seedbed preparation is a desired objective, it is preferable to leave some duff cover and not to burn down to mineral soil. Duff removal depends on the moisture content of the lower duff layers and on the amount of small woody fuel (smaller than 7.5 centimeters diameter) above it. At moisture contents below 30 percent, duff will burn independently of surface fuels. Above 120 percent, duff is virtually fireproof. At intermediate moisture contents, duff only burns under the influence of external heat supplied by surface fuel (Sandberg 1980). This means that underburning should be done a few days following rain or, in snow climates, early in spring following snowmelt so that the lower duff layers are protected while the surface is dry enough to burn. Surface fuel moistures must be below 30 percent if the fire is to spread and above 5 percent if the fire is to be controllable. Within this range the prescription should be governed by the amount of dead fuel present. As a rough rule of thumb, the surface fuel moisture for underburning should be twice the surface fuel volume (fuels < 7.5 cm only) in tonnes per hectare. Wind is a critical element in underburning. Wind controls the rate of advance of the fire, affects the residence time, and reduces the heat that reaches the crowns. A minimum windspeed of one meter per second within the stand is needed to prevent excessive crown scorch. Windspeeds above 5 meters per second pose grave risks of spot fires. The most desirable windspeed within this range depends on the ignition pattern selected. Slope can be substituted for wind on the basis that each 15 percent slope is equivalent to 1 meter per second in windspeed. Susceptibility to crown scorch, and thus the production of additional dead fuel is directly proportional to ambient air temperature. Underburning should only be conducted when temperatures are below 10° C. Relative humidity affects the moisture content of very fine fuels and the exposed surfaces of larger fuels. To ensure relatively rapid fire spread with a minimum chance of spot fires, underburning should be conducted when ambient relative humidity is in the 30 to 50 percent range.

In the United States underburning is usually accomplished by crews on foot spreading a continuous line of fire from drip torches (Mobley et al. 1973). Control of the fire, and of the fire effects, is obtained by varying the spacing between the lines of fire, the speed of lightning, and the direction of fire spread relative to the wind direction or slope. A backing fire (spreading against the wind or downslope) is generally used in heavy fuels or when the overstory stand is usually susceptible to fire injury. Backing fires have the slowest spread rates, the narrowest burning zones, and the shortest flame heights. Each backing fire must be started from a prepared fireline (Figure 4.7), whereas headfires (burning into the wind or upslope) need only have prepared lines around the perimeter of the area to be burned (Figure 4.8). Because of the need for interior firelines and because of their slow rates of spread, backing fires are considerably more expensive than underburning with other ignition techniques. Headfires have the advantage of needing no interior firelines. Fire intensity is controlled by the distance between the strips. Strip headfires are the most common ignition technique for underburning. Other, more complex, techniques for special purposes are discussed in the chapter on managing fire use.

In Australia, where underburning is initiated from aircraft, spot fires are ignited in a grid pattern. Intensity is controlled by spacing the spots so that they do not coalesce until evening when burning conditions have abated. Aerial ignition has the advantage of being able to burn very large areas in a short period. Australians average 4200 hectares per aircraft-day when underburning jarrah forest in western Australia (Packham and Peet 1967). When days with weather conditions meeting prescription are infrequent, aerial ignition may be the only way to meet the land manager's objectives for rotational hazard reduction with the use of fire. Spot firing is not as controllable as strip firing and acceptance of some degree of scorch of crop trees is necessary when using aerial ignition. In Australian experience overstory damage ranges from 5 to 35 percent with 20 percent considered acceptable.

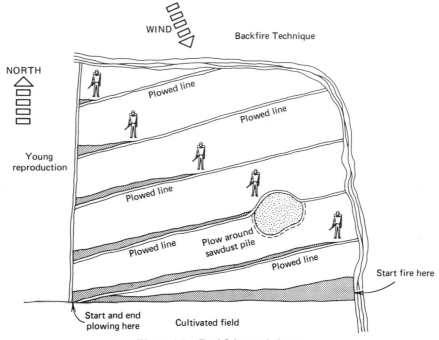

Figure 4.7. Backfiring techniques.

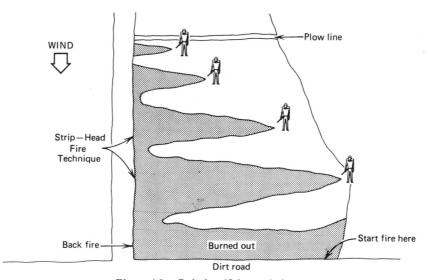

Figure 4.8. Strip headfiring technique.

When there is no desirable overstory to worry about, burning for fuel removal is much simpler. The objective is to develop a fire of sufficient intensity for complete combustion of all unwanted material while minimizing the chances of fire escaping from the prescribed area. There are numerous fuel manipulation and ignition techniques to accomplish this and they are described in Chapter 9.

In Canada, the operational use of prescribed burning has been almost entirely to reduce the potential fire hazard in logging slash and incidentally to improve the ease of replanting. A high proportion of such burns are done in the coastal forests of British Columbia although the practice has spread eastward to some degree (Chrosciewicz 1978, Kiil 1969, 1970, 1971, Muraro 1971, Stocks and Walker 1972).

In concert with the expanding interest in the use of fire to reduce the hazard in Canadian forests, increased emphasis has been placed on the preparation of guidelines designed to assist the fire management officer in preparing an effective prescription (Muraro 1975), in recommended procedures for achieving the desired results (McRae et al. 1979), and in methods of measuring fuel loading on the area to be burned (Van Wagner 1968).

Physical removal is an acceptable alternative to burning for reducing fuel loading, but it deprives the site of nutrients and is prohibitively expensive unless there is some market for the material removed. Forest managers can achieve some measure of hazard reduction by cutting to diameter limits below those considered marginal from the standpoint of timber production economics alone. The amount to which the organization is willing to subsidize intensive utilization depends on their perception of the value added from increased hazard reduction. Another worldwide method of achieving fuel removal is to permit the public to gather dead material for fuelwood at no cost or for a nominal charge. The amount of material removed depends heavily on accessibility, but since the most accessible locations are also those of highest fire risk, fuelwood gathering can be a very effective way to reduce the overall fire hazard. A "free" firewood program is not without its costs, however. Without guidance and control, the public will often fail to distinguish between fuelwood and crop trees. Many forest managers feel that unrestricted public access instills a sense of common proprietorship and leads inevitably to the *tragedy of commons* as outlined by the economist Ricardo in the eighteenth century. In many parts of Africa and even in some areas of southern Europe, unrestricted fuelwood gathering has resulted in virtually total denudation.

Controlling Fuel Compactness and/or Continuity

Sometimes the fuel hazard may be too great for isolation to offer an acceptable degree of protection but fuel removal may be impractical or unwarranted. This is often the case following a light partial cutting or after timber stand improvement operations such as pruning or thinning. In these instances hazard can often be reduced to an acceptable level by simply rearranging the fuel. Lopping and scattering slash serves the triple purpose of breaking up concentrations of hazardous dead fuels, reducing the height of fine fuels and, by bringing the fine fuels closer to the ground, enhancing their rate of decay (Williams 1955). Lopping and scattering can be done by hand or by tractor crushing, sometimes aided by specialized equipment (Roby and Green 1976). In heavier slash concentrations chipping may be economically feasible, particularly if the area is accessible by truck and there is an available market for chips. Pruning the lower branches of all residual trees (and scattering the prunings away from the base of the tree) will markedly reduce the chance of crown fires. In young stands pruning is often prerequisite to underburning.

Species Manipulation

Although it has been a longstanding dream of foresters in fireprone parts of the world to alleviate their problems by introducing and nurturing "fireproof" or at least less flammable vegetation, the realities of history tend to point in exactly the opposite direction. Almost universally, the most desirable and valuable forest species tend to be fire types, and the successful importations such as *Pinus sylvestris* in Lower Saxony or *P. radiata* in New Zealand have vastly increased rather than lessened the fire hazard (Otto 1981). Even when introductions are accidental rather than deliberate such as the *Melaleuca* invasion of southern Florida, the species that flourish in a climate favoring fire are usually more flammable than are the native species they displace (Wade et al. 1980). On the other hand, even massive attempts to introduce fire-resistant species, such as the planting of 1300 hectares of succulents (primarily *Mesembryanthemum*) in southern California between 1928 and 1936 resulted in equally massive failures (Ilch 1937).

Robert Mutch in a widely quoted and quite perceptive paper theorizes that fire-dependent plant communities burn more readily than nonfire-dependent communities because natural selection has favored development of characteristics that make them more flammable (Mutch 1970). More recent evidence would seem to go one step further than Mutch's hypothesis and suggest that vegetation will evolve towards the most flammable plant community that the climate will support.

Despite the fact that the search for a fireproof species seems foredoomed to failure, the forester has several options that can reduce the probability of large, extensive conflagrations (Rico Rico 1977). Planting mixed stands rather than monocultures, encouraging perennial grasses over shrubs, and the careful use of fire with a timing and intensity that inhibits rather than encourages fire-adapted species can delay if not reverse the evolutionary trend toward ever more flammable ecosystems.

BIBLIOGRAPHY

Bentley, J. R., C. C. Chandler, and V. E. White. 1962. *Guidelines for fuel-breaks in southern California*. Calif. Div. For. Fuel-Break Report No. 7, 15 pp.

Brown, A. A. and K. P. Davis. 1973. *Forest fire: control and use*. 2nd ed., McGraw-Hill, New York, pp. 327–357.

Byram, G. M. and G. M. Jemison. 1948. *Some principles of visibility and their application to forest fire detection*. U.S. Dept. of Agric. Tech. Bull. 954. 78 pp.

Cecil, G. H. 1934. *Firebreak study*. U.S. For. Serv. Unnumbered Report, 32 pp.

Chrosciewicz, Z. 1978. *Large-scale operational burns for slash disposal and conifer reproduction in central Saskatchewan*. Can. For. Serv. Info. Report NOR-X0201, 11 pp.

Davis, L. S. 1965. *The economics of wildfire protection with emphasis on fuelbreak systems*. State of Calif. Res. Agency Unnumbered Report, 166 pp., illus.

Grace, H. T. 1951. Intensive pre-planning for fire suppression. *Fire Contr. Notes* 12(2):37–46.

Green, L. R. 1977. *Fuelbreaks and other fuel modification for wildland fire control*. U.S.D.A. Ag. Handbook No. 499, 79 pp., illus.

Hirsch, S. N. 1962. *Possible application of electronic devices to forest fire detection*. U.S. For. Serv. Res. Note INT-91, 7 pp.

Ilch, D. M. 1937. *Some limitation on the use of succulents for erosion control*. U.S. For. Serv. Unnumbered Report, 10 pp.

Karlikowski, T. 1981. *Systems for forest fire detection*. Paper presented at Seminar on Forest Fire Prevention and Control, Warsaw, May 1981, 9 pp.

Kiil, A. D. 1969. Fuel consumption by a prescribed burn in spruce-fir logging slash. *For. Chron.* 45:100–102.

Kiil, A. D. 1970. *Effects of spring burning on vegetation in old partially cut spruce-aspen stands in east-central Alberta*. Can. For. Serv. Info. Report A-X-33, 12 pp.

Kiil, A. D. 1971. *Prescribed fire effects in subalpine spruce-fir slash*. Can. For. Serv. Info. Report NOR-X-3, 30 pp.

Kourtz, P. H. 1973. *A visual airborne forest fire detection patrol route planning system*. Environment Canada, Forest Fire Res. Inst. Info. Report FF-X-45, 22 pp.

Latter, M. 1980. Fire wars and the new technology. *Can. Pulp and Paper Ind.* 33(6).

Maloney, J. E. 1974. *Wildland fire game (role-players manual and trainers manual)*. Can. For. Serv., Unnumbered Misc. Pub.

Martell, D. L. 1975. *Contributions to decision-making in forest fire management*. Ph.D. Diss., Dept. Ind. Eng., Univ. of Toronto, Toronto.

McRae, D. J., M. E. Alexander, and B. J. Stocks. 1979. *Measurement and description of fuels and fire behavior in prescribed burns—a handbook*. Can. For. Serv. Unnumbered Pub., 44 pp.

Middleton, L. J. 1974. *Users manuals for forest fire equipment inventory and personnel programs*. Can. For. Serv. Info. Report FF-X-63.

Mobley, H. E. and others. 1973. *A guide for prescribed fire in southern forests*. U.S. For. Serv. Unnumbered Report, 40 pp., illus.

Muraro, S. J. 1971. *Prescribed-fire impact in cedar–hemlock logging slash*. Can. For. Serv. Pub. 1295, 20 pp.

Muraro, S. J. 1975. *Prescribed fire predictor*. Can. For. Serv. Misc. Pub.

Mutch, R. W. 1970. Wildland fires and ecosystems—a hypothesis. *Ecol.* 51(6):1046–1051

National Fire Protection Association (USNFPA) 1975. *Telecommunications systems: principles and practices for rural and forestry fire services*. 28 pp., illus.

Office of Emergency Planning (U.S.) 1967. *Communication in the fire services*, 32 pp.

Otto, H. 1981. *Measures to reduce forest fire risk and restoration of damaged areas in Lower Saxony.* FAO-ECE-1LO Document TIM/EFC/WP.1/SEM.10/R.4, 5 pp.

Packham, D. R. and G. B. Peet. 1967. *Developments in controlled burning from aircraft.* CSIRO Unnumbered Report, 18 pp.

Rico Rico, F. 1977. *Policy regarding forest fires.* FAO/UNESCO Technical Consultation on Forest Fires in the Mediterranean Region, FO:FFM/77/2.0, pp. 87–99.

Roby, G. A. and L. R. Green. 1976. *Mechanical methods of chaparral modification.* U.S.D.A. Ag. Handbook No. 487, 46 pp., illus.

Sandberg, D. V. 1980. *Duff reduction by prescribed underburning in Douglas-fir.* U.S. For. Serv. Res. Paper PNW-272, 18 pp.

Sharkey, B. J. 1976. *Fitness and work capacity.* U.S. For. Serv. Eqpt. Dev. Center Pub. No. 7661 2811, 81 pp., illus.

Sharkey, B. J., A. H. Jukkala, and R. Herzberg. 1977. *Fitness trail: how to build the trail, sign the trail, use the trail.* U.S. For. Serv. Eqpt. Dev. Center Pub. No. 7761 2612, 29 pp., illus.

Stocks, B. J. and J. D. Walker. 1972. *Fire behavior and fuel consumption in jack pine slash in Ontario.* Can. For. Serv. Info. Report O-X-169, 19 pp.

U.S. Forest Service. 1977. *FIRESCOPE implementation plan.* 46 pp.

Van Wagner, C. E. 1968. The line intersect method in forest fuel sampling. *For. Sci.* **14:**20–26.

Wade, D., J. Ewel, and R. Hofstetter. 1980. *Fire in south Florida ecosystems.* U.S. For. Serv. Gen. Tech. Report SE-17, 125 pp., illus.

Williams, D. E. 1955. *Fire hazard resulting from jack pine slash.* Can. Dep. North. Aff. Tech. Note 22, 14 pp.

Youngner, V. B., T. E. Williams, and L. R. Green 1976. *Ecological and physiological implications of greenbelt irrigation.* Calif. Water Res. Center Contr. No. 157. 104 pp., illus.

CHAPTER FIVE

Forest Fire Equipment

The success of any wildfire suppression method depends on a combination of people, equipment, and training. Since people first attempted to exert their will over wildfire, they have needed tools of some kind to help them. The first such tools were probably green branches torn from nearby trees and used to beat out or smother the flames. Indeed, such primitive, yet effective, tools are still used in some parts of the world and a simple modification, the fire broom, is a modern equivalent used against grass and other light-fuel fires.

Whatever the tool used, its purpose is to reduce combustion in any one of several different ways or by some combination of them. First, the person–tool combination may reduce combustion by removing potential fuel from the path of the fire—such as a rake to remove leaf or needle litter. Secondly, a tool can be used to cool the burning fuel and the fuels directly in front of the fire to a temperature that will no longer support combustion—water or sand applied to the flaming fuel will do this. Thirdly, a tool can be used to "smother" a fire, that is, prevent it from obtaining the amount of oxygen it needs to sustain combustion. The green branch was used in this way as well as the fire broom and swatters of various kinds.

Some tools, as noted, can be used effectively on a fire in a combination of the ways just discussed. For example, the shovel can be used as a swatter to smother a fire, it can be used to spread sand or soil on a fire to cool it, and it can also be used to remove fuels from the path of a fire by preparing a line across which the fire cannot spread. A good firefighter may, in the course of fighting a single fire, use the shovel in all three ways depending on the fuel types and fire intensity being encountered.

All forest fire fighting tools, no matter how simple or how complex, are used to attack the fire in any one or combination of the three ways just described. In addition, there are a number of auxiliary tools that are not used directly on the fireline but support the firefighters' attack efforts. One example of this category of tools would be the power saw which has many uses along the fire line. It may be used, for example, to help remove downed trees in the path of a firebreak, to fell burning stubs into the fire, or to clear landing spots for helicopters.

There are, of course, many different tools for forest fire suppression in use around the world and individual preference plays a role in deciding which are habitually used in any particular forest area. Probably more important, however, are the surface conditions existing in that forest area. The term *surface conditions* is meant here to include such factors as fuel type and quantity, living vegetation, soil type and roughness, and slope. These and other factors determine the type of person–tool combination that will most effectively do the job of suppressing fire.

Regardless of the type of tool, there are a number of important points that should be considered when new tools are selected or old ones replaced. First, the quality of the tool is crucial. Because of the emergency nature of the work required of these tools, it is essential that they perform satisfactorily when the need arises. Many times equipment must be transported over long distances at significant expense—often by aircraft. Under these circumstances, it is obvious that only high quality equipment should be used.

The same argument can be made for equipment maintainance. Fire fighting is an arduous and dangerous task. Every effort should be made to ensure that the firefighter is provided with effective, well-maintained equipment.

One system used by many forest fire control agencies to help ensure that newly purchased equipment will be of acceptable quality is the preparation and maintainance of standards. These standards may be formal or informal. Their main purpose is to provide firm guidelines for those making purchases for the agency. This is particularly important for those agencies, mainly governmental, who have a low bid policy. In such circumstances, the purchasing agent is under pressure to accept whatever equipment is being offered at the lowest price. If there are no clear standards to use as guides, the agent will be hard-pressed to accept low cost items regardless of quality.

Most standards, formal or informal, are prepared by a panel of experts and may include test procedures to be used to ensure that the item meets the agreed-upon standard. In many countries, standards associations or societies have been established. They have the responsibility for developing and maintaining standards on request and, usually, for maintaining facilities to test the equipment as required by the standard. In other instances, standards may consist simply of a description of the piece of equipment that would be acceptable to the agency.

Another advantage of standardization is that it facilitates the exchange of equipment and personnel between districts, regions, or agencies. Firefighters will be much more effective if given equipment with which they are familiar. There is a limit, however, to the extent to which standardization should be applied. Obviously, there must be some flexibility in equipment usage based on varying conditions between areas.

Another criteria that must be considered in selecting equipment is portability. As was noted earlier, most fire equipment must be transported long distances and under difficult conditions, often by aircraft. Heavy, awkward, or bulky equipment will increase transport difficulty and increase the frustration level of those responsible for the job. With air drops, or any air transport, consideration has to be given to the size of the drop hatch or doorway on the type of aircraft that is normally used for the purpose. In many fire management agencies some items of equipment are prepackaged to facilitate transportation and possible air drop.

In summary, because of the special demands placed on forest fire fighting equipment of all kinds, it is vital that it be of excellent quality, be well maintained, and, through standardization and training, be effective in the hands of a broad spectrum of firefighters. It is true that to achieve those goals is expensive, and all fire management agencies must be conscious of the economics of their operation. Some balance must be achieved between high-cost equipment and funds available, but an agency must be very careful to ensure that any reduction in cost of equipment does not result in the lowering of the quality of that equipment to the point where it may fail to function on the fireline.

The range and variety of equipment now used to combat wildfires is extremely broad and is increasing almost daily as new technology is adapted to this task. To discuss all this equipment and the many add-ons and modifications that have evolved would be impossible in one chapter or even in one book. What is attempted here is a description of the major types of equipment used, the conditions under which they are most effective, and in some instances a short discussion on how they evolved.

HAND TOOLS

In fire fighting, as in many other unusual skills, the basic hand tools have not changed much over the years. Since people first decided they might do something about wildfire rather than let it have its way, they found that under the right conditions and with simple beating or scraping tools, they could stop the spread of a fire. Presently used hand tools are, for the most part, relatively simple modifications of the originals. Some, such as various rakes and shovels, are used directly on the fireline in ways described at the beginning of this chapter and in Chapter 6. Others serve an auxiliary or support role. Examples of these are the axe and the saw which are used to cut trees and brush to facilitate line building and to provide openings in forests for such uses as campsites and helispots (Figure 5.1).

The principal line-building tools are the shovel, the Pulaski tool (a combi-

Figure 5.1.   Common hand tools used in forest fire control: (from left to right) shovel, Pulaski, axe, brush hook. Photo by San Dimas Equipment Development Center, U.S. Forest Service.

nation axe and grub-hoe), various types of rake–hoe combinations such as the Rich and McLeod tools, leaf rakes and various brush hooks used to cut underbrush and roots from the fire line. For beating out or smothering light surface fires there are a number of swatters or beaters. Descriptions of these tools are given in various handbooks and training guides as well as in *Forest Fire: Control and Use* by Brown and Davis (1973) and *Bushfires in Australia* by Luke and McArthur (1978).

Although there have been great technological advances in the equipment used to combat wildfires in some parts of the world, in many others simple hand tools are still the only equipment used. Even in those countries where fire management has been developed to a high professional level, people with hand tools still play the major role in the suppression of small fires (and most fires do remain small), in controlling parts of large fires, particularly in accessible areas, and in the inevitable mop-up job.

Backpack Pumps

Along with hand tools, the application of water has always been a basic method of fire fighting. Any handy container, including the hat, has been used to scoop up available water to be splashed on the fire, cooling and smothering the flames. Fire buckets are currently used in some areas and are often effective when employed by the well-known bucket brigade. The back-pack pump, like the stirrup pump designed for building fires, was a significant advance on the bucket. It was designed to eliminate serious draw-backs of the fire bucket when dealing with wildfires. First, the water is carried in a closed container on the fire fighter's back thus improving com-fort and mobility both from the water source to the fire and along the fireline. Secondly, it is equipped with a hand-operated pump and nozzle system that allows a firefighter to increase the effectiveness of the limited amount of water (approximately 20 liters) in the container. A number of different units are available. The original backpack pump used a metal tank, but new mod-els use rubber or plastic-lined collapsible bags, or fiberglass or plastic tanks to reduce weight and corrosion. In the USSR a pressurized backpack pump has been developed (Kourtz 1973). Once the tank has been filled, it is charged with sodium bicarbonate and the operator controls the application of water on the fire by using a trigger-type valve. In the United States a small gasoline-powered pump has been designed to operate with a backpack tank. Both the Russian and United States types have the advantage of relieving the operator of the necessity of working a hand pump. However, they suffer from additional complexity, expense, and weight.

The effectiveness of backpack pumps can be increased by using chemical retardants or wetting agents although, again, this adds to the complexity of what is intended to be a simple device and, for the most part, backpack pumps are used with water only.

Backfiring Tools

Backfiring or burning-out is a frequently used fire control technique. Ignition may be achieved from the air, from a ground vehicle or by the use of handheld devices. The first two are discussed later. One of the most com-monly used manual devices is the drip torch, which consists of a metal fuel tank filled with kerosene or a mixture of diesel oil and gasoline, and a relatively large metal tube with a drip nozzle or wick on the end. A handle on the side of the tank allows the firefighter to carry the torch in such a manner that a trail of burning fuel may be laid along the route of the desired burnout. A variety of coils may be incorporated to prevent flash-back, thus making the drip torch a relatively safe tool (Figure 5.2). A number of other torches are available, some having backpack tanks for the fuel and some pres-surized. Various fuels are used in pressurized tanks including propane, gasoline, and kerosene. In general, pressurized torches are more complex and hazardous to use than the popular drip torch. They are quite useful, though, in igniting heavy logging slash or dense brush when rapid firing is desired.

Figure 5.2. The handheld drip torch is the most common tool for backfiring and prescribed burning. Photo by W. R. Tikkala.

Solid fuel ignition devices, sometimes referred to as fusees, are also used in backfiring. Their burning period is usually limited to about 10 minutes, but they have the advantage of not requiring a supply of flammable fuel. Other solid fuel ignition devices take the form of a hand-thrown grenade.

Tool Packages and Caches

A long-standing problem concerning hand tools is that of ensuring that they remain reserved exclusively for use in fire control. As a first step, all fire control tools should be marked and identified as such. This alone, of course, won't ensure that they are not "borrowed" from time to time to dig a hole or fell a tree. Many agencies package a set of tools for each crew of a certain size in a bundle or carton, seal them, and store them in a cache where they will be intact when needed. Whether prepackaged or not, all fire tools should be kept separate from other tools and should be frequently examined to ensure that they remain in good condition.

MECHANIZED EQUIPMENT

The various adaptations of mechanical equipment to fire fighting are far too numerous to cover in one chapter, but a number of them have developed in different parts of the world and, because they have been found to be effective, are widely used. These are discussed here in general terms because of the great variation in machines around the world.

Many of the points noted for hand tools also apply to mechanical equipment. They must be dependable, of high quality, and well maintained. The conditions under which wildfires are often fought will place a heavy strain on both the equipment and the firefighter. Failure of equipment at crucial times during suppression operations can have disastrous effects on the success of the effort and the safety of the firefighters.

Fireline Plows

One of the most commonly used pieces of mechanical equipment is the fireline plow. It is essentially an adaptation of the familiar farm plow. The purpose of the plow in forest fire work is like that of many other tools, to break the fuel continuity by clearing a line or furrow down to mineral soil. To be more effective in this task, the farm plow has been modified and strengthened to meet the rugged conditions of forest and wildland, to widen the furrow it produces, and to allow it to be attached to a wide range of vehicles used in the forest. Fireline plows range from self-contained or sulky units that must be towed behind a tracked or wheeled tractor or truck, to hydraulically operated units attached as an integral part of the prime mover (Figure 5.3). Normally, the depth of furrow of hydraulic plows can be controlled and the unit can be lifted clear of the ground when not building firelines.

Figure 5.3.   Hydraulic plow unit mounted behind a small tanker. Photo by Canadian Forestry Service.

Figure 5.4.   The fire plow creates a flat furrow with earth mounded on each side. Photo by U.S. Forest Service.

In order to widen the furrow so that the result is an effective fire guard, most fireline plows are designed so that the blade throws the sod and soil to either side creating a flat bottomed furrow with earth mounds on each side (Figure 5.4).

Obviously, the more the terrain resembles farm land, the more effective a plow will be in building fireline. Best results are obtained in relatively level, open, sandy, or loam sites. On the opposite side of the scale, plows are seldom effective in steep, rocky terrain or in dense bush or underbrush. As with any other type of fire equipment, the best plow units are those that are sturdy and simple, easily transported, and readily attached to their prime mover. The depth of plow blade penetration must be readily adjustable and the plow must be capable of riding over rocks, stumps, or other obstacles without damage and without serious disruption to its building continuous line. The unit should also be capable of reversing without difficulty. This is often necessary when the vehicle becomes bogged down and a new start or direction is required. The sulky-type plows have a disadvantage in this regard whereas those attached to the vehicle may be lifted out of the soil to facilitate reversing. Since, as was said earlier, the fireline plow is an adaptation of the farm plow, many variations have arisen from the fertile minds of local fire "equipmenteers." Many of these are, of course, particularly adapted to meet local conditions and if one is interested in acquiring a good plow for a certain region it is usually wise to begin by looking at what has been developed locally.

The Bulldozer

The bulldozer, for the uninitiated, is a heavy-tracked vehicle with a wide adjustable blade that it pushes in front of it. There are as well wheeled tractors with bulldozer blades and a modification known as the front-end loader where the blade takes the form of a wide bucket that can be used to load or transport material. These types of equipment were designed originally for roadbuilding in rough terrain and are, therefore, not only ideal for fireline building but are frequently available in forested areas. The bulldozer has another advantage in that it does not need modification to do effective work in fire control. In the hands of a skilled operator, the bulldozer can do many jobs in fire management where the terrain is too rugged for other equipment such as the fireline plow. One of the more frequent uses of the dozer is in the construction of permanent fire breaks and access roads through brush and forested areas. On large fires, it is used to build fireline, prepare roads, and clear areas for campsites, helispots, and the like. In a sense, the bulldozer is the "Hercules" of the large fire organization and can accomplish an impressive variety and amount of work on a fire. However, in recent years, there has been much environmental concern expressed about the damage that can result from inordinate or indiscriminate use of bulldozers, usually in the form of soil erosion caused by rains after the fire has been extinguished. As a result, more care is being exercised in the use of bulldozers, particularly in parks and other areas that may be susceptible to such damage. In far northern areas where permafrost is common, care must also be taken in the use of any heavy equipment since it can leave scars that may remain for many years.

In a large fire organization, bulldozers are often used in pairs (Anon. 1976), the first machine being used to clear a rough route through the forest while the second clears the fireline. The two machines are often accompanied by firefighters assigned to locate a route for the machines and to burn out from the cleared line.

As with the fireline plow, there have been many modifications of the bulldozer. Tracked all-terrain vehicles have been equipped with dozer blades as well as with torch systems for burning out and backfiring. Others have been fitted with water tanks and hose and nozzle systems for direct fire attack. In the USSR one type of all-terrain vehicle has been equipped with a bulldozer blade on the front and a fireline plow on the back. Again, these interesting modifications are usually the reflection of local conditions and needs.

There are many examples of specialized heavy equipment that have been developed to meet a local fire problem. One such example is the *brushbuster* used in Massachusetts in the United States. Another is the *Dragon-wagon* designed and constructed by the U.S. Bureau of Land Management. Experience has shown, however, that such specialized developments are not widely accepted outside their local area and there is no doubt that the most widely used piece of heavy equipment is the unmodified bulldozer.

The all-terrain vehicle, apart from its use with a dozer blade in line construction, is also used for the transport of firefighters and their supplies and equipment in roadless and rugged terrain. Some such vehicles, equipped with wide low-pressure tracks, are capable of traversing swamps and muskeg.

Lightweight Mechanical Equipment

The mechanized equipmnent discussed to this point is expensive, very heavy, and often presents difficulties in transporting it to a fire. Many attempts have been made to transpose the mechanical advantages to lighter weight machines that can be more readily transported, even by air, and more easily handled and serviced on the fireline. Examples are various types of trenchers and flails powered by small gasoline engines, or leaf-blowers designed to clean a line through hardwood litter fuels. The aim of the development of such machines is to speed up the rate of line construction and increase the amount of line each firefighter can build. Other machines such as the powered wheelbarrow have been designed to transport supplies and equipment over trails or along a fire guard.

Power saws, generators, and pumps are other examples of lightweight mechanical equipment frequently found on fire control operations. The power pump is discussed in more detail later in this chapter.

WATER-HANDLING EQUIPMENT

Probably since people first learned to use fire for their benefit, they have known the powerful effect of water in extinguishing fire. It does this by both cooling and smothering, and is more effective on flaming fire than on a smoldering fire—a point that has had an important influence on the development of various types of water-handling equipment. A factor of equal importance is the availability of water.

Pumps and Hose

The portable mechanical fire pump was first developed in the 1920s utilizing an early outboard motor as the power source. The complete fire control pumping system consists of a suction hose, the pump, lengths of specially designed forestry hose, and a nozzle or series of nozzles. Such systems have been widely used in forested areas having a good availability of usable water sources. Over time, many advances have been made in forestry pumping systems. Currently, high-performance, high-pressure centrifugal pumps are most generally used. They are rugged yet lightweight and are designed to withstand many hours of continuous operation under rough conditions. The centrifugal pump has several advantages over the earlier positive displacement or gear pump. It can pump dirty or sandy water for longer periods with less resulting wear and it is able to continue running when the water flow has been stopped. This allows firefighters to close off the water flow when they wish to add or substitute a length of hose, change nozzles, and so on. An additional advantage of centrifugal pumps is the ability to use them in tandem, the first pumping directly to the second, where increased pressure is needed.

As with the pumps themselves, there have been numerous developments in the hose used with them. The suction hose is a semirigid hose about three to four meters in length with a foot valve and strainer on the intake end. It is usually somewhat larger in diameter than the outlet hose. The latter has been designed to provide effective transport of water yet be light in weight to facilitate transport to the fire. For many years the type most used was a lightweight woven linen hose. One of its major advantages was in its ability to remain wet through seepage. This reduced the likelihood of its being burned should it come in contact with burning embers or be subjected to high levels of heat radiation near the fireline. Linen hose has now been largely replaced by hoses made with synthetic fabrics. Hoses having a smooth impermeable inner lining such as rubber are able to deliver more water because of reduced friction loss but they lose the ability to remain wet. This type of hose is generally used where it is not likely to be close to the fire. Another type, the lined percolating hose, was designed to combine the advantages of the linen hose and the lined hose. The lining has small slits in it to allow enough water to seep through to keep the outer jacket wet.

There are also many variations in such ancillary equipment as couplings, nozzles, and valves. In some countries, threaded couplings have largely given way to what is known as quick-connect couplings. These can be connected with a simple twist and have the added advantage of being interchangeable, that is, having neither male nor female fittings. Originally most fittings were brass, but in recent years other materials such as aluminum and high-strength plastics have been used, partly to reduce the weight of the fittings and partly because of the high cost of brass.

Commonly used nozzles consist of a barrel with a set of interchangeable tips of various orifice size. Different diameter tips will give different patterns of spray and different droplet sizes and an operator is able to select the most desirable effect for the particular fire situation. The larger the nozzle orifice diameter, the greater the volume of water being delivered and the less the nozzle pressure, hence the less the length of stream. For light surface fires, a fine spray is more effective than a straight stream whereas the latter is more effective when dealing with a fire in heavier fuels. At times a wide variety of fuel types are encountered on the same fire segment and, to meet this challenge, variable stream nozzles have been designed. Using these nozzles, an operator is able to change the application rate from a straight stream to a fine spray or to anything in between at the turn of a dial. The so-called fog nozzle where a high pressure fog is produced has not been found effective against wildfires. A portion of the fog tends to drift away from the target in the wind and, in addition, the entrained air with the high pressure fog may actually fan the fire.

Depending on the source of water, it is frequently crucial that it be applied sparingly, the objective being to achieve a fine balance between under and overapplication. Tables have been constructed to show the amounts of water applied through various nozzle tips (Luke and McArthur op. cit.), but it is really through experience with the equipment on going fires that an operator can understand the principles of water application and become expert at getting the most out of the least or the "greatest lick for the liter."

Fire Engines

In many parts of the world there are adequate natural sources of water such as lakes, rivers, and streams that allow the frequent use of pump and hose systems in wildfire suppression. In many other areas, however, water sources are few and far between and in some places, of course, there is no readily available water. In areas such as these, if pump and hose systems are to be used, water must be brought to the equipment in one way or another. The method most commonly used to do this is to use some sort of mobile tank. A great deal of ingenuity has been demonstrated in modifying various types of carriers to use as fire engines or *ground tankers*.

What has generally happened in the development of these machines is the equipping of some commonly used vehicle with tanks to contain a quantity of water consistent with the load capability of the vehicle (Figure 5.5). To this is usually added some system of pump and hose with which to apply the water or water plus fire retardant to the fire. The vehicles used are usually those that have been found to be able to negotiate the roads, trails, and terrain of the area. In other examples, the vehicle may be one that becomes available as surplus military equipment. A simple example of this is the modification of a surplus military four-wheel drive truck where the box is removed and replaced with a tank and pumping system. Since trucks of this type were designed for rough off-road operations, they frequently prove to be very useful as ground tankers. The variety of vehicles that have been converted to ground tankers is wide, ranging from the famous jeep through all types of trucks, tractors, all-terrain vehicles, and even heavy bulldozers.

Similarly, the pumping system used has many variations but the more common features are: (1) a high-pressure pump operating either from a power take-off from the vehicle's power plant or with its own small gasoline engine, (2) a *live* reel of hose, live meaning that water can be pumped through the hose when it is still on or partially on the reel, and (3) a nozzle

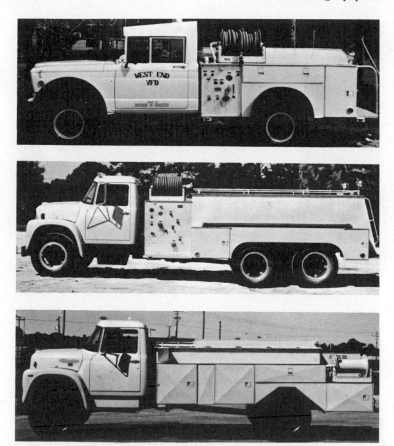

Figure 5.5. Firetrucks converted from excess military equipment carry from 1000 to 5000 liters of water. Photo by Florida Division of Forestry.

that is equipped with a shut-off valve so that the nozzle operator can conserve water.

These may be looked on as minimum requirements for a tanker–pumper system. Many additional features have been designed to improve the effectiveness of such systems for fire suppression under various conditions. Examples are methods for injecting into the system chemicals for reducing friction loss, for reducing surface tension (wetting agents), and for enhancing the suppression effect of the water (retardants).

One adaptation of the tanker concept that has received wide acceptance is the so called "slip-on" tanker (Figure 5.6). This is a tank and pumper unit designed to fit on an available vehicle normally used for some other purpose. For example, some of the earliest such tankers were designed to fit into the box of a pickup truck, the object being to keep the unit filled and ready on an elevated stand so that, when it was needed on a fire, it could be readily

Figure 5.6.   Small slip-on tanker used on forest fires in Italy. Photo by Italian Ministry of Agriculture and Forestry.

slipped onto any available pickup truck of the required size. This concept has been applied in many parts of the world and to many types of vehicles including logging trucks, forewarders, and even aircraft as in the Modular Airborne Firefighting System (MAFFS) which fits into any Hercules C-130 airframe.

Many types of tank trailers have also been developed, again with major factors being the availability of equipment that can be modified and the utility of such tankers in the local terrain.

In many parts of the world (e.g., Australia, Portugal, and Sweden) wildfire control is the responsibility of rural fire departments. In other areas, where it is not their direct responsibility, rural and municipal fire departments are frequently called to help in the control of wildfires that threaten the communities for which they are responsible. These departments are frequently equipped with tanker–pumpers specifically designed for fire control whether it be building fires or wildfires. Most of those vehicles are designed for use where good road systems exist and, of course, fill a role in wildfire control only insofar as they can operate from a road.

Apart from their use as tanker–pumpers, most tankers of the types discussed are also used to supply water and retardants to pumps and other tanker–pumpers on the fire. This is usually done through the transfer of their contents to a holding tank located near the fireline. Portable holding tanks have been developed for this purpose, many utilizing light strong fabrics. Some of these are self-supporting and can be used to convert any flat bed truck to a tanker.

EXPLOSIVES

Explosives have been used for many years in the construction of roads and ditches in rural areas. It is not surprising, then, that techniques have been developed for the use of explosives in fireline building. In the USSR this form of line construction has been operationally used for a number of years in areas inaccessible to fireline plows or ground tankers. Two methods are used. In heavy peaty soils, holes are drilled about one meter deep and two meters apart along the line to be blasted. A charge of one-half kilogram of ammonium nitrate explosive is dropped into each hole and a detonating cord is used to connect all charges in the line. The line of charges is then detonated using a blasting cap and fuse.

A second technique used by the Russians for building fireline in lighter soils utilizes a continuous tube or hose of explosive that is laid along the surface of the ground or buried in a small slit trench. This technique is also used to a limited extent in both the United States and Canada (Lott 1975). As with most other fireline building methods, the success of explosives depends largely on the fuel and soil conditions encountered. Line building with explosives is not effective where there are very heavy fuels, slash, or dense underbrush, or where the soil is rocky. Another important factor is the availability of the right type of explosive. It must be able to do a good trenching job without starting fires.

Explosives are also used, under certain conditions, for falling snags and to prepare water holes as a source of water for pumps or tankers. In muskeg and swampy areas where no clean open water is available, explosives can prepare a hole or pond quickly and effectively.

Development of improved fireline explosives is underway at several equipment development centers. At Missoula, "water gel" explosives were found to be a safe and effective method of preparing fireline for prescribed burning (Ramberg 1978). In his report, Ramberg points out that the major factors presently limiting the use of these explosives are the lack of certified blasters and suitable explosives storage facilities at fire management centers. This, no doubt, applies in other countries where there is an interest in the use of explosives.

FIRE-RETARDANT CHEMICALS

There are several principal ways to inhibit combustion: (1) lower the temperature of the burning fuel below its ignition temperature, (2) dilute the combustible gases above the fuel until they are below their lower flammability limit, (3) coat the fuel surface with a nonflammable material to exclude oxygen and/or reduce heat transfer, and (4) catalyze the pyrolysis process to favor char formation over tar formation. Water is quite effective in the first three of these processes—which is why water has been the most widely used fire-retardant chemical since humans began extinguishing fire. However, water is not a perfect combustion inhibitor, and many other chemicals are available that will substitute for or enhance the ability of water as a fire suppression agent.

In order for a material to lower the temperature of burning fuel, the material must first reach the fuel surface. Water often fails to meet this test under two quite opposite circumstances. When water is sprayed or cascaded onto a fire, the smaller droplets are often caught in the rising convection currents and never reach the fuel surface. This difficulty can be overcome by increasing the viscosity of water so that it will not disperse into small droplets. At the other extreme, deep-seated smoldering fires such as those burning in inorganic soils or deep layers of duff can be extinguished only after water has penetrated the overlying layer of ash and charred material. If the overlaying material is tightly packed, capillary attraction may prevent the water from penetrating to the burning surface beneath the char and ash. In these instances, the addition of surfactants, or wetting agents, will reduce the capillary attraction and increase penetration by five to eight times. Dozens of wetting agents are commercially available and are widely used in forest fire control, particularly for mop-up when extinguishment of deep-seated glowing combustion is the primary objective.

Viscosity agents have seen less use in forest fire ground operations than wetting agents. There are several reasons for this. Most of the viscosity agents that have been tested for forest fire use are industrial gums or polymers that form gels at very low concentrations—typically one-tenth percent to one-half percent by weight. They are very sensitive to water properties such as pH, temperature, hardness, and impurities (Stechishen et al. 1982). Consequently, the concentration of chemical required to achieve a given viscosity must be recalibrated with each new water source. This is difficult for ground tankers which may use several different water sources while operating on a single fire. It is easier when servicing air tankers where the mixing base is usually a permanent installation, or at least one that remains fixed for the duration of the fire operation. Another disadvantage of viscosity agents in ground operations is that they are extremely slippery, which is potentially dangerous to firefighters on the ground but of little concern to the air tanker pilot whose feet remain tens of meters above the target. Lastly, many viscosity agents are subject to spoilage or chemical changes unless used within a few hours. Purging and flushing the system is more time-consuming and difficult for the ground tanker than for the air tanker with its less complex plumbing system.

To act effectively as a coolant in gas phase combustion, a chemical must have a high heat of vaporization and a boiling point lower than 280°C, the temperature where exothermic reactions predominate in wood pyrolysis. For practical use in forest fire control the vapors produced must also be nonflammable and nontoxic. To date, no chemical can compete successfully with water which has a heat of vaporization of 540 calories per gram and a boiling point of 100°C.

Water is also unbeatable as a diluent to flame gases. Water vapor at saturation occupies 1700 times the volume of liquid water at 100°C, and expands to 4300 times its original liquid volume when heated to 700°C. Liquid nitrogen, on the other hand, only expands 175 times at its boiling point of − 196°C and has a volume half that of water vapor at 700°C. Frozen carbon dioxide (dry ice) is even less efficient than liquid nitrogen. Nevertheless, there are advantages to inert gas extinguishing systems that make them preferable to water under some circumstances. Water is a good conductor of electricity. The electrical resistance of natural water supplies ranges from 700 to 5500 ohms per cubic centimeter depending on the amount and nature of impurities (NFPA 1976). Use of water on fires involving electrical equipment may cause severe damage to the equipment and the use of water on or near lines carrying more than 600 volts to ground is dangerous to firefighters. This subject is discussed in more detail in Chapter 10. Several inert gas extinguishing agents such as chlorinated hydrocarbons (Halons) are available for use on electrical fires. Inert gases may also be preferable to water on fires where valuable materials susceptible to damage by soaking may occur. Since all water applied to a fire is never totally converted to vapor, some liquid will always be residual at the fire scene. Chemicals such as liquid nitrogen or dry ice, whose boiling points are below normal ambient temperatures, leave no residue and hence reduce ancillary damages. These factors are rarely a consideration in forest fire control and the use of inert gas extinguishers is confined to urban fire situations.

Water will coat fuel surfaces and exclude oxygen, but water evaporates readily and the effect is temporary. One chemical, long used in forest fire control, that operated on the principle of surface coating, was sodium calcium borate. Applied in slurry form, hydrated borate with a melting point of 75°C precipitated out as the water carrier evaporated. The molten hydrated borate flowed over fuel surfaces. As the water of hydration was removed, the melting point of the salt increased to 750°C, effectively coating the fuel in an impervious glass. Because of its residual toxicity to emergent vegetation, sodium calcium borate fell out of favor as a wildland fire retardant and is no longer in use. Intumescent coatings consisting of a flame retardant such as ammonium phosphate mixed with urea and paraformaldehyde are often used to protect interior surfaces in structures. When heated, the coating boils and swells to form a foam char layer one to three centimeters thick. This layer acts to insulate the underlying surface. Intumescent coatings have not been used in forest fire control largely because of cost.

The action of water in fire suppression is purely physical in nature; water plays no role in the pyrolysis process. There are several chemicals that do, however. When cellulose is heated, water vapor is driven off as soon as the fuel surface temperature reaches 100°C. At 200°C, the cellulose itself begins

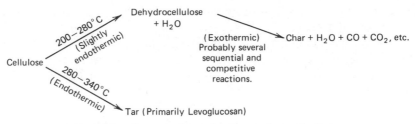

Figure 5.7.   General scheme for the pyrolysis of cellulose.

to dehydrate, a process as yet poorly understood but catalyzed by several inorganic salts. At a temperature of 280°C, the dehydrocellulose decomposes to form char, water vapor, carbon monoxide, carbon dioxide, and low molecular weight gases such as methane and ethane. Flaming is minimal and the primary reaction upon heating to higher temperatures is the glowing combustion of the residual char. At 280°C, the cellulose that has not been dehydrated during the earlier heating period dissociates to form levoglucosan which, in turn, reacts to produce several high molecular weight tars (Figure 5.7). These are ejected in the gas stream and burn readily in the flame zone. Any chemical that acts to enhance the dehydration reaction of cellulose will increase the ratio of char to tar resulting from pyrolysis, encourage glowing over flaming combustion, and reduce fire intensity by lengthening the burning time per unit mass of fuel. Many chemicals are known to act in this manner. The two classes most commonly used in forest fire control are ammonium phosphates and ammonium sulphates.

Ammonium phosphates are produced commercially as agricultural fertilizers. They are labeled according to the relative proportions of nitrogen, phosphorus, and potassium, respectively. For example, diammonium phosphate, a popular forest fire retardant known as DAP, is 21-53-0 or 21 percent nitrogen, 53 percent phosphorus, and no potassium. Other commonly available fertilizers range from 12-61-0 to 8-24-0. The fire-retarding qualities come solely from the phosphorus; the nitrogen content and other ingredients are irrelevant except as they may affect the mixing and handling properties of the chemical. The usual mixture for both ground and air application is eight percent P_2O_5 equivalent in water. This requires from 150 to 380 grams per liter depending on the chemical selected. The criteria of choice is largely one of cost at the mixing site since the lower concentration salts are less expensive to purchase but require higher transportation costs. The ammonium phosphates must be mixed with viscosity agents if they are to be used on intense fires or heavy fuels in order to maintain enough salt on the fuel surface for effective retardancy. It is not possible to increase the P_2O_5 content of aqueous solutions much above eight percent because of the tendency for the salt to precipitate at low temperatures or in water with impurities.

Ammonium sulphate has about two-thirds the fire-retarding efficiency as an equal weight of diammonium phosphate. However, it is much more soluble and will form 25 percent solutions with a minimum of agitation. Consequently, an equal volume of 25 percent sulphate will have twice the effectiveness of an 8 percent phosphate solution. Again, the choice depends largely on cost.

The forest fire control chemical industry has expanded rapidly since its inception in the mid1950s. Many specialty additives as well as specialized mixing and handling equipment systems are available. In the United States, the National Fire Protection Association regularly revises a handbook on chemicals for forest fire fighting (Hardy 1977).

AIRCRAFT

The history of the use of aircraft in forest fire control is discussed in detail in Chapter 6. It is safe to say that one of the first and most successful applications of aircraft after they had "won their wings" in World War I was in forestry work of various kinds. This included their use in detecting forest fires and in transporting equipment and firefighters to the fire or, more precisely, in the case of the early flying boats and float planes, to the nearest lake. It was not until after the second World War that serious thought was given to the dropping or *cascading* of water and various chemical retardants on or in front of a fire from the aircraft itself. Early experiments involved relatively light planes and small quantities of water. These early demonstrations were not particularly impressive and were frequently met, as a result, with a considerable amount of skepticism. Proponents of the technique fortunately persisted and by the 1950s a number of forest fire management agencies, particularly in North America, had adopted the *airtanker* as one more operational tool to use against wildfire.

Airtankers

The first airtankers were fixed-wing aircraft equipped with either wheels or floats. In the latter type, some of the planes utilized the floats as tanks. Thus there developed two distinct types of fixed-wing airtankers; those operating from airstrips and those operating from a water surface. Many of the early land-based airtankers were modifications of forestry or agricultural spray aircraft (Figure 5.8). These smaller airtankers are still used where conditions call for low volume, highly maneuverable aircraft. The majority of the larger land-based airtankers that followed were surplus military aircraft such as the CS2F "tracker" or the American TBM fitted with various configurations of tanks and drop gates. Others are modified commercial transport aircraft such as the DC-6.

It is not, of course, any aircraft that can be successfully converted to an airtanker. It must meet the government regulations for airworthiness and safety of the country in which it is to operate. To do this, it must be able to

Figure 5.8. "Snow Commander" agricultural spray aircraft dropping 1100 liters of "Gelgard" retardant during tests in Alberta, Canada. Photo by B. Hodgson.

withstand stresses associated with the airtanker role (i.e., many take-offs and landings), the effect of the sudden release of its load, and low-level operation under poor flying conditions. A listing of those aircraft that have "stood the test" and are used as airtankers in North America and in many other countries is provided in *Air Operations for Forest, Brush and Grass Fires* (NFPA 1975) and by Simard and Young (1977).

In the midyears of airtanker development, the 1960s, tests with current airtankers and tank systems indicated that best results would obtain when the load was released in the shortest time possible. The objective at that time was to design a system where the bottom literally dropped out of the tank to release the load. As airtankers became larger with a consequent increase in load-carrying capacity, it was inefficient to release all of the load at once. Various sophisticated combinations of tanks, gates, and activation mechanisms have been developed to enable an airtanker to lay down a pattern that covers a maximum amount of retardant necessary for extinguishment under the prevailing fuel and weather conditions. Determining the optimum level of coverage involves consideration of several variables including both the aircraft and the retardant being carried. For a complete discussion of the subject the reader should consult Swanson et al. (1975).

Water-based airtankers, either float-equipped (Figure 5.9*a*) or of the flying-boat type (Figure 5.9*b*) evolved from forestry or military aircraft. During the course of their development, a very useful feature was in-

Figure 5.9. (*a*) A turbo-Beaver equipped to carry 635 liters in its floats. Photo by T. P. M. Cooper-Slipper. (*b*) The PBY—a reconnaissance aircraft in World War II and the mainstay of the firefighting fleet in the early 1960s. Photo by Field Aviation.

117

troduced in the form of a method for taking water into the tanks as the aircraft moved across the water surface. This was accomplished through the design of retractable probes that are lowered as the aircraft taxis and, through the momentum of the aircraft, water is forced through the probes and into the tanks. Airtankers equipped with these probes became known as *scooper* or *skimmer* airtankers. In areas where there are numerous lakes or other usable bodies of water, they are able to make frequent drops, scooping up a new water supply in a few seconds as they skim the water surface. The largest airtanker yet developed, the Martin Mars, with a capacity of 27,000 liters is of this type. Also, the first aircraft designed and built specifically as an airtanker, the Canadair CL-215 (Figure 5.10), is a scooper as well as an amphibian which can also be loaded from a land base.

Land-based airtankers have an advantage over scoopers in their ability to use long-term chemical retardants. Various types of mixing, storage, and loading facilities for these retardants have been designed for installation at air bases used by these airtankers (Anon. 1980). With these operations it is

Figure 5.10. The Canadian CL-215 was the first aircraft designed specifically for forest fire control. Photo by Canadair Ltd.

important that the aircraft be refueled and reloaded as quickly and as efficiently as possible.

The selection of the best airtanker to use in a specific area depends on a number of factors including the availability of usable water sources, the presence of suitable airstrips, the fuel type to be dealt with, the fire history of the area, and, of course, the budget available. The smaller airtankers with a tank capacity of up to 1500 liters such as the Snow or the Twin Otter can be effective on small fires within about 20 kilometers of their base or water source, particularly in support of a ground crew. The larger machines with tank capacities of 2,000 to 10,000 liters have a greater range and a greater line-building capability.

An adaptation of the slip-on tank concept for aircraft, the Modular Airborne Fire Fighting System (MAFFS) was developed by the U.S. Forest Service for use with the Lockheed C-130 Hercules military transport, although the system can be adapted for use with other aircraft having a rear loading door through which the system can be mounted and from which it discharges its load over a fire. It is a self-contained slip-in unit and is called "modular" in that it may contain a number of interconnected pressurized tanks. The system used for the C-130 (Figure 5.11) is made up of five 1900-

Figure 5.11. The C-130 MAFFS unit in action. Photo by U.S. Air Force.

liter tanks whereas that for the DeHaviland DHC-5 Buffalo uses a single tank. A three-tank system has been designed for the CH-47C Chinook helicopter.

A significant advantage of the MAFFS is that it is mounted on its own palletized cradles allowing it to be slipped into a variety of cargo aircraft without requiring any modification to the aircraft. This means that several types of military and commercial transport aircraft located in many countries may be temporarily converted to airtankers on relatively short notice and with a minimum of disruption to their primary role.

Because airtankers are highly photogenic (as well as highly effective when used as an integrated part of a modern forest fire organization), there has been something of a stampede on the part of countries that are just beginning to establish forest fire agencies to lease or purchase airtankers. In our view this trend is unfortunate. The airtanker is the most expensive piece of equipment in the firefighter's tool kit. To be effective, airtankers must be backed by an infrastructure that includes a detection and communications system capable of dispatching airtankers to all fires while they are still small enough to be controllable, a training and transportation system capable of placing skilled firefighters on the ground in time to follow up the aerial suppression efforts, and a fire command organization capable of prioritizing targets and directing a coordinated fire suppression campaign.

Fixed-wing aircraft, of course, also have roles in fire control other than as airtankers. We have already discussed their importance and increasing use in fire detection. As a means of transporting firefighters, equipment, and supplies to or near a fire control operation, both land-based and float-equipped aircraft have been invaluable to fire managers for many years. Large transport aircraft are used where long distances are to be covered with lighter aircraft being used to carry people and materials to smaller airports or landing points as close to the fire as possible. Specially designed *bush* planes such as the DeHaviland Beaver and Otter were produced with forest fire control requirements very much in mind.

Helicopters

The helicopter continues to assume an increasingly prominent role in wildfire control mainly because of its ability to operate without elaborate landing strips, its maneuverability, and its ability to hover and move at low speed when required. As an airtanker, helicopters have been fitted with various types of tanks and suspended containers, usually called *buckets,* that may be dipped into a water source for refilling (Figure 5.12). A National Fire Protection Association publication (NFPA 1975) lists those helicopters commonly used in North America with remarks on their various attributes as well as specifications for 16 different buckets available for use with those helicopters. The advantages of the suspended bucket are, first, that it can be

Figure 5.12.   Typical fiberglass bucket used in helitanker operations. The circles are plastic plugs that can be inserted or removed to control the water level and thus the weight of the load. Photo by Canadian Forestry Service.

filled quickly if a suitable source is available—sources may include a holding tank set up for the purpose as well as lakes, ponds, or rivers—and second, the bucket can readily be removed, freeing the helicopter for other tasks. Helitankers having fixed tanks are mainly retardant airtankers and are handled in essentially the same way as are fixed-wing airtankers. The primary advantage to a fixed-tank helicopter is that it can drop accurately at higher airspeeds, thus minimizing the dangers of rotor downwash.

Apart from their use as helitankers, helicopters perform many important jobs in wildfire control. Using slings, cargo racks, and interior space, they are effective and versatile in transporting firefighters, equipment, and supplies close to the action at fire camps or on the fireline. As observation aircraft they excel because of their ability to pick up fire officers from their bases and allow them to observe the fire with a greater degree of speed and flexibility than is possible using fixed-wing aircraft. In transporting firefighters to various positions on the fireline helicopters have become invaluable. In this role, several important developments have increased their usefulness. In one technique developed in the United States fire attack crews have been specially trained and equipped for helicopter transport. Members of the "helitack" crew exit from a helicopter as it hovers as close as possible to the ground. Special equipment includes visored helmets, padded jump suits, and special boots to protect crew members in their unorthodox exit from the helicopter.

Another variation of the helitack crew is used in the USSR and Canada as well as in the United States, and by many military services around the world. Crew members use a technique known as rappeling to lower themselves from a hovering helicopter to the ground. Again, the crews are equipped with protective clothing and use a form of harness and a mechanical device to control their descent down a rope or cloth tape. In the USSR a high-strength webbing is used in place of the rope. The webbing is wound on a reel strapped to the chest of the firefighter and is rewound on reaching the ground. A brake on the reel is used to control the rate of descent. The same piece of equipment is used, with the reel remaining in the helicopter, to lower supplies and equipment. In most other countries a winch is used for this function.

The helicopter also has played a valuable part in many rescue operations on wildfires where, again, its maneuverability comes into play.

In view of its unique attributes, it is not surprising that the helicopter has become an invaluable tool to so many wildfire management agencies. As new techniques are developed and with advancing technology, it is likely that their use will continue to increase. Helicopters, for example, are limited in their night operation capability. To reduce this limitation, the U.S. Forest Service has promoted the development of a night vision system for helicopter pilots that, in effect, turns night into day (Anon. 1981; Figure 5.13).

Figure 5.13.   Night vision goggles amplify starlight sufficiently for night navigation. Photo by San Dimas Equipment Development Center, U.S. Forest Service.

Smokejumping

Another method of aircraft delivery, first used for equipment and later for firefighters, to the vicinity of a wildfire is by use of the parachute. The development of this technique took place largely in North America prior to World War II, with the greatest operational advance taking place after the War as trained paratroops returned to civilian life. Since that time, use of the method has diminished in favor of the increased use of helicopters. Many different aircraft types have been used to transport and drop parachute-equipped firefighters (smokejumpers) and materials. Requirements for such aircraft are that they be able to operate from rough landing strips, that they have a low stall speed so that they can be flown at a low groundspeed over the target area, and that they have the power required to climb rapidly when flying in mountainous areas.

The parachutes used by smokejumpers and for cargo dropping have been largely military-type chutes or modifications of them. Because of the conditions under which they are used (i.e., rough terrain and uncleared landing sites) smokejumper parachutes must be large enough to ensure a low landing velocity and steerable to allow the smokejumper as much flexibility as possible in selecting his or her landing spot. Nevertheless, smokejumpers do on occasion make a landing in a tree and become suspended above the ground, an uncomfortable predicament especially in the vicinity of a wildfire. To alleviate this problem, smokejumpers are equipped with some type of rappeling rope that they may use to descend to the ground.

Smokejumping is obviously a high-risk occupation requiring a high level of physical and operational training as well as specialized clothing and protective equipment. Details on these and on other aspects of smokejumping are given in Chapter 6.

Aerial Ignition Devices

Under the section on hand tools, mention was made of various types of fire starting devices that are used to "fight fire with fire." With their usual flair for doing things in a big way, the Australians designed a device for igniting fire from the air over large areas (Luke and McArthur op. cit.). The objective of the technique is to achieve the burning of a large area in a short period of time or to ignite a long burnout line, again in a short period of time. The device injects plastic containers of potassium permanganate with ethyleneglycol, and drops them to the ground where the reaction between the two chemicals causes the container and contents to burst into flames. The Canadians adapted the concept for use in that country (Lait and Muraro 1977) with a device that uses ping-pong-type balls of the chemicals and may be mounted on a helicopter as well as a light aircraft. They are now widely used throughout North America as well as in Australia for both prescribed burns and in backfiring to help curtail wildfires.

Another helicopter-mounted ignition device is the so called "flying drip torch" (Fielder 1975). It is essentially a large drip-torch suspended beneath a helicopter with fuel flow and ignition controlled remotely from the helicopter cockpit. It has been particularly effective in slash burning operations on the west coast of North America.

Fire Mapping

Fire mapping using infrared or similar electronic detection devices is another increasing role for both fixed-wing aircraft and helicopters. The principles of these types of equipment were outlined in Chapter 4 with reference to detection. Currently, their most important use is in fire mapping, that is, the obtaining of a "picture" map showing the location of the fire perimeter, indicating sectors of high fire intensity, and location of any spot fires in the vicinity of the main fire. The advantage of these instruments over aerial cameras lies in their ability to "see" and record the fire through smoke and at night. The infrared scanner, however, cannot penetrate cloud or fog but similar mappers using other wavelengths such as microwave have this capability. There seems to be no doubt that future airborne mappers will be able to transmit fire perimeter information direct to ground stations under any atmospheric and light conditions.

There are several means of transmitting the fire map data to the ground varying in complexity with the type of system being used. These range from the dropping of a photograph in a container to the use of television or other electronic transmission. At some time in the future we may see remotely controlled robot aircraft or lighter-than-air craft positioned over a major fire continually providing atmospheric information as well as data on the location and intensity of the fire perimeter to the fire boss who may then feed the information into a computer to obtain guidance on what action should be taken. The technology for this and many other developments of significant potential to wildfire management exists today. It remains only to work out applications that will be within the budgetary range of fire management agencies. Aircraft themselves are very expensive fire control tools whatever their role and are rapidly becoming more so. This increasing cost linked with increasing utility has given rise to a number of complex studies and computer models designed to provide guidance on the more economic use of aircraft (Simard 1979).

Infrared measuring devices also have an important application when used on the ground as a handheld instrument. Several such compact portable infrared detectors have been developed for fire control use (Niederleitner 1976). They are primarily used during mop-up to detect and locate smoldering spots along the fire edge and in the burned-over area that are not visible to the mop-up crew. The devices are similar to and sometimes adaptations of those developed for medical use in locating abnormal "hot spots" in the human body. The fireline devices are, of course, more ruggedly constructed, more portable, and have a different temperature response range. In addition, they are usually equipped with some type of audible or visible signal to indicate when a hot spot has been "seen."

BIBLIOGRAPHY

Anon. 1976. *Handbook on use of bulldozers on forest fires*. For. Prot. Handbook No. 8, British Columbia For. Serv. For. Prot. Div., Victoria, B.C., 63 pp.

Anon. 1980. *Airtanker base planning guide*. Nat. Wildfire Coord. Gr., Fire Equip. Working Team, 29 pp.

Anon. 1981. *Night vision goggles—alive and well*. U.S. For. Serv. For. Fire News No. 16, July 1981, pp. 20–21.

Brown, A. A. and K. P. Davis. 1973. *Forest fire: control and use*. McGraw-Hill, New York, pp. 397–456.

Fielder, R. L. 1975. *The development and use of a remote control helicopter sling torch*. British Columbia For. Serv., For. Prot. Div., Victoria, B.C.

Grigel, J. E. 1974. *Role of the helitanker in forest fire control*. Canada Dept. of the Environ., Can. For. Serv., Edmonton, Atla., NOR-X-123, 41 pp.

Hardy, C. E. 1977. *Chemicals for forest fire fighting*, 3rd ed., Nat. Fire Prot. Assoc., Boston, 87 pp.

Kourtz, P. H. 1973. *The U.S.S.R. forest fire control operation as seen by the 1973 Canadian fire control delegation*. Environ. Canada, Can. For. Serv. Misc. Report FF-Y-2, 46 pp.

Lait, G. R. and S. J. Muraro. 1977. *The PFRC aerial ignition system Mark II*. Can. Dept. Fish. and the Environ., Can For. Serv. Info. Report BC-X-167, 27 pp.

Lott, J. R. 1975. *An operational system for constructing fireline with explosives*. U.S. For. Serv. Equip. Dev. Cent., Missoula, Mont. 7 pp.

Luke, R. M. and A. G. McArthur. 1978. *Bushfires in Australia*. C.S.I.R.O. Div. For. Res., For. and Timber Bureau, Canberra, 359 pp.

NFPA. 1975. *Air operations for forest, brush and grass fires*. Nat. Fire Prot. Assoc., Boston, 59 pp.

NFPA. 1976. *Fire protection handbook*, 14th ed., Nat. Fire Prot. Assoc., Boston, 1263 pp.

Niederleitner, J. 1976. *Detecting holdover fires with the AGA Thermovision 750 infrared scanner*. Environ. Can., Can. For. Ser. Info. Report NOR-X-151, 37 pp.

Ramberg, R. G. 1978. *Water gel explosives for building fireline*. U.S. For. Serv. Equip. Dev. Cent., Missoula, Mont., 7 pp.

Simard, A. J. 1979. *AIRPRO: an airtanker productivity computer simulation model, air tanker systems*. Environ. Can., Can. For. Serv. Info. Report, FF-X-67, 38 pp.

Simard, A. J. and A. Young. 1977. *Air tankers: a bibliography*. Canada Dept of Fish. and the Environ., Can. For. Serv. Info. Report FF-X-62, 79 pp.

Stechishen, E., E. C. Little, and M. W. Hobbs. 1982. *Laboratory-determined characteristics of several forest fire retardants and suppressants*. Environ. Can., Can. For. Serv. Info. Report PI-X-11.

Swanson, D. H., C. W. George, and A. D. Luedecke. 1975. *User guidelines for fire retardant aircraft: general instruction manual*. Honeywell Inc., 83 pp.

CHAPTER SIX

Forest Fire Suppression

SUPPRESSION PRINCIPLES AND METHODS

The Fire Triangle

The combustion process can be considered as the interaction of three essential components: fuel, oxygen, and heat. Combustion can proceed only when all three are linked together in a triangle. Fire suppression is aimed at removing any one of the three sides.

Oxygen can be excluded by smothering the fuel with dirt, or by diluting the combustible gases either with water vapor (steam) or inert gases (nitrogen or carbon dioxide). Oxygen removal is a very common method of fire extinguishment in enclosed spaces but of limited applicability in forest fire suppression for two reasons. Outdoor fires have almost unlimited access to a fresh air supply both from natural winds and from convection currents set up by the fire itself. Consequently, inert gases must be continually supplied until the heat production has dropped below the point where further flammable volatiles are being produced. This requires many times the volume of extinguishing agent that would be needed for a fire of the same size and intensity in a room with limited ventilation. The other limitation to oxygen exclusion is that smoldering combustion requires a much smaller proportion of oxygen in the immediate atmosphere than does flaming combustion. If the fire has been burning long enough for fuel surfaces to have become deeply charred, the flames may be quickly quenched by an inert gas, but will be as quickly reignited by smoldering material as soon as the gas has dissipated. It is this problem of rekindling that makes inert gas extinguishing systems impractical for forest fire use (Pirsko and Steck 1961) and limits their utility in urban fire control (Rasbash 1966). In fact, the entire topic of flame kinetics is of only academic interest to forest fire managers and is not covered in this book. Readers interested in pursuing the subject should start with Fristrom's (1967) monograph, an old but excellent introduction and review.

Fires, or at least flames, can also be extinguished by putting extra air into the combustion zone. This can dilute the involved volatiles below their lean limit thus quenching the flame or, as a more usual case, high velocity air can stretch the flame so far from its fuel base as to prevent reattachment. This is what happens when one blows out a match or extinguishes an oil well fire with explosives. One of the earliest and most primitive methods of fighting forest and grass fires was beating out the flames with a green bough, an example of extinguishment through air enhancement.

Heat can be removed from a fire either by cooling the flames or by cooling the fuel surface. Water is by far the most common cooling agent used in fire fighting. A thorough discussion of the use of water in forest fire management is found later in this chapter, but some of the basic principles are pertinent here.

Although water, when vaporized to steam, does displace significant amounts of air from the volatile mixture, the principle action of externally applied water on a fire is in cooling, not in oxygen displacement (Rasbash 1962). In outdoor fires an equal volume of water is more than four times as effective in cooling the fuel surface as it is in cooling the flames above the surface. Consequently, the optimum use of water involves delivering the minimum amount to the fuel surface that will result in complete extinction. A lesser amount will result in the fire's rekindling, whereas a greater amount will waste water. One way to conserve the amount of water applied to a unit area of surface is to distribute the water in small drops rather than in a straight stream from a hose or a great glob from a bucket. Theoretically, a charcoal fire can be quenched by 0.04 grams of water applied to each square centimeter of charcoal surface. Thus 1 liter of water is sufficient to extinguish $2\frac{1}{2}$ square meters of burning surface and only 4000 liters should be sufficient to completely suppress a 1-hectare fire.

Unfortunately, it is never possible to achieve theoretical maximum efficiency with water, primarily because the drops must travel from the nozzle of the hose through the air to the site of the fire and then through the rising convection column to the burning fuel surface. Since the mass of a drop is proportional to the cube of its diameter, whereas the surface area of a drop (which determines its air resistance or drag) is proportional to the square of its diameter, the penetrating power of a drop is inversely proportional to the size of the drop. The smaller the drop size, the greater the chance of being blown away and never reaching the burning fuel surface. This difficulty can be partially overcome by increasing the pressure with which the spray is ejected from the nozzle, and high pressure fog is widely used for fighting fires in closed compartments. However, high pressure sprays also entrain large volumes of air; about half the initial thrust is transferred into air momentum for coarse sprays (2 to 4 millimeter drop diameter), and for fine sprays (drop diameter < 1 millimeter), virtually all of the thrust is converted into momentum of the airstream by the time the stream is 2 meters from the nozzle (Rasbash 1962). In outdoor fires the increased oxygen supply from the high velocity airstream is more effective in enhancing combustion than the cooling effect of the entrained fog droplets are in suppressing it and, rather than being extinguished, the fire burns hotter.

Another phenomenon also limits the size of droplets that can be effectively used on cellulosic fires. Have you ever put a few drops of water on a very hot griddle or frying pan? The drops do not spread out, but skitter about over the surface growing smaller and smaller until, one by one, they disappear with an audible pop. This is because the lower surface of the drop vaporizes before the liquid ever touches the metal of the pan and the drop is, in effect, cushioned by its own steam. This will occur whenever the temperature at the junction of the solid and liquid surfaces exceeds 100°C, the boiling point of water. The temperature at the junction, known as the *instantaneous interfacial impingement temperature,* is a linear function of the temperature of each of the two substances and an exponential function of their thermal diffusivities. Figure 6.1 shows the temperatures of water and charring wood required to achieve an instantaneous interfacial impingement temperature of 100°C. At the temperature of glowing charcoal (850°C), the water temperature must be below 38°C in order to avoid exceeding the critical instantaneous interfacial impingement temperature. If a water droplet with a temperature above 38°C arrives at the glowing surface, it will never touch the

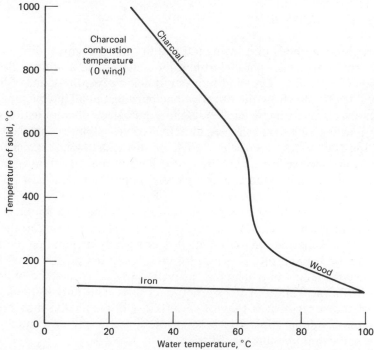

Figure 6.1.   Temperatures required for an instantaneous interfacial impingement temperature of 100°C.

charcoal and cooling must be accomplished by a much smaller mass of steam at 100°C rather than the greater mass of water at much lower temperature. The temperature of the water droplet depends on the time it takes to travel through the hot combustion gases and on the surface/volume ratio of the drop. Since both these factors decrease linearly with droplet size, droplet temperature will be inversely proportional to droplet size and drops smaller than a certain size will contribute little to cooling the fuel.

From a practical standpoint, water is generally most effective on forest fires when applied as very coarse sprays, and the most optimum results to be expected in practice are about 1 liter per square meter, or about $2\frac{1}{2}$ times the theoretical minimum (Stechishen 1970).

Breaking the third, or fuel, leg of the fire triangle is by far the most common method of suppressing forest fires. Usually, the fuel is simply removed from in front of the advancing flames, physically by scraping or bulldozing for low-intensity fires, and by burning out when wider lines are needed to check high-intensity fires. Fuels can be altered in other ways than removal, however; lopping branches and scattering debris piles affects vertical and horizontal continuity, wetting down in advance of the fire raises the fuel moisture content, and applying fire-retardant chemicals alters the fuel chemistry. Each of these techniques is discussed in its appropriate section later in this chapter.

Fire Suppression Methods

There are three methods of bringing a forest fire under control: direct attack on the burning fire edge, parallel attack by constructing a fireline close by and parallel to the fire edge, and indirect attack by locating control lines a considerable distance from the fire edge and burning out all intervening fuel.

Direct attack, as its name implies, is the suppression of combustion of the actively burning fire front. Direct attack involves suppressing flames by cooling the fuel with water, chemicals, or dirt and then scraping a line completely around the fire edge. Direct attack is normally used on very small fires that can be suppressed and completely mopped up as a unit, on low-intensity fires where heat and smoke do not preclude workers remaining at the fire edge, and on the rear of more intense fires where the smoke is being blown into the burned area. Because direct attack is always undertaken in a relatively high radiation environment, it is physically demanding work and crews must be rotated often. It is, however, the most positive method of control, leaving a cold line behind it, as well as the safest method of control because of the proximity of the burned-over area, and direct attack is the method of choice when fire behavior permits it. Direct attack is most feasible when water handling apparatus is available since water is a much more effective flame suppressant than dirt.

Parallel attack is used whenever the fire is too intense for direct attack or when the fire edge is so irregular that direct attack would result in excessive length of line. In parallel attack a fireline is constructed as near to the fire edge as possible while still allowing for crew comfort and ensuring that the line can be completed before the arrival of the fire. A wider fireline is needed in a parallel attack since flame suppression is not undertaken as the fire meets the line. Parallel attack requires that the line be fired out as the work progresses or that firefighters be dropped off to patrol the line to ensure that it is not breached when the main fire hits it. Parallel attack requires a larger force per unit of held line than does direct attack, but this is compensated for by the fact that the easier working conditions make it possible to sustain productivity for longer periods, and because the line may often be shorter than that required in a direct attack. Heavy equipment such as fire plows and bulldozers usually use parallel attack since it is difficult for them to work directly on the fire edge without the risk of scraping or throwing burning material outside the fireline. This form of attack is often used on the flanks of intense fires, but it is potentially dangerous in these situations since an unexpected wind shift can turn a flank into the head of the fire with not enough distance between the fire and the line to permit the crew an orderly withdrawal.

Indirect attack is used when the fire is too intense for safe use of any other method or when the values protected are insufficient to justify a large firefighting expenditure. In indirect attack the firefighter force is withdrawn to roads, trails, fuelbreaks, or natural barriers and all fuel within this connected network is burned out. Indirect attack trades off increased area burned against reduced cost of operation. It is the least certain of success of the three methods since it usually requires the longest firelines and requires the most time. Long firelines mean more potential places for breakover and longer times mean more chances for unanticipated weather changes. If all intervening fuels cannot be burned clean, either because adverse weather makes backfiring too dangerous or because easing burning conditions precludes the spread of backfires, then nothing has been accomplished and the main fire still remains to be controlled. In the worst possible case, when backfires have been lit but fail to spread as anticipated, firefighters will have two fires rather than one to suppress. Successful indirect attack requires experienced personnel thoroughly knowledgeable about weather and fire behavior in similar fuel and topographic situations. Neophytes are better served by undertaking a parallel attack along the flanks and waiting for burning conditions to ease before attacking the head.

Principles of Initial Attack

Although conflagrations make the headlines and the television screens, more than 90 percent of all forest fires are extinguished while small by the original individuals or small crews who were dispatched to control them. Although every fire is different is some way than any of its predecessors and requires something different in the way of strategy or tactics, there are certain universal principles followed by all wildland fire management organizations in taking effective initial action on forest fires.

The firefighter should travel to the fire by the shortest, quickest route compatible with his or her mode of transportation. For sedans or loaded engines, for example, a somewhat longer trip by paved road may be safer and more certain than several miles over unimproved dirt. Upon approaching the fire, its smoke should be studied whenever possible to make an initial assessment of the direction of spread. The arrival spot should be the closest feasible location nearest the head of the fire.

Immediately upon arrival the firefighter in charge should scout the fire before initiating any suppression action. This initial reconnaissance is called *size-up* and is the most critical single decision process made during the life of a fire.

The first decision to be made during size-up is whether the fire will be controlled with the force at hand or whether reinforcements will be necessary. This decision needs to be made known to the dispatcher as soon as possible. Since the fire will be moving as suppression efforts are taking place, making a judgment on the probability of successfully stopping the head may require evaluation of the fuels and topography some distance in front of the fire.

If the fire can be controlled with the forces available, start work immediately and aggressively at the most vital point of the fire. This is usually the head, but may be at some other point in order to keep the fire away from a particularly valuable area or some particularly hazardous fuel accumulation. The most important sector should be handled first before fatigue reduces the rate of line construction.

If reinforcements will be needed for complete control, work should be organized so as to be of the greatest assistance to the reinforcement crews when they arrive. This may mean a hotspotting attack in order to give the reinforcements the minimum of fire intensity and area to contend with upon arrival, or it may mean a flanking attack with the rear of the line anchored to a road or clearing. Building line without an anchor point is practically useless since the line will inevitably by outflanked by fire burning around it. If the initial attack force consists of more than one firefighter, a line can be anchored in the center by splitting the force and working the fire edge simultaneously in both directions. This is normally done at a rear corner of the fire with the weaker force working the rear and the stronger force the flank.

Once the fire has been contained by having itself burned out against natural or artificial barriers, the job of mopping up begins. Mopping up is necessary to prevent rekindling and the extent to which it is required is dictated by the anticipated weather conditions over the next few days and weeks. As an absolute minimum, all unburned areas within the perimeter should be burned out or lined, all burning snags should be felled, all smoldering materials including stumps and roots within 20 meters of the fireline should be extinguished or covered with earth, and all heavy fuels such as large limbs and logs dragged back 10 meters into the burn. If the fire danger is expected to remain steady or worsen, all material within 40 meters of the perimeter should be completely extinguished, not merely covered with earth; all heavy fuel accumulations that could possibly throw sparks across the line should be scattered; unburned logs, stumps, and snags should be cleared at their bases to prevent ignition; all areas of heavy duff should be dug out and scattered or thoroughly soaked with water and thoroughly mixed and churned throughout their full depth.

After mop-up is complete, the area should be patrolled on foot at least twice a day until it is certain that all fire is out.

There are several excellent manuals on initial attack firemanship written for the technician level practitioner. Readers interested in the subject may refer to Gaylor (1974), the Florida Division of Forestry Training Manual (1975), ICONA (1981), the British Columbia Handbook on Forest Fire Suppression (1969) or Ontario's Forest Fire Suppression (1979).

Crew Organization

The crew, two or more firefighters trained to work together as a team, is the basic unit of any fire suppression organization for any fire that escapes initial attack. Crews can be organized around a specific job for which they are trained (line-building crews, backfiring crews) or around a specific piece of equipment (engine companies, tractor plow units). In both instances the crew consists of individual specialists under the supervision of a single leader who is responsible for their performance, safety, and welfare.

Historically, the unqualified term *fire crew* has been thought of as a hand line crew and most of the early literature on crew organization was developed on the basis of experience with such crews (U.S. Forest Service 1963). Even today with the routine use of power equipment and aircraft for forest fire fighting, the hand line crew is indispensable in steep or rocky terrain and the lessons learned in the 1930s and 1940s are as appropriate today as they were then.

Proper tool selection is the single most important factor in determining the productivity of a given hand line crew in a given cover type (Figure 6.2). To prepare a fireline in most forest fuels requires a certain amount of cutting, a certain amount of digging, and a certain amount of scraping. The rate of the crew as a whole will be determined by the slowest rate of production of the three tasks. To take an extreme example, a six-person crew building line in light grass with three double-bit axes and three McCleod tools will produce line at half the rate, or less, of the same crew with six McCleod tools. In tests in Oregon with 45-person crews, simply changing tools on 5 firefighters resulted in a 50 percent increase in the rate of line construction (Campbell 1938). The first important job of the crew leader is to make sure that the proper mix of tools is available for the fuel complex in which the crew will be expected to work.

Figure 6.2. A proper mix of cutting, digging, and scraping tools is vital to maintaining hand crew productivity. Photo by C. B. Lyon.

Crew size itself affects productivity. This is inherently true because the area of fireline that must be cleared is the same regardless of the number of firefighters in the crew, whereas the length of line that will be walked by the crew is directly proportional to the number of firefighters. Walking time is nonproductive. In a careful series of studies over a five-year period, Matthews (1940) shows that line production rates per man hour could be predicted by the equation

$$R = \frac{K}{\sqrt{N}}$$

where R = Rate of line construction
        N = Crew size
        K = Fuel type constant based on resistance to control

Consequently, doubling the size of a crew only results in a 40 percent increase in total line production rate and, theoretically, splitting a crew and sending it in two directions simultaneously would accomplish the same result. The latter result is seldom realized in practice because the crew has been trained to function as a unit and is not divisible as is an amoeba. Nevertheless, the optimum size crew is the smallest-sized unit that can handle the tasks assigned to it. Most forest fire organizations have standard hand line crews sizes ranging between 6 and 25 firefighters depending on the prevailing fuel types.

The effect of fuel type (Matthews' constant K) in determining hand line production rates cannot be overemphasized. Murphy and Quintilio (1978) in Northern Canada develop a system for rating and difficulty of line construction in any fuel type by measuring the stand density and height of trees and understory separately and adding a rating for quantity of down, dead material, and depth of duff. The resulting indices showed that production rates could vary by a factor of 70, and limited field trials showed rates varying by a factor of 21.

The effect of fatigue or length of shift on line production rates depends very largely on the leadership, training, and conditioning of the crew. Brown and Davis (1973) state that the output in the last hour of a 12-hour shift is only 25 percent of the initial rate, whereas most earlier writers (Matthews op. cit.) find very little difference in rates over shifts of 3 to 10 hours in length.

The *method* of hand line construction will also affect the *rate* of construction. There are two general methods of hand line construction with seemingly endless variations of each. Both were adequately described in the earliest forest fire control manual of which the authors are aware (Headly 1916) and both have been rediscovered and redescribed several times since.

In the *man-passing-man* method, sometimes called in less sexist but less self-explanatory jargon, the *hand-over-hand* method, each worker is assigned a particular task such as cutting brush or scraping away duff, and a particular area of fireline. Upon completing the task the worker walks to the head of the fireline, passing other workers on the way, and is assigned another section of line by the crew leader. The method has the advantage of simplicity and ease of supervision. Each worker knows exactly what the assignment is, and the crew leader can easily keep track of the productivity of each worker. It is also an easy method to use with untrained crews since individual variations in productivity can be accommodated by varying the amount of line assigned to each worker. Its disadvantage is inefficiency. Much time is spent in simply walking and receiving orders. While passing other workers there is always the temptation to pause for a few moments of polite conversation. And in steep country or heavy brush where the fire trail itself may be the only access there is the risk of injury when one worker carrying a sharp tool passes another worker using a sharp tool.

In the *progressive* method of hand line construction each crew member keeps an assigned place in line. Each firefighter can be assigned a particular length of line, as in the man-passing-man method, but in this instance when the first crew member to complete his or her assignment reaches the completed portion of the firefighter ahead, the crew member shouts "step up" and all crew members ahead advance to the next section of uncleared line and resume work. The step-up method is more efficient than man-passing-man, but it tends to spread the work unevenly with the first firefighter always facing an unbroken stretch of uncleared country, the last firefighter responsible for leaving nothing but manicured line behind, while the firefighters in the middle have an opportunity to shirk, since when the "step up" call comes someone else will move in to complete their task.

The *one lick* method of hand line construction differs from the step-up in that no one is assigned a particular section of line. Instead the firefighters are spaced a safe distance apart and start moving at a slow pace, each taking a few "licks" at the line as they go. By proper pacing, the result of all the cumulative licks is a completed fireline when the last crew member passes by. The one lick method is ideally suited to cover types requiring a variety of tools but it requires highly skilled leadership and a dedicated crew, each member willing to do an equal share of the work.

Probably the ultimate in hand line construction methods was the *variable lick* method. As described by its originator (McIntyre 1942):

> The digging crew of hazel-hoe men work as a unit, step by step, blow by blow, regimented by a count, spoken aloud by picked individuals, which causes a foot to be placed ahead along the line or a working blow to be struck by each tool. For example, a hazel-hoe crew of 20 men, spaced at intervals for four feet, face the fire and will build control line to their right. Count "five" has been called for all to hear by the line locator. The pacer begins his count, "one" and the left foot of each individual is placed ahead to the right along the fire line. On count "two" each man lifts his right foot in such a position as to give him working stance. Counts "three, four, five" are now called slowly, and the tool of each man in unison rises and falls for three working blows on the soil before him. Counts "one, two," ring out again, and feet are placed into position; on counts "three, four, five," three more blows are struck by each man in the crew.

> The line specifier may find that the quality of control line exceeds specification; if so, he signals the pacer orally for a "count four." The count is now changed and the men, keeping in mind that counts "one, two" are walking counts, proceed with line buiding at a faster rate because one working count has been eliminated.

> If tougher going is encountered, the line locator calls for a count of "six." Now for this stretch of line the crew moves ahead more slowly than before because of the addition of two working counts. The "Variable Lick Method" thus makes possible the building of a control line to certain specifications that can be controlled by the line specifier who inspects the work of and follows behind the digging crew.

Although this description of the variable lick method seldom fails to evoke memories of Cleopatra's galley slaves pulling their oars to the beat of the overseers drum or kulaks hauling barges up the Volga towpath to the crack of a cossack whip, it produced rates of hand line construction that have yet to be exceeded. The specialized hand line crew fell into disuse after World War II, perhaps because of the increasing use of bulldozers, fireline plows, and other motorized equipment or, perhaps, in the words of the inventor of the variable lick method, "although skilled woodsmen adapt themselves well to the method, skid road bums and fruit tramps show up poorly."

Backfiring

Backfiring in fire suppression is the process of intentionally starting a fire in advance of a head fire or along the forward flanks of a rapidly spreading fire. The decision to backfire is a serious one, not to be undertaken lightly. Backfiring always involves the sacrifice of additional burned area and often involves an increased safety risk for firefighters. The decision to backfire should be based on careful calculation of the probability of success, not out of blind desperation or as a last resort when all else has failed. It is better to simply hang on to the flanks of a fast running fire and wait for weather conditions to improve than it is to accelerate the fire's spread by unsuccessful backfiring.

Backfiring is most successful in light, uniform fuels. Heavy fuels increase the danger of spot fires and, because of their longer burning times, increase the number of firefighters needed to hold each unit length of line. Patchy fuels make it difficult to obtain a clean burn when burning against the wind from a cleared fireline. Backfiring success is inversely proportional to wind velocity and backfiring against adverse winds greater than five meters per second should be strictly avoided.

Backfiring is usually undertaken under two quite different circumstances: when trying to stop, slow, or break up the head of a fast running fire, or when trying to obtain a clean burn between a line or natural barrier and a quiescent fire whose perimeter is too long or too ragged for direct attack to be feasible. Since quite different tactics and techniques are required for each situation, they are discussed separately.

With a fast running headfire, spotting is the main concern. In order to hold the fire successfully the backfire must be burned clean at least twice the spotting distance of the headfire at the time the two meet. If the spotting distance cannot be estimated, the backfire must be planned to be burned back from the line at least 30 meters. If at all possible, it is preferable to set the backfire between two firelines and allow the intervening strip to burn out before the arrival of the headfire. This avoids the extreme convective turbulence that occurs when two active fires merge and greatly reduces the chance of fire spotting over the line. Backfiring should never be undertaken unless there is an adequate firefighting force to assure control of the set fire. A backing fire alone will seldom spread fast enough to provide an adequate safety strip within reasonable time limits and it is usually necessary to resort to strip headfires, flanking fires, or spot firing to gain the necessary area. If the backfire is lost before the main fire arrives, the situation is worse than it would have been with no firefighting effort whatever.

In mountainous terrain, the preferred location for backfiring is a short distance below the crest of the ridge opposite the slope where the main fire is burning. This location allows the set fire to run upslope, takes advantage of any upslope winds that may be present, and also uses the upslope component of the lee eddy that is formed whenever a strong wind blows across a ridge. This not only lets the backfire spread faster and thus create a wider barrier in a shorter time, it makes it more likely that the convection column will merge with that of the main fire at a greater distance from the line and thus reduce the probability of spot fires downwind.

Backfiring is a line building technique that uses combustion rather than a shovel to remove fuel from the path of the fire. In backfiring, just as in hand line construction, it is necessary to have the line securely anchored to avoid having it breached or flanked. Again, as in hand line construction, it is possible to anchor a backfire by starting in one spot and firing the line out in two directions simultaneously. This is not always possible in mountainous terrain since backfires must generally be carried downhill to avoid rapid uphill runs that can hook and threaten the fireline above. Consequently, when the fireline crosses a saddle or narrow valley it is usually necessary to split the firing and holding crews and fire downhill from both sides. This is a dangerous and delicate maneuver and must be done carefully with experienced people in charge at all times.

An even more dangerous technique called *blowhole firing* is used to break up the runs of fast moving fires burning with narrow fronts in light fuels. In blowhole firing one or more torchmen string fire at right angles to the fireline, starting at the line and moving towards the main fire. When he has advanced as far as safely possible, the torchman returns to the line by crossing in front of the newly created backfire. When the main fire arrives, one or more V-shaped areas will have been burned out and serve to split the head fire and blunt its force. The technique is dangerous because the torchman has fire between himself and the fireline throughout the operation. A twisted knee or sprained ankle could prove fatal.

When trying to backfire toward a dormant main fire, the fire manager's problems are the reverse of those encountered when trying to stop a rapidly moving head. Usually, the manager is faced with a situation where burning conditions are poor or marginal but expected to worsen later. The challenge is to cleanly burn out a sufficiently wide strip to stop the main fire when fire danger increases and the fire begins another run. Timing is critical because if the job is begun too soon the backburn will be patchy and consume only the fine fuels. The residual material will be impossible to backfire again later, but still contain enough fuel to allow a headfire to burn through. On the other hand, if backfiring is delayed too long, the main fire may commence its run before backfiring can be completed. Many of the techniques of hazard reduction burning have direct application under these circumstances and firefighters with experience with prescribed fire are indispensable advisors. Mass ignition is often desirable and aerial ignition devices are extremely useful.

USE OF WATER AND CHEMICALS

Water is the firefighter's best friend and most precious asset. The specific heat of water is five times that of most soils, thus giving the firefighter five times as much cooling power for each kilogram thrown on the fire. In addition, water expands to 1700 times its liquid volume when it vaporizes and this water vapor displaces oxygen from the flame zone, at least momentarily. At most forest fire operations, water is scarce. At all operations it is heavy. The key to successful firefighting with water is to suppress the most fire with a minimum application of water.

Hydraulics

Because water is usually applied to a fire by being expelled under pressure from the nozzle of a hose, every fire manager needs to know some basic principles of hydraulics.

Pure water weighs 1 kilogram per liter. The pressure exerted by water resting in a container without flow is called the *static pressure* and is measured in kilopascals. The pressure exerted by a column of water 1 meter high is 9.8 kilopascals (kP). The term *head* is often used instead of pressure. Head is the equivalent height of water required to produce an observed pressure; 9.8 kilopascals of pressure equals 1 meter of head. Pressure is sometimes measured in centimeters of mercury rather than meters of water. One centimeter of mercury equals 1.33 kP or 0.136 meters of water. Normal atmospheric pressure at sea level is 101.4 kP, or 10.34 meters of water, or 76 cm of mercury.

The velocity produced in a mass of water by pressure acting upon it is the same as if the mass were to fall freely, starting from rest, through a distance equivalent to the pressure head in meters. Thus

$$V = \sqrt{2gh}$$

where V = Velocity in meters per second
   h = The head in meters of water
   g = Acceleration due to gravity (9.8 meters/second^2)

This is a reversible relationship. Just as pressure head produces velocity, so can velocity be converted into an equivalent head of pressure. Consequently, $h = V^2/2g$ for a head measured in meters of water, or $P = 9.8V^2/2g$ = $0.5V^2$ for pressure in kilopascals.

As a stream of water leaves a hose or pipe, all pressure is converted into velocity pressure. Therefore, there is a direct relationship between nozzle pressure, exit velocity, and flow rate for any given size of hose. For flow rates in liters per minute, velocity in meters per second, pressure in kilopascals, and nozzle diameters in centimeters, these relationships are:

$$F = 1.5 \pi D^2 V = 6.66 D^2 \sqrt{P}$$

$$V = \frac{F}{1.5 \pi D^2} = \sqrt{2P}$$

$$P = 0.5 V^2 = \frac{0.0225 F^2}{D^4}$$

Since nozzle diameter is known or easily measured, any two of the other three variables can be calculated if one of the three is known or measured.

In forest fire fighting operations, pressure is supplied by the pump and by gravity when the water supply is higher than the nozzle of the hose (pumping downhill) and pressure is lost by friction as the water passes through the hose and by gravity when the water is being pumped uphill. When using long hose lays in steep terrain, the pump operator must have a good understanding of the balance of forces in order to supply sufficient water at the nozzle to control the fire without creating sufficient pressure to rupture the hose anywhere along the lay.

Pressure gains and losses due to gravity are, of course, constant at 9.8 kP per meter of elevation change. Since the optimum nozzle pressure for most forest fire operations is about 700 kP and forestry fire hose should not be stressed beyond 1700 kP to avoid its rupturing, this limits single pump hose lays to roughly 100 meters elevation difference in either direction. If the fire is more than 100 meters above or below the water source it is necessary to set up a relay tank and a second pump.

Friction losses vary with the type of fire hose being used, the diameter of the hose, and the flow rate through the hose. Of the three factors, diameter is by far the most important. Friction loss varies inversely with the fifth power of the diameter: doubling the diameter of the hose decreases friction loss 32 times. Volume flow affects friction loss by about the 1.8 power of the flow rate: doubling the flow increases friction loss $3\frac{1}{2}$ times. Hose types may vary by up to a factor of five for the same diameter and volume. Rubber-lined hose has about half the friction loss of unlined hose of the same diameter. Table 6.1 gives some typical friction loss values for typical forestry hoses, flow rates, and volumes.

The distance to which a stream of water will carry once it leaves the nozzle is, in the absence of wind, a function of the nozzle diameter (not the hose diameter) and the nozzle pressure. As a rule of thumb, the effective distance in meters is equal to one-half the nozzle diameter in centimeters times the square root of the nozzle pressure in kilopascals. Thus a 2-centimeter nozzle at 400 kilopascals pressure would be expected to throw an effective stream out to 20 meters.

Consider some practical applications of these hydraulic formulas. You are considering a hose lay from a lake 1 kilometer from a fire and 150 meters below it. For the sake of safety and for the ability to knock fire out of snags you insist on a 10-meter effective stream at the nozzle. You have a choice of

Table 6.1.   Friction Loss in Forestry Fire Hose

Flow Rate (l/min)	Hose Diameter (cm)			
	2.0 lined	2.54 lined	4.0 lined	unlined
	Friction loss (kP/m)			
25	1.4	0.4	0.06	0.1
50	5.0	1.3	0.2	0.4
75	10.4	2.7	0.4	0.8
100	17.5	4.6	0.7	1.3
125	26.2	6.8	1.0	1.9
150	36.3	9.4	1.4	2.7
175	48.0	12.5	1.8	3.4
200	61.0	15.8	2.3	4.4
250	91.1	23.7	3.5	6.6
300	—	32.9	4.9	9.3
350	—	43.4	6.4	12.1
400	—	55.2	8.1	15.4
450	—	68.2	10.1	19.2
500	—	82.5	12.2	23.1
550	—	97.9	14.5	27.5
600	—	—	16.9	32.1
700	—	—	22.3	42.4
800	—	—	28.3	53.8
900	—	—	35.1	66.7
1000	—	—	42.4	80.6
1200	—	—	58.9	—
1400	—	—	77.8	—
1600	—	—	98.8	—

an unlimited length of lined or unlined 4-centimeter hose, each type tested at 1750 kP, 4 pumps rated at 3000 kP, and an assortment of nozzles ranging from 0.5 to 3.5 centimeters in diameter in 0.5-centimeter increments.

Since the availability of water is not a limiting factor, your objective should be to get the maximum rate of flow on the fire within your constraint of a 10-meter effective stream. The 150 meters of lift needed to get the water to the fire means you have 150 × 9.8 = 1470 or about 1500 kP of gravity head to contend with. Since the bursting point of your hose is 1750 kP, this leaves only 250 kP available if the lay is made without relay. A glance at Table 6.1 shows that unlined hose is out of the question since delivery of even 50 liters per minute would exceed the allowable pressure. However, if the lake were 150 meters *above* the fire, unlined hose might well be a practical choice since friction loss would reduce the excess gravity head.

With lined hose, you can safely deliver 50 liters per minute, or perhaps a little more, to the fireline in each of four separate hoselays. But will this give you a 10-meter effective stream? Take a quick look at the requirements for three candidate nozzles: 0.5, 2.0, and 3.5-centimeter diameters.

Since distance $= 0.5D \sqrt{P}$, then $P =$ (Distance)^2/$0.25D^2$ or, for this example $P = 100/0.25D^2$. For the three nozzles, this works out to 1600 kP, 100 kP, and 33 kP for the 0.5, 2.0, and 3.5-centimeter nozzles respectively. Since $F = 6.66 D^2 \sqrt{P}$, the required flow rates are 67, 266, and 469 liters per minute and not even the smallest nozzle will produce a 10-meter effective stream. You will have to relay water. The only choices are one hoselay with three relay stations or two hoselays with one relay station.

A 3-relay hose lay will cut the gravity head to 370 kP, leaving 1380 for friction loss. Since each lay will be 250 meters, you can operate with 5.5 kP friction loss per meter. With lined hose this means a flow rate between 300 and 350 liters per minute. You already know that a 2.0-centimeter nozzle needs 266 liters per minute for a 10-meter effective stream, but what about a 2.5 cm one? $100/0.25 (2.5)^2 = 64$ kP pressure. $6.66 (2.5)^2 (\sqrt{64}) = 333$ liters per minute. With one 3-relay hoselay you can put 333 liters per minute on the fire.

But what about two lines with one relay per line? That would give you the advantage of two working nozzles on the fire. The gravity head will be 750 kP and the allowable friction loss 2.0 kP per meter. The flow rate must be held to 175 to 200 liters per minute. A 1.5-centimeter nozzle will require 200 liters per minute which is too high for safety, whereas a 1-centimeter nozzle will only deliver 133 liters per minute. The decision on whether it is preferable to put 333 liters per minute on the fire with one line or 266 liters per minute with two lines will depend on the tactical situation.

On the opposite side of the fire you have a different hydraulics problem. A road runs adjacent to the fire and four 1000-liter engines are available to assist in direct attack on the flanks. Each engine carries 4-centimeter hose and 1.5-centimeter nozzles and each is also equipped with a 2.5-centimeter live reel with a 0.5-centimeter nozzle. It is 16 kilometers to the nearest resupply of water and you expect the round trip plus refilling time will take nearly an hour. What orders do you give the crews? If you hadn't already calculated that a 10-meter effective stream from a 0.5-centimeter nozzle takes 67 liters per minute and the same stream from a 1.5-centimeter nozzle requires 200 liters per minute you would do so now. Since using the main hose would empty the tank in 5 minutes and even the live reel alone will only operate continuously for 15 minutes, you tell the crews to leave the hose on the truck, operate one at a time with the live reel only, and don't dawdle when refilling!

Tactics

In actual practice water is most often used in mop-up and as backup assistance for hand line crews rather than in direct attack. In these situations the effective use of water and water conservation depends more on tactics than on hydraulics. When water is scarce, and on forest fires it usually is, the objective should be to use water sparingly, and on the points of the fire where it is most needed. Water is most effective at knocking down flames, thus reducing radiation levels so that firefighters with hand tools can move in and build fireline or break up concentrations of fuel. Water sprays should be applied to the base of the burning area nearest the nozzle, not sprayed directly on the flames themselves, and then fanned back as rapidly as flames are extinguished until the area is cool enough to advance the hose to a new trouble spot. This technique minimizes the amount of spray that is carried off in the convection currents, maximizes the amount reaching glowing combustion at the fuel surfaces, and maximizes steam production. The nozzle should always be shut off when walking between hot spots. Intermittent operation not only saves water, it allows the firefighter to observe whether the fire rekindles and thus judge the minimum amount of water required for permanent extinguishment.

Water is usually the only way to knock fire out of the upper part of a snag or the crown of a tree without taking the time and effort to fell the tree. This requires a straight stream rather than a spray application, both to obtain better accuracy and to ensure enough force to reach smoldering pockets underneath the bark. Use the highest pump pressure and smallest practical nozzle size. Start at the base of the burning area and work up.

In mop-up, water is most useful for quenching roots burning underground, cooling deep smoldering pockets of duff for easier mixing with hand tools, and for drenching the crevices in logs where limbs meet the main stem which would otherwise require extensive chopping. Water and hand tools should work together on mop-up (Figure 6.3). Physical manipulation of fuels is needed in addition to wetting them down if complete extinguishment is to be guaranteed.

Weather Modification

At one time or another practically every forest fire management officer, facing an impossible fire situation, has prayed for rain. With the discovery in 1946 that frozen carbon dioxide (dry ice) and silver iodide smokes could induce precipitation in certain types of supercooled clouds, some fire managers attempted to do more than pray. Cloud seeding as a suppression technique, that is, attempting to induce precipitation directly on going fires in order to assist in their extinguishment has been attempted in Australia, Canada, the United States, and the USSR. Only the Russians claim to be continuing the practice on an operational basis.

Precipitation enhancement methods are based on the Bergeron–Findeisen theory that precipitation from cumulus clouds occurs when ice crystals and supercooled water droplets coexist in certain proportions within a cloud, and the water vapor is transferred from the droplets to the crystals by the process of sublimation. The theory further presupposes that the ice crystals

Figure 6.3.   Water and hand tools work together on mop-up. Photo by U.S. Forest Service.

are formed around nuclei of small particles of chemically active agents such as sea salt derived from the evaporation of windborne spray, whereas the supercooled water droplets are formed by condensation without such a nucleating agent. When clouds are deficient in condensation nuclei, there are too few ice crystals to produce significant precipitation. With too many nuclei there is too little free water to produce crystals large enough to fall out of the cloud. Introduction of additional nuclei through cloud seeding can produce rain if, and only if:

1.   There are clouds present whose tops are above the freezing level.
2.   The clouds have a deficiency of ice-forming nuclei.
3.   The clouds have bases sufficiently low that raindrops will not evaporate before reaching the ground.

To be useful in forest fire suppression, clouds with these characteristics must be present above or immediately upwind of a forest fire.

Experimental trials in Alaska (Sierra Research Corp. 1972) and in Canada (MacHattie et al. 1976) show that during the normal fire season suitable seeding opportunities were not present often enough to justify the expense of keeping aircraft and cloud-seeding equipment on stand by. The Russians, however, report that such clouds are present in the Siberian and Far Eastern forest fire regions 50 percent of the time and that their occurrence can be forecast with 90 percent accuracy (D'yachenko et al. 1972). Thirty percent of all seeding operations are judged "successful" in assisting in control of the fire and an operational program has been adopted using both aircraft and ground-based rockets to introduce silver iodide, lead iodide, and copper sulfide as nucleating agents into the clouds (Artsybashev 1973).

In the Russian method, silver or lead iodide is mixed with propellant (15 grams of each) and loaded into a 26-millimeter cartridge which is fired from a Very pistol. Since copper sulphate requires about 10 times as much chemical to produce the same nucleation as the iodides, it is placed in special containers equipped with a delay fuse and dropped by aircraft into the cloud from above. Cloud thickness (base to top) must exceed 2500 meters and cloud top temperatures must be below $-7°C$. However, results are achieved if the seeding agent is introduced at the $-7°C$ isotherm regardless of the minimum temperature at the cloud top. Optimum cloud thickness is 3100 to 3500 meters. Clouds greater than 4000 meters thick are not seeded due to the extreme turbulence associated with strong vertical development. The amount of seeding is determined by visual observation with seeding stopped as soon as heavy virga appears below the cloud.

Every active large fire produces a convection column that is, in effect, a cumulus cloud and may often reach 4,000 to 15,000 meters, well above the freezing level. One then wonders why experiments have not been conducted to seed convection columns independently of any adjacent cloud formations. This is particularly true since there are rare but documented instances in all parts of the world of rain falling naturally from forest fire convection columns.

The Russians report three such trials with poor success (Artsybashev 1973). In all three cases cloud thicknesses were less than 2500 meters indicating relatively low fire intensity and/or stable air aloft. There are two reasons why fire managers have been reluctant to experiment with active convection columns. On theoretical grounds, because of the large volumes of smoke and ash entrained into the column we should expect an excess of condensation nuclei rather than a shortage, and artificial seeding would reduce rather than enhance the probability of precipitation. On more practical grounds, the energies displayed by the convective activity over a large forest fire are awesome, riveling those of a fully developed thunderstorm. The possibility that seeding could produce significant downdrafts is not negligible and such a result would imperil every firefighter on the fire as well as practically ensuring a major fire run. For these reasons, no fire agency has been willing to pioneer such an experiment.

Chemicals for Forest Fire Fighting

Although water is the best and cheapest natural substance for fighting forest fires, water has its drawbacks. Over time, water evaporates completely leaving no residual fire-suppressing or retarding effect. Because of its high surface tension, water does not penetrate rapidly into the interior of semiporous fuels. Because of its low viscosity, it drips readily from aerial fuels and runs rapidly down the sides of vertical fuels. Water passes easily from laminar to turbulent flow, and turbulent flow rather than true friction causes 90 percent of the "friction loss" in pumping water through fire hose. Each of these deficits can be overcome or reduced by chemical additives.

A fire retardant, as its name implies, is a chemical used to slow or stop the spread and/or intensity of a fire. In the earlier literature a distinction was made between a fire retardant and a fire suppressant with the former referring to chemicals used to pretreat fuels ahead of the fire and the latter to chemicals used in direct attack on the burning front. This distinction has become blurred, largely because many of the same chemicals are now used for both purposes, and the term fire retardant is now used for all chemicals used in forest fire fighting to enhance fire extinguishment.

There are two types of forest fire retardants: short term, which simply enhance the extinguishing power of water by retaining more of it on the fuel or by retarding evaporation or both, and long term, which leave a residue of combustion-inhibiting agent on the fuel after all the water has evaporated. Short-term retardants include a variety of clays, gums, and natural or artificial gelling agents. Rheology is the most important consideration in selecting a short-term retardant. The material must be pumpable, flow through hose without undue friction loss, divide into coarse drops after leaving the nozzle or aircraft tank, and adhere to fuel surfaces immediately upon impact. Abrasiveness, susceptibility to spoilage, and, of course, cost are also major considerations when selecting a short-term retardant.

Surfactants (surface active agents or wetting agents) should technically be considered to be short-term retardants. However, because their use is more widespread and occurred earlier than the thickeners, wetting agents are usually considered in a class by themselves. A good wetting agent will reduce the surface tension of water by more than half (from 73 dynes per centimeter to 30 to 35) and increase penetration into wood or charcoal from 5 to 8 times. Surfactants are widely used in mop-up because of their superior penetrating ability. They are widely available commercially, and, other than cost, the only major consideration when selecting a wetting agent for forest fire use is its ability to resist foaming. Foaming is undesirable because it increases wind resistance and decreases the distance of the stream for a given nozzle pressure.

Firefighting foams are widely used by urban fire services to fight fires in flammable liquids, but have little forestry application. Foams act to blanket the burning surface and exclude oxygen. Since the individual foam bubbles are water coated, water is also released on the fuel as the foam breaks down. The primary problem with foam in forest fire fighting is its tendency to be blown away by wind or by the convection currents of the fire itself. However, in the United States, the Texas Forest Service has successfully used low expansion foam on low-intensity fires and for constructing *wet line* for backfiring in light fuels (Ebarb 1978). High expansion foam is also used in tundra fires in the USSR under burning conditions similar to those in Texas.

Selection of long-term retardants involves more complex considerations than is true for wetting agents or short-term retardants. The relative ability of various chemicals to suppress fire in forest fuels has been known since the mid1930s when a series of carefully controlled tests were made at the U.S. Forest Products Laboratory (Truax 1939).

With the exception of sodium calcium borate, the tests included every chemical that has since been used or tested for operational use. Table 6.2 shows the results of these tests. Because of cost, corrosivity, or toxicity, all

TABLE 6.2. *Extinguishing properties of concentrated water solutions of chemicals compared with water (Tests made under quiet air conditions; liquid applied at rate of 26 cc per minute)*

Chemical	Concentration of Solution by Weight (%)	Superiority Factor[a] Based on Volumes Used	
		Flame Extinction	Total Extinction
Acid, citric	25	0.90	0.75
Acid, phosphoric	26	1.50	2.40
Acid, tartaric	25	0.75	0.60
Aluminum sulphate	23	1.00	1.40
Ammonium carbonate	28	0.95	1.50
Ammonium nitrate	25	0.80	0.80
Ammonium nitrate	29	1.10	1.00
Ammonium phosphate, di-	26	1.30	2.10
Ammonium phosphate, mono-	26	1.20	2.00
Ammonium sulphate	26	1.10	1.70
Calcium chloride	26	1.10	1.50
Cobaltous chloride	25	1.00	1.30
Lithium chloride	27	1.25	1.80
Magnesium chloride	25	1.20	1.70
Magnesium sulphate	30	1.10	1.30
Potassium acetate	30	1.75	1.80
Potassium bicarbonate	25	1.70	1.55
Potassium carbonate	25	1.90	1.70
Potassium chloride	25	0.90	1.20
Sodium acetate	27	1.50	1.60
Sodium chloride	25	1.10	1.50
Sodium phosphate, mono-	24	1.00	1.50
Sodium silicate	22	1.00	1.20
Stannous chloride	25	1.10	1.50
Zinc chloride	30	1.30	1.70

[a] Calculated by dividing the average volume of water by the average volume of chemical solution used in extinguishing similar fires.

the chemicals listed except for the ammonium phosphates and sulphate have never been used in field practice or have been tried and fallen out of use.

The effectiveness of a long-term fire retardant depends very markedly on the amount of salt deposited per unit surface area of fuel. Salt content can be increased by using a more concentrated solution or by increasing the viscosity of the solution so that more retardant adheres to each fuel particle. Highly concentrated solutions are more difficult to mix and, generally, more corrosive than dilute solutions, whereas increasing viscosity decreases the area covered per unit amount of solution applied. A great deal of research effort has been spent trying to reach an optimum trade-off between concentration and viscosity (George et al. 1976, Stechishen et al. 1982).

All long-term retardants are corrosive to a greater or lesser degree. Some degree of corrosivity can be tolerated in ground equipment where failure of a pump is exasperating and expensive, but rarely fatal. However, with retardants applied from aircraft where retardant mists drift onto control surfaces and interior crevices, corrosion cannot be tolerated. It is extremely difficult to design standard tests for corrosivity since a chemical will have different effects on different metals and/or different effects on the same metal depending on whether the metal is being stressed (flexed) or static, and different effects on two metals in contact than it will on either metal alone. Corrosion inhibition has also been the subject of intensive research (George et al. op. cit.).

Toxicity of long-term fire retardant compounds has been an occasional problem. Sodium calcium borate failed to hold its market largely because it was moderately toxic to many commercial tree species. Used on fires in southern pine plantations, the results resembled the often-quoted Vietnamese village after the Tet offensive—we had to destroy the plantation in order to save it. The presently used ammonium compounds have been largely immune from criticism since they are widely used as agricultural fertilizers. There have been some questions about possible nitrate poisoning to mammals (Dodge 1970) but the evidence shows this possibility to be highly unlikely. All the ammonium fire retardants are toxic to fish through the release of free ammonia when applied directly to lakes or streams, but such releases are always inadvertent and the effects are localized, transitory, and predictable (Norris et al. 1978). Questions have also been raised about possible toxic effects from various dyes, corrosion inhibitors, and spoilage inhibitors that are found in small amounts in various commercial long-term fire retardants. These are referred to the manufacturers and to appropriate public health authorities for screening. Based on experience to date, forest fire retardants pose less of an environmental safety and health problem than do most chemicals used in agriculture and forestry.

In the late 1940s, the Union Carbide Corporation working with the New York City Fire Department discovered that long chain, linear polymers would greatly increase the velocity at which water switches from laminar to turbulent flow within a hose or pipe. Applied at 1 cubic centimeter of polymer to 6 liters of water, ethelene oxide will increase flow rates 40 percent for a given pressure and hose diameter. Several commercial "friction reducers" are available based on the long chain, linear polymer technology and they should be useful for long hose lays in forest fire operations.

Attempts to improve the firefighting capabilities of water have been documented as far back as the fourth century, B.C. (Broido 1973). Yet, with the exception of aerially applied retardants (covered in some detail in the next section) and except in the USSR where all initial attack vehicles are equipped with chemical retardant dispensers (Zinov 1975), chemicals have played a very minor role in forest fire fighting although their efficacy has been noted and their use advocated for nearly 50 years. It has been suggested that this is because firefighters are an inherently conservative lot. To a certain extent this is true—firefighters and soldiers are both conservative in the adoption of new methods and equipment because they both stand to lose their lives should their new acquisition prove to be a failure in practice. But there are also some rational reasons why forest fire fighting chemicals have been slow to win acceptance.

More than 90 percent of all forest fires are fought by workers on foot or in fire engines using direct attack on the fire edge. When using water in direct attack, proper tactics and methods of application are vital. In early tests of water vs. water containing wetting agents for direct flame suppression, wet water was twice as effective as plain water in laboratory tests, $1\frac{1}{2}$ times as effective on outdoor test fires when applied by specially trained crews, and statistically showed no advantage whatever when applied in practice by regular fire crews (Fons 1950). The differences in efficiency of water use among crews overshadowed any differences between the chemical and non-chemical applications.

Many types of firefighting chemicals are only needed in special situations. Because the logistics on forest fires are difficult at best, firefighters are reluctant to carry materials or equipment that will not be needed most of the time and tend to use what they carry whether or not the situation requires it. Crews using chemicals on all fires tend to remember the many times they could have done as well with plain water and forget the few fires that could only have been stopped with chemicals.

Equipment that uses chemicals requires more housekeeping than equipment that uses only water. Most forest fire fighting chemicals, compared to plain water, are either corrosive, abrasive, film forming, sticky, slippery, smelly, toxic, or some combination of these. A crew or a fire agency that is not convinced that chemicals are worth the extra inconvenience will seldom keep them in use for long.

Despite these difficulties, chemicals have a place on the fireline and can be nearly indispensable for certain operations. Their use can be expected to increase over time.

For more detailed information on chemicals used in forest fire control, the NFPA handbook (Hardy 1977) is recommended.

THE USE OF EXPLOSIVES, WIND MACHINES, AND OTHER EXOTICA IN FOREST FIRE CONTROL

Explosives can be used to fell snags, dig shallow wells, and even to build fireline in some soils and cover types. In the USSR explosives are used extensively in fireline construction (Shchetinsky 1975). The explosive equipment consists of a slow fuse ignitor, a primacord initiator, and 250 gram sticks of *ammonite* (pressed ammonium nitrate with tetryl booster) explosive. Two techniques are used in preparing fireline depending on the soil type and density of ground cover.

In one technique, holes are drilled with a light power auger and one to three sticks of ammonite, again depending on soil conditions, are placed vertically in each hole. The charges are connected by primacord tied to the top ammonite stick. A one-minute slow fuse is used to detonate the primacord. The resulting explosion in a light sandy soil creates a trench about 30 centimeters deep with a dirt berm extending up to a meter on each side of the trench.

In the other technique, both sticks and primacord are packed in a polyethelene tube. The tube is then rolled out along the preplanned fireline and the primacord ignited by slow fuse. This technique is preferred for rapid line building; a trained team of six firefighters can build line at a rate approaching one kilometer an hour under ideal conditions, but it produces a narrower line than the auger method and, occasionally, individual sticks of ammonite will fail to explode and be thrown off to the side of the line for varying distances (Figure 6.4).

In the western United States the development of fireline explosives was slow because of the tendency of primacord and other common explosives to start fires when tested under low humidity conditions (Banks and Fenton 1957). This problem has been overcome by embedding the explosive in a casing of diammonium phosphate (Lott 1975).

Air blowers of various types, sizes, and configurations have been used to prepare fireline in forests in the eastern United States where understory vegetation is absent and ground fuels consist only of leaf litter. In southern California wind machines with fans two meters in diameter, originally designed to produce motion picture special effects, have been used to assist in backfiring and to project high-pressure fog streams for protecting structures against encroaching brushfires (Controlled Airstreams Inc. 1964; Figure 6.5). One disadvantage of all blowers when used to project a flow into an opposing wind is the tendency to produce traveling eddies at the shear line between the natural and the induced flow. Burning embers may be picked up in these eddies and deposited behind the machine and its operator.

Halogenated hydrocarbon flame suppressants have had very little acceptance in forest fire management outside the USSR. There, freon emulsions ($C_2Br_2F_4$ and C_2H_5Br) are widely used in backpack sprayers in direct attack with handcrews (Artsybashev 1974). The enhanced flame-suppressing qual-

Figure 6.4. Line built by ammonite tube method, Irkutsk, USSR. Photo by John Deeming.

ities of freon allow firefighters to work closer to the fire edge and permit direct attack tactics to be used where they would be impossible using water alone as a suppressant.

Deep-seated fires in peat, muck, or other organic soils are often immune to any firefighting tactic except raising the water table to a level higher than the zone of active burning. Since it takes 10,000 liters per hectare to raise the water table one millimeter, this requires high-volume water-moving equip-

Figure 6.5. Air blowers used to project fog streams. Photo by Craig Chandler.

ment (Dorman 1954), continuous sprinkling systems (Johnson 1970), well drilling technology (Ritter 1949), and a host of techniques more often associated with irrigation agriculture than with forest fire management.

AIR OPERATIONS

Because the key to successful fire control is rapid detection and initial attack, and because forest fire managers must protect large areas with generally poor accessibility, it should not be surprising that forest fire fighters adopted the airplane almost as soon as it was invented. Because forest fire fighting is a paramilitary operation, it is not surprising that the history of aerial forest fire control in every country that employs it is a history of cooperation between foresters and Air Force pilots and officers.

In the United States, aircraft were first used for forest fire detection patrols in the summer of 1915 when an experimental Navy flying boat provided detection coverage for the forests around Puget Sound. In 1919 a cooperative agreement between the U.S. Forest Service and the Army Air Corps expanded aerial fire detection to the entire western United States during the fire season. By 1926 airplanes were being used to drop supplies to fire camps and 10 years later aerial photographs of large fires were being developed in the aircraft and dropped to fire headquarters to aid in planning for the next work shift. Smokejumpers made their United States debut in 1939. The use of airplanes in direct attack by dropping water or chemical bombs has been attributed to forest rangers as early as 1919 (Driggs 1921) but some of those early stories sound suspiciously apocryphal. The first serious efforts to develop water bombing equipment and tactics by the United States occurred in 1947–1948 when the Army Air Force and the Forest Service tested a wide variety of military aircraft, containers, and fuses for extinguishing incipient fires. Later tests included self-propelled firefighting rockets. Despite reasonable success in controlled tests, the inherent safety hazard associated with propelling heavy containers at high velocity onto the landscape precluded operational use of aircraft in direct attack until the technique of freely cascading liquids directly from the aircraft was developed during Operation Firestop in 1954. This technique was rapidly adopted as standard operating practice worldwide.

The first use of rotary wing aircraft in forest fire management took place in 1932, only three years after the production of the first commercial models. It was not until 1946, however, that the helicopter became sufficiently reliable and had sufficient lift capacity to be used for more than occasional reconnaissance missions.

The aircraft has had a very short but dramatic history in forest fire control in Canada. On the 23rd of February, 1909, a Mr. J.A.D. McCurdy, who was a member of Alexander Graham Bell's "Aerial Experiment Association" successfully piloted an aircraft which he had built himself, the "Silver Dart" in Baddeck, Nova Scotia. This was the first aircraft flown in Canada and, following this initial success, McCurdy attempted to interest the military in the possibilities of his machine. Unfortunately, the plane crash-landed on its first military demonstration, convincing the high-ranking observers that it would be of little use in warfare. However, the first World War changed the picture drastically. During the war, Canadian Aeroplanes Limited built some 2900 JN-4 (Curtis Jennies) in Toronto for war use and, following the war, they produced the Felixstowe flying boat. At the same time the provincial government of British Columbia commissioned local boat builders to design and build a flying boat for forest fire patrol use. The aircraft was built but, unfortunately, it too crashed during demonstration flights.

Also in 1919, the Laurentide Company of Quebec borrowed two HS-2L flying boats from the Navy and experimented with them as fire patrol aircraft with the cooperation of the Quebec government. This time the flights were successful and much interest was created throughout the forestry community. In 1920 an interdepartmental conference convened by the Air Board, set up the year before, recommended the establishment of airbases in British Columbia, Alberta, Ontario, and Quebec to assist in forestry and survey work.

On the 4th of July, 1921, R.N. Johnson, assistant provincial forester in Ontario, reported to the Air Board what was likely the first full air operation in forest control in Canada. The fire in question was first observed by the air patrol on June 24th. The aircraft returned to its base, reported on the location and condition of the fire, and then arranged to fly firefighters to the fire. Later reinforcements and additional equipment were flown in and the entire operation was declared a great success. This again created a wave of interest on the part of forest managers and, by 1924, about 60 percent of all flying in Canada was being done in support of forestry.

The demand for aircraft spurred the Canadian Vickers Company to set up an aircraft plant in Montreal; the forerunner of the present Canadair Limited. Vickers produced the much-used Viking and Vedette flying boats designed for forest fire patrol and aerial photography. In 1927 De Haviland Aircraft of Canada built a factory in Toronto to produce the Moth and the DH-6l, both of which were used in forest fire control work. In 1935 Nordwyn Aircraft Ltd. of Montreal produced another famous forestry workhorse, the Norseman, designed for forestry work of all types.

The second World War struck Canada in 1939 and, again, the development and production of aircraft was greatly accelerated to meet wartime requirements. At the same time, a large number of trained pilots were turned out, many of whom returned at the end of the war with a desire to continue their flying careers in a civilian capacity. They again focused the attention of forest managers on the potential use of aircraft in many aspects of forestry, including forest fire control. In 1948 De Haviland Aircraft of Canada, working closely with the staff of the Ontario Provincial Air Service and applying their specified performance requirements as well as those of many other "bush pilots," designed and produced the famous Beaver aircraft which became the backbone of the Ontario government fleet. It proved to be an excellent aircraft for forestry use in Canada as well as around the world. De Haviland followed the Beaver with the larger Otter and, later, with the Turbo-Beaver and the Twin Otter.

During the war period, the use of aircraft in forest fire control expanded greatly in many directions. One of the most spectacular developments was the application of aircraft in direct attack on fires—the dropping of water or retardant chemicals onto or in the path of a fire. Beginning in 1944, experiments were undertaken in Ontario using a Stinson seaplane modified to enable it to drop water from valves built into its floats. The following year, these experiments were continued using a Norseman aircraft of the Ontario fleet. Because of the limited capacity of the float tanks and concern about the effect of the additional weight on aircraft performance, these experiments were discontinued, but in 1949 a system was designed and tested employing latex-lined paper bags filled with water dropped in salvos from a Beaver. After a short period of use, this system was also discontinued as being ineffective, and special tanks were designed for the Beaver and Otter aircraft. It has been recognized that, because of the speed of the aircraft, it was essential to release the load in as short a period as possible. The new tanks were open at the top and, when the pilot wished to release the load, the pilot pressed a lever that caused the tanks to rotate, dumping the water or chemical very quickly. The success of this led to the modification of many other aircraft, particularly, military surplus aircraft such as the PBY Canso, the TBM Avenger, A-26, B-26, and the Tracker (Figure 6.6).

During this period airtankers, or water-bombers as they were called, developed along two main lines—the water-scoopers and the land-based machines. The water-scoopers are float planes, amphibians, or flying boats with systems designed to allow them to fill their tanks while skimming the surface of a body of water. This usually takes about a half a minute or less. The land-based airtankers, by contrast, must be filled at a base adjacent to a landing strip. Obviously, the water-scoopers can be used effectively only in areas where sufficiently large bodies of water are readily available, although a number of amphibians can load in either way.

During the 1950s and 1960s these airtankers saw increasing use and success in Canada, the most heavily used being the Beaver, Otter, and Canso in the east and the Avenger, A-26, and B-26 in the west. An interesting development in British Columbia was the conversion in the early 1960s of the huge Martin Mars flying boat. Three of these surplus monsters were purchased by a consortium of forestry companies located on Vancouver Island and modified into water-scooping airtankers with the unheard-of capacity of 27,500 liters (6,000 Imp. gallons). They saw more than 20 years service on Canada's west coast.

In the early 1960s growing concern was expressed about the life expectancy of surplus military aircraft in the role of airtankers, particularly, the

Figure 6.6.   Canadian Canso on fire duty in Quebec. Photo by Canadian Forestry Service.

Canso. The cost of overhauling them was steeply escalating and parts were becoming scarce. In response to these concerns, the Associate Committee on Forest Fire Protection established a workshop to discuss the feasibility of designing an aircraft specifically for forest fire suppression. The workshop included experts representing many aspects of aviation and met in December of 1963. These experts concluded that design and development of an airtanker would be practical and that, for best general use, it should be a twin-engined amphibian capable of both scooping water and filling from an airstrip. The workshop also identified a number of other operational specifications that were then submitted to various aircraft manufacturers. The challenge was taken up by Canadair Limited and in 1969 the first CL-215, as the new airtanker was designated, entered service with the Quebec government. The CL-215 is a multipurpose twin-engined amphibian with a capacity of 5350 liters of water or retardant. It can also be used as a transport or aerial spray aircraft (Figure 6.7).

Although the CL-215 faced some difficulties competing against the low cost of converted surplus military aircraft, there were, by 1981, some 18 operating in Canada and many more in various countries around the world.

In Europe airtankers were first employed in 1963 when the French tested two Cansos operationally along the southern coast. The operation was quite successful and by 1966, six Cansos were deployed throughout southern France. These were replaced by 10 Canadair CL-215s and in the early 1970s Spain, Greece, and Yugoslavia also acquired CL-215s for forest fire suppression in their coastal areas. Portugal contracts for smaller airtankers from pri-

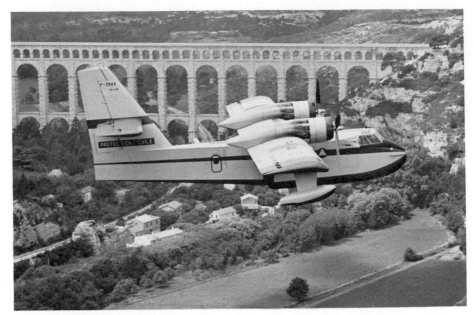

Figure 6.7.   The CL-215 over southern France. Photo by Canadair Ltd.

vate agricultural aviation services, whereas the Italian Forest Service operates its own helitanker fleet and uses military C-130s with a modified
MAFFS system for larger campaign fires.

In the USSR the use of aircraft in forest fire management was a compara-
tively late development, but when it came, it came in a rush (Nesterov 1939).
The first experiments with aircraft for fire detection and reconnaissance
were not begun until 1932, but by 1938 the Russians had an operational
forestry air arm complete with smokejumpers, chemical bombers, and a
unique airborne sprinkling system. The extent of coordination between the
Russian forestry and military services in these developments is not documented, but in view of their rapid progress in the field it was undoubtedly
close, as it was elsewhere in the world.

Following World War II the USSR began experimenting with helicopter
rappeling as an alternative to smokejumping and by the mid1970s they had
the largest trained force of helicopter fire specialists in the world (Moody
1976).

Aircraft for Fire Detection

The first use of aircraft in forestry was for fire detection and this remains one
of the most important functions of a forestry organization's aircraft fleet.
Aerial detection has already been discussed in the chapter on presuppression, but some of the fundamental points relating to air operations bear
repeating here.

In contrast to the fire lookout who provides constant surveillance of a limited geographic area, the aerial observer offers intermittent but flexible coverage of a much larger territory. In addition, the aerial observer can function in a scouting role, obtaining and relaying information on fuels, fire behavior, and any signs of activity on or around the fire. However, the advantages of flexibility are always gained at the price of increased detection time. Over the course of a fire season, lookouts will always have shorter average detection times than aerial patrols.

Many types of aircraft are suitable for forest fire detection missions as long as they provide good visibility for the observer (wing over cabin and a minimum of struts forward of the observer's seat) and relatively high stability during bank and turn maneuvers. The selection of cruising speed involves a trade-off between area covered and probability of detecting a small smoke since increasing airspeed decreases the time available for scanning any individual area.

In planning detection patrols in mountainous topography, the manager must remember that the field of view from the aircraft flight path contains blind spots just as does the view from a lookout tower. Routes should be chosen to complement the fixed detection system, so that those areas blind to the one are seen by the other.

Flying techniques for detection patrols involve more than simply maintaining course and altitude. The pilot must maneuver the aircraft to take advantage of light and shadow so as to facilitate the detection of small smokes. It is also helpful to change the heading by a few degrees every two to three minutes resulting in a slightly zigzag flight path. This keeps the observer's attention from becoming fixed on one spot or direction.

There are several available handbooks covering aerial detection procedures in detail. One of the best is that of the British Columbia Forest Service (1976).

Paracargo Operations

Aircraft can deliver supplies and equipment to remote fire locations faster and with less damage than occurs with other means of transportation provided that proper precautions are taken in packaging the material to be dropped. Incompressible materials such as hand tools can be *hard packed* for free fall by binding or taping the coverings as tightly as possible so that the load reacts as a solid unit on impact, much like dropping a brick. Fuel, canned goods, motors, and other easily damaged materials must be *soft packed* with an outer covering of honeycomb material sufficient to absorb and dissipate the impact forces. Although it is possible to soft pack most items to withstand the impact of a free-fall delivery, it is usually simpler to deliver soft pack items by parachute. Parachute delivery reduces the impact velocity by at least a factor of 10 thus reducing the packaging requirements.

One very important consideration in cargo delivery by parachute is that the normal rigging and deployment system for paracargo is the reverse of

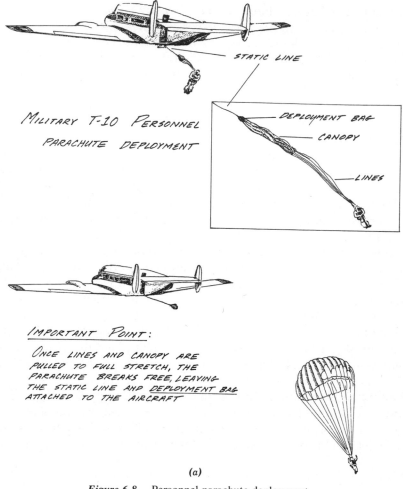

MILITARY T-10 PERSONNEL
PARACHUTE DEPLOYMENT

STATIC LINE

DEPLOYMENT BAG

CANOPY

LINES

IMPORTANT POINT:

ONCE LINES AND CANOPY ARE
PULLED TO FULL STRETCH, THE
PARACHUTE BREAKS FREE, LEAVING
THE STATIC LINE AND DEPLOYMENT BAG
ATTACHED TO THE AIRCRAFT

(a)

Figure 6.8.   Personnel parachute deployment.

that used for parachuting human beings. In both instances the parachutes are stowed in deployment bags attached at one end to the aircraft by static line and at the other end to the cargo or parachute. In dropping personnel the deployment bag remains attached to the static line and the parachute is pulled down from the bag by the weight of the parachutist (Figure 6.8). This is done so that there will be no interference with the parachutist when manipulating shroud lines. In dropping paracargo, on the other hand, the static line is tied to the apex of the parachute, whereas the deployment bag is anchored to the cargo. The parachute is pulled up from the bag by the weight of the cargo (Figure 6.9). This is done to minimize the risk of premature chute opening and subsequent entanglement with aircraft control surfaces. Should the rigging sequence inadvertently be reversed so that the static line is attached to the cargo and the cargo line to the parachute, when the cargo is

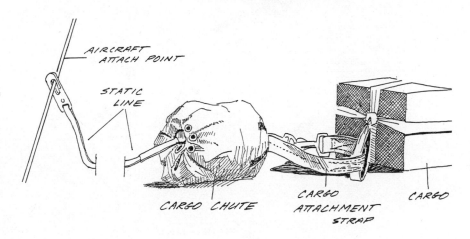

CORRECT PARACARGO ATTACHMENT
SEQUENCE

AIRCRAFT ATTACH POINT

STATIC LINE

CARGO CHUTE

CARGO ATTACHMENT STRAP

CARGO

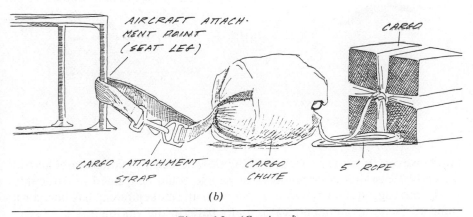

APPARENT ELY ACCIDENT
ATTACHMENT SEQUENCE

AIRCRAFT ATTACH-MENT POINT (SEAT LEG)

CARGO

CARGO ATTACHMENT STRAP

CARGO CHUTE

5' ROPE

(b)

Figure 6.8. (*Continued*)

dropped and the parachute opens the aircraft becomes, in effect, the cargo (Figure 6.10). This error can have dire consequences.

Smokejumping

The idea of dropping firefighters by parachute to remote forest fires where access by foot or horse might take days is as old as the airplane itself. It was

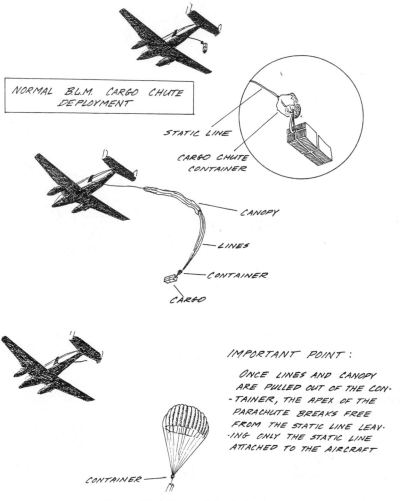

Figure 6.9. Cargo chute deployment.

not, however, until the perfection of the slow descent, steerable parachute in the early 1930s that large numbers of people could be trained to parachute safely into rugged timbered forests. Since then, smokejumping has become a standard tactic for initial attack in many parts of the world.

Each fire management agency has its own standards, equipment, and procedures for its smokejumping program. Since the USSR operates the largest and most complex program with 2600 full-time smokejumpers, we will use the Soviet technology as a model. Smokejumping in most other countries is conducted along similar lines.

The Russian smokejumper is an experienced firefighter specially trained and equipped for this particular method of transport. Once down and working on a fire, the smokejumper is indistinguishable from any other firefighter.

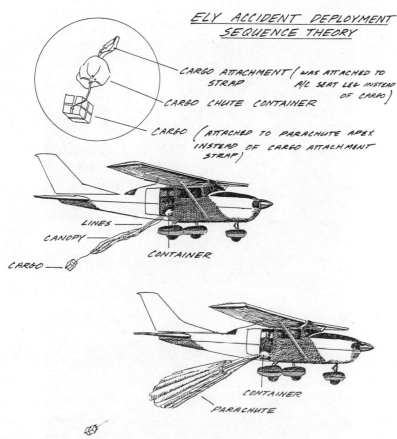

ELY ACCIDENT DEPLOYMENT
SEQUENCE THEORY

CARGO ATTACHMENT (WAS ATTACHED TO
STRAP   A/C SEAT LEG INSTEAD
                          OF CARGO)
CARGO CHUTE CONTAINER

CARGO (ATTACHED TO PARACHUTE APEX
INSTEAD OF CARGO ATTACHMENT
STRAP)

LINES
CANOPY
CONTAINER
CARGO

CONTAINER
PARACHUTE

Figure 6.10.   Incorrect cargo chute deployment.

A typical smokejumping mission begins when a squad of three to eight jumpers is dispatched for initial attack on a fire. Quickly, the jumpers don their gear which consists of a one-piece canvas suit with a zipper down the front, padded for protection against branches and with a high collar for the same reason; a fiberglass "motorcyclist" type helmet with a detachable wire mesh facemask; long gauntlet gloves; high boots for ankle support (Figure 6.11). On arrival at the aircraft the crew first load their fire equipment, already packed in bags ready for dropping. A typical fire bag contains axes, shovels, a saw, backfiring devices, radio, signal flares, a tent, mess gear, rations, and a first-aid kit. Kits for building line with explosives are packaged separately but carried in the same airplane with the jumpers. After the gear is stowed the jumpers "chute up."

The smokejumpers' parachute assembly is actually an integrated assortment of parachutes and associated equipment. The main chute weighs about 13 kilograms and opens to a diameter of approximately 8.5 meters. By varying the porosity of the cloth, the chute is designed to maintain a forward

Figure 6.11.   Soviet smokejumper, Karelia, USSR. Photo by John Deeming.

speed of one to two meters per second if no attempt is made by the jumper to control the descent. The chute is fully controllable with a maximum forward speed of four meters per second, reverse speed of two meters per second, descent rate of five meters per second, and the capability of executing a 360° turn in five to six seconds. This main chute is packed in a three-meter long cloth sleeve which is, in turn, packed into the canvas bag strapped to the smokejumper's back. The sleeve is hooked to a two-meter diameter pilot chute also stowed in the back pack. The pilot chute is, in turn, hooked to a two-meter static line which remains outside the back pack and can be released by a manual rip cord, a timing device, or an aneroid barometer release system.

A smaller reserve parachute is worn on the chest. This chute can only be opened manually by a ripcord. A *letdown* package consisting of a 30-meter nylon strap, a braking device, a set of tree-climbing spurs, and a two-meter climbing rope is attached to the harness below the reserve chute.

On entering the aircraft the smokejumpers anchor their static lines to the aircraft and take their seats. They are now under the command of the jump-master who sits at the front of the plane next to the pilot. When the aircraft arrives over the fire, the jumpmaster selects the most suitable landing spot and directs the pilot to circle at an altitude of 600 meters above terrain. The jumpmaster then signals the senior smokejumper to drop streamers. The streamers are strips of crepe paper five meters long and weighted at one end with wire designed to fall and drift with the same characteristics as the main chute. The jumpmaster selects the proper jump spot relative to the landing spot by observing the descent of the streamers. While the aircraft is maneu-vering to the jumpspot, the crew is given a final briefing on their assignments by the senior smokejumper. Approximately six to eight seconds before arriv-ing over the selected jumpspot the jumpmaster signals the senior smokejump-er to open the cabin door. Two jumpers then move up to their exit position: left foot forward, semicrouched, and grasping the near door firmly with one hand. At the jumpmaster's signal the senior smokejumper slaps the first jumper firmly on the shoulder. Two seconds later the procedure is repeated and the second jumper exits.

As the jumpers leave the aircraft they cross their arms over their chests above the reserve chute with their right hands grasping the main chute ripcord (see Figure 6.12). The static line plays out and deploys the pilot chute and also activates the five-second timing device. The pilot chute serves to slow and stabilize the jumper in a vertical position but does not activate the main chute. The jumper activates the main chute by pulling the ripcord. If the jumper fails to do so within five seconds of pilot chute deploy-ment, the timer automatically deploys the main chute. Should the timer malfunction, the aneroid barometer device deploys the chute at a pre-selected altitude (normally 150 meters). After the main chute has deployed, the jumper visually checks the canopy and that of his or her partner. In case of malfunction the reserve chute is deployed.

In smooth level country smokejumpers will attempt to land on the ground in a clearing to avoid the time and trouble of retrieving themselves and their equipment from the treetops (Figure 6.13). In rough and rocky terrain, how-ever, hanging the parachute in a tree is preferable to slamming into a rock or down a steep hillside at five meters per second. After landing the jumpers retrieve and loosely stow their equipment and await the arrival of the full crew.

Meanwhile, in the aircraft, the sequence of passing over the jumpspot is repeated until all have exited save the pilot, jumpmaster, and senior smoke-jumper. The latter then drops the fire bags attached to cargo chutes and jumps. The jumpmaster then retrieves the last static lines, closes the cabin door, and watches for the senior smokejumper's signal that the crew is safely down. The pilot will generally remain in the vicinity of the drop until radio communication has been established and the jumpmaster and senior smokejumper have conferred on fire behavior, tactics to be used, and the probable need for reinforcements. After that, the smokejumpers become just another fire crew and the aircraft returns to base.

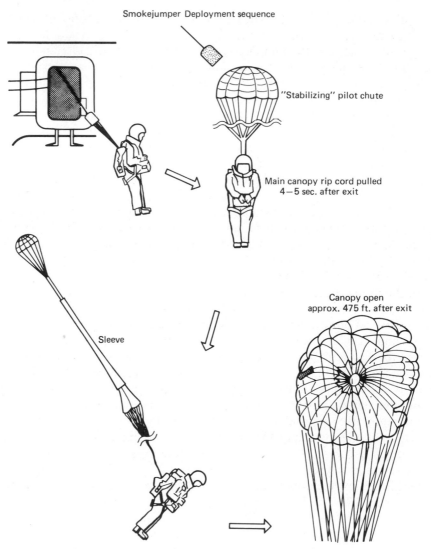

Figure 6.12. Smokejumper deployment sequence. Illustrations by Barry George, NCSB.

Airtanker Operations

Fixed-wing aircraft are routinely used to drop water and/or chemicals on forest fires in many countries of the world. In the United States alone, airtankers dropped an average of 75 million liters per year on wildfires during 1970–1979 (Figure 6.14). The vast majority of airtankers are surplus military or civilian aircraft modified by the installation of watertight tanks, gates, and venting systems. A good review of the principles of tank and gate design can be found in Grigel et al. (1975). Only three aircraft have been specifically

Figure 6.13. A treetop landing requires rappeling down by rope. Photo by U.S. Forest Service.

Figure 6.14. Most airtankers are surplus military aircraft. A B-17 drops on a fire in Oregon. Photo by U.S. Forest Service.

designed for airtanker work: the Canadian CL-215 (Canadair 1965), probably the most widely dispersed airtanker worldwide; the Shinmeiwa SS-2A (Shinmeiwa Ind. 1977), a four-engine amphibian holding 12,750 liters which has seen little use outside of the Far East; the C-130 MAFFS (Bussey and Harrington 1975), a pressurized system designed for the U.S. Air Force. Only eight MAFFS units were ever built and their use is restricted by military policy to catastrophic forest fire situations when all available civilian airtankers have been utilized. There are many advantages to operating an airtanker specifically designed for forest fire missions, as many CL-215 and MAFFS users will attest, but the availability of surplus military aircraft and the cost differential between new and used airplanes has greatly limited the market.

Although virtually every type and style of propeller-driven airplane from the Stearman Agro-Cat to the Martin Mars has at one time or another been forced into duty as an airtanker, the trend in recent years has been the displacement of smaller (under 4000 liter capacity) airtankers in favor of helicopters and the utilization of ever-larger capacity airtankers. This is partially due to the greater versatility of the helicopter, whose tanks or buckets can easily be jettisoned making the aircraft available for other work, and partly inherent in the airtanker mission itself.

Aerial delivery of retardants or suppressants can never be relied upon to completely control fire since there is no mop-up capability from the air. Air attack on forest fires is undertaken in two modes: initial attack on small fires where the objective is to suppress the entire fire until the arrival of a ground crew, and in direct support of ground crews on larger fires where the objectives is either to retard the spread of selected sections of the fire in order to allow ground crews to complete firelines or to reduce fire intensity so that fire crews can make a direct attack.

The ground pattern of material dropped from an airtanker depends on the material dropped, the altitude and airspeed of the aircraft, the wind velocity and direction relative to the drop, the tank and gating characteristics of the airplane, and the overstory through which the material must pass to reach the ground. A detailed discussion of these determinants is beyond the scope of this book and the interested reader is referred to Swanson et al. (1975). However, the general shape, under most circumstances, is that of a lozenge with the highest concentration of material in the center and progressively lesser amounts at the side and ends. In the literature, concentration of material from airtanker drops is measured in U.S. gallons per hundred square feet of land surface (abbreviation gpc). One gpc is equivalent, roughly, to 1 liter per $2\frac{1}{2}$ square meters. In more common terms, 1 gpc is equal to 0.4 millimeters of rain. The amount of material needed to stop a fire depends on the fuel, burning conditions, and the material used. For long-term retardants one to five gpc are adequate under most circumstances. The most efficient airtanker pilot is the one who maximizes the area covered by the lowest effective concentration of material. Numerous techniques and tactics have been devised to improve airtanker efficiency, and handbooks on the subject have been available since the 1960s (Linkewich 1966).

Because airtankers are the single most costly weapon in the forest firefighter's arsenal, a great deal of sophisticated attention has been devoted to optimizing their use. Operations research techniques have been used to determine the number and size of airtankers needed to cover a specific district, optimize their basing requirements, and even specify their tactics (Simard and Young 1978).

Helicopter Use

Because of their versatility, hoverability, and ability to land in confined spaces, helicopters are rapidly displacing fixed-wing aircraft in many forest fire management operations. In the United States and the USSR the initial attack is made by helicopter on five fires for every fire attacked by smoke-jumpers. Reconnaissance of large fires has become almost exclusively a helicopter show. Even the airtanker is losing ground to aerial delivery of water and retardants from helibuckets. During the period 1975–1979, 25 percent of the retardant dropped on fires in the United States was dropped from helicopters.

Initial attack by helicopter, known as helitack, is the principal job of the helicopter firefighters. In the U.S. Forest Service, 3500 fires a year are helitack fires (in the USSR there are more than twice as many) compared to 700 first attacked by smokejumpers, 4000 by airtankers, and 4500 by ground crews. Normally, the helicopter will land and discharge passengers at a clearing near the fire. If no clearing is available but the ground has only brush or low ground cover, the pilot may hover while one or two specially trained and equipped firefighters jump out and construct a helispot for landing. If dense timber prevents either landing or jumping, firefighters are rappeled to the ground on ropes. Rappeling requires dual-engined rotorcraft for safety and is rare in the United States where most helicopters used in forest fire control are single motor. In the Soviet Union, however, where the K-28 helicopter is the forest fire workhorse, rappeling to fires is the rule rather than the exception. The Russian rappeling device is unique. Fifty meters of 700-kilogram test nylon tape are wound on a metal drum about 40 centimeters in diameter and about 7.5 centimeters thick. The drum is hooked to a body harness and worn in front of the rappeler about waist high. The entire assembly weighs 8.5 kilograms. In use, the end of the tape is snapped to the aircraft, the same as a smokejumper's static line, and the rappeler exits. The speed of descent is controlled manually by a handle-type brake which is spring-locked to "no rate of release" unless pulled. Maximum rate of descent is reached when the brake is pulled down 90 degrees. It locks again if pulled 180 degrees. Thus the rappeler's descent is stopped if he or she either releases the grip on the control handle or pushes too hard against it in a panic situation. The maximum rate of descent is controlled at six meters per second by an internal friction brake. Any intermediate rate can be achieved, but the usual descent is three to five meters per second. On landing, the jump-master in the aircraft unhooks the tape and drops it. The rappeler then reels in the loose tape using a hand crank on the front of the drum. Operating from a hover 30 meters over dense timber, six rappelers can be landed in three minutes.

The British Columbia Forest Service is faced with the control of wildfire in some of the most rugged and inaccessible terrain in Canada. The major problem of fire managers in this terrain is that of getting fire crews and equipment to remote lightning fires. To help overcome this problem, they developed in 1977 a rappel-attack system known as *Rapattack* (Morgan 1981) which places a small, highly trained initial attack crew close to the fire site using a helicopter and rappeling technique. The size of the crew depends on the size of the helicopter being used. Normally, a rapattack crew consists of the pilot, a spotter, and three rappelers. A cargo bag slung under the helicopter contains all the equipment the crew will need in their first attack on the fire. It is lowered to the crew after they have reached the ground.

Equipment for Rapattack includes a rope attachment point on the helicop-ter (certified by the Department of Transport), a 70 to 80-meter continuous fiber nylon rope, and a device by which the rappeler controls descent on the rope. Special clothing and equipment include a helmet, heavy gloves, a jumpsuit, and reinforced boots. Each rappeler also carries a small bag for personal needs.

The most commonly used helicopter is the Bell 206L-1 although other machines such as the Bell 205 may be used when larger crews are required.

Apart from their use as initial attack firefighters, the Rapattack crew is frequently used as an advance crew to prepare a landing site to be used by helicopters for more conventional unloading of crew and equipment.

The second greatest use of helicopters, in terms of flight hours, is drop-ping water or retardants. The material is carried in fiberglass open-topped *helibuckets* sling-loaded beneath the helicopter with an electrical connection from the pilot's control system to release a metal gate at the bottom of the bucket (Figure 6.15). Because helicopters have a much greater range of permissible airspeeds during dropping operations than do fixed-wing air-craft, drop patterns from helicopters can be more closely controlled and more fireline can be built per liter of material dropped (Grigel et al. 1974). Another advantage to the use of helicopters for delivering suppressants is that, with the aid of forward looking infrared equipment or light amplification goggles, drops can be made at night when burning conditions are poorest and water is the most effective in extinguishing fire.

Helicopters can also be useful in backfiring and prescribed burning opera-tions, especially when center firing is required, and in other situations where it would be dangerous to send firefighters on foot. Several special devices have been developed to dispense incendiary materials from helicopters. These have already been discussed in Chapter 5.

Figure 6.15. Typical helibucket operation. Photo by Los Angeles County Fire Department.

BIBLIOGRAPHY

Artsybashev, E. S. 1973. *Forest fire suppression with artificially induced precipitation from clouds,* Ezdatelestvo Lesnaya Promichlennost, Moscow, 88 pp.

Artsybashev, E. S. 1974. *Forest fires and the fight against them,* Lesnaya Promichlennost, Moscow, 151 pp.

Banks, W. G. and R. H. Fenton. 1957. Primacord tested for blasting fireline. *Fire Contr. Notes* 18(4):164–167.

British Columbia Forest Service. 1969. *Handbook on forest fire suppression.* For. Prot. Handbook No. 3, 81 pp.

British Columbia Forest Service. 1976. *Handbook on aerial detection of forest fires.* For. Prot. Handbook No. 9, 33 pp.

Broido, A. 1973. Flammable—whatever that means. *Chem. Tech. J.* 3(1):14–17.

Brown, A. A. and K. P. Davis. 1973. *Forest fire control and use.* McGraw-Hill, New York, 686 pp.

Bussey, A. H. and J. J. Harrington. 1975. *Modular airborne fire fighting system (MAFFs).* Air Force Weapons Lab. Report AFWL-TR-73-271, 56 pp., illus.

Campbell, J. F. 1938. Developments in the one-lick method. *Fire Contr. Notes* 2(4):25–29.

Canadair, Ltd. 1965. *Certification standard for Canadair model CL-215 special purpose aircraft.* Report No. RAO-215-100, 42 pp.

Controlled Airstreams Inc. 1964. *72-inch fog machines versus wild fire and wind.* Glendale Conf. Report No. 100-1, 15 pp., illus.

D'yachenko, L. N., P. S. Y. Lu, and N. S. Shiskin. 1972. Studies of artificial control of precipitation relative to the problem of extinguishing forest fire. *Trudy v Vsesoyuznogo Meterologicheskogo S"Yezda.* V.4:37–44.

Dodge, M. 1970. Nitrate poisoning, fire retardants, and fertilizers—any connection? *J. Range Manage.* 23(4):244–247.

Dorman, L. A. 1954. Use of irrigation pipe in fire suppression. *Fire Contr. Notes* 15(3):9–13.

Driggs, L. L. T. 1921. Fighting fires from the air. *The Outlook,* Jan. 1921, pp. 138–142.

Ebarb, P. 1978. Texas snow job. *Fire Manage. Notes* 39(3):3–5.

Florida Division of Forestry. 1975. *Fire fighters guide.* Fla. Div. For., 127 pp., illus.

Fons, W. L. 1950. *Wet water for forest fire suppression.* U.S. For. Serv. Calif. For. Exp. Sta. Res. Note No. 71, 5 pp.

Fristrom, R. M. 1967. Combustion suppression. *Fire Res. Abs. and Rev.* 9(3):125–161.

Gaylor, H. P. 1974. *Wildfires: prevention and control,* Robert J. Brady Co., Bowie, Md., 319 pp., illus.

George, C. W., A. D. Blakely, and G. M. Johnson. 1976. *Forest fire retardant research—a status report.* U.S. For. Serv. Gen. Tech. Report INT-31, 22 pp.

Grigel, J. E., R. J. Lieskovsky, and R. G. Newstead. 1974. *Air drop tests with helitankers.* Nor. For. Res. Centre Info. Report NOR-X-7, 77 pp., illus.

Grigel, J. E., R. G. Newstead, and R. J. Lieskovsky. 1975. *A review of retardant delivery systems used in fixed wing airtankers.* Nor. For. Res. Inst. (Canada) Info. Report NOR-X-134, 66 pp., illus.

Hardy, C. E. 1977. *Chemicals for forest fire fighting,* 3rd ed., Nat. Fir. Prot. Assoc., Boston, 106 pp.

Headley, R. 1916. *Fire suppression.* U.S. For. Serv. Dist. 5 Unnumbered Report, 58 pp.

ICONA (Instituto Nacional para la Conservation de la Naturaliza). 1981. *Teconicas para defensa contra incendios forestales.* ICONA Monog. No. 24, Madrid, 200 pp.

Johnson, V. J. 1970. *A water curtain for controlling experimental forest fires.* U.S. For. Serv. Res. Paper NC-48, 7 pp., illus.

Linkewich, A. 1966. *Pilot's notes for fire bombing.* Canadian Copyright, P.O. Box 857, Red Deer, Alberta, 89 pp., illus.

Lott, J. R. 1975. *An operational system for constructing fireline with explosives.* U.S. For. Serv. ED&T 2004, 28 pp.

MacHattie, L. B., G. A. Issac, and N. R. Bobbitt. 1976. *Prospects for economic suppression of large forest fires by induced showers.* Canada For. Fire Res. Inst. Info. Report FF-X059, 22 pp.

Matthews, D. N. 1940. Effect of size of crew on firefighting efficiency. *Fire Contr. Notes* 4(3):136–141.

McIntyre, R. N. 1942. The variable lick method—an approach to greater efficiency in the construction of fire-control line. *J. For.* 40(8):609–614.

Moody, W. D. 1976. *Technical report US–USSR rappelling.* U.S. For. Serv. Unnumbered Report, 48 pp.

Morgan, D. G. 1981. B.C.'s rapattack. *Can. Aviation,* July 1981, pp. 38–39.

Murphy, P. J. and D. Quintilio. 1978. *Handcrew fire-line construction: a method of estimating production rates.* Nor. For. Res. Centre Info. Report NOR-X-197, 27 pp.

Nesterov, V. G. 1939. *The nature of forest fires and how to deal with them*, NVILLKh, Moscow, 154 pp.

Norris, L. N. and others. 1978. *The behavior and impact of chemical fire retardants in forest streams.* U.S. For. Serv. For. Sci. Lab., Corvallis, Ore. Unnumbered Report, 261 pp.

Ontario Ministry of Natural Resources. 1979. *Forest Fire Suppression.* Toronto, 115 pp.

Pirsko, A. R. and L. V. Steck. 1961. Liquid nitrogen and solid carbon dioxide as forest fire suppressants. *Fire Contr. Notes* 22(4):120–122.

Rasbash, D. J. 1962. The extinction of fire by water sprays. *Fire Res. Abs. and Rev.* 4(1,2):28–53.

Rasbash, D. J. 1966. *The use of liquid gases to extinguish fires.* J.F.R.O. Fire Res. Note No. 637, 14 pp.

Ritter, E. 1949. Driven wells for fire protection. *Fire Contr. Notes* 10(1):43–46.

Shchetinsky, E. A. 1975. *Cooperation of aviation and ground forest protection*, Rosselichozez-dat, Moscow, 28 pp.

Shinmeiwa Ind. 1977. SS-2A airtanker. *Seaplane News (Japan)*, pp. 23–26.

Sierra Research Corp. 1972. *Cloud-seeding in Alaska: a program to aid in the control and prevention of forest fires.* Unnumbered Pub., 16 pp., illus.

Simard, A. and A. Young. 1978. *AIRPRO: an air tanker productivity simulation model.* For. Fire Res. Inst. Info. Report FF-X-66, 191 pp.

Stechishen, E. 1970. *Measurement of the effectiveness of water as a suppressant.* For. Fire Res. Inst. Info. Report FF-X-23, 16 pp., illus.

Stechishen, E., E. C. Little, and M. W. Hobbs. 1982. *Laboratory determined characteristics of several forest fire retardants.* Can. For. Serv. Info. Report II-X-11, 47 pp.

Swanson, D. H., C. W. George, and A. D. Luedecke. 1975. *User guidelines for fire retardant aircraft: general instruction manual.* Honeywell Corp., U.S. For. Serv. Contract 26-3332, 19 pp.

Truax, T. R. 1939. *The use of chemicals in forest fire control.* U.S. For. Serv. Unnumbered Report, 23 pp., illus.

U.S. Forest Service 1963. The interregional suppression crews. *Fire Contr. Notes* 24(4):93.

Zinov, G. I. 1975. *Forest fire chemical stations*, Rossel'khozizdat, Moscow, 24 pp.

CHAPTER SEVEN

Large Fire Organization

It is important that certain basic principles be recognized. The organization on any fire must be fitted to that particular fire. Furthermore, during the process of suppression, the organization must be constantly adjusted to the changing requirements. Every Forest Officer must be familiar with the duties of each position so that when the Fire Boss selects a man, he knows without being told just what his duties, responsibilities and authority are. To go further than this and create a preliminary paper organization, specifying the men who shall fill each position on a paper fire, is to do important organization work in the wrong way at the wrong time. Welding men into a suppression organization is a duty which can be properly discharged only at the time of the fire and by the Fire Boss. To attempt to relieve him of this duty only cramps him by overorganization.

> Roy Headly
> Fire Suppression Manual
> U.S. Forest Service 1916

In 1916 when fighting a large fire involved merely rounding up a few dozen volunteers, equipping them with hand tools, and trying to ensure that they did not starve to death in the next few weeks, on-the-spot organization was both practical and necessary. Today, however, the manager of a large forest fire may be responsible for thousands of personnel in dozens of specialties, several hundred million dollars worth of equipment, and have scores of reporters and journalists scrutinizing every decision. Under these conditions creating "a paper organization for each position on a paper fire" is the only way to avoid chaos.

The overall strategy for fire suppression on any forest unit is established by the forest land manager during the development of the fire plan for the

173

unit. The manager decides the relative priority for firefighting resources to be allocated to the various cover types and land uses within the district. The manager determines which areas are sufficiently valuable to warrant extraordinary measures such as sustained air attack and in which areas hectarage can be sacrificed to reduce suppression costs. When a large fire is in progress on lands under his or her jurisdiction, the land manager will consult frequently with the fire boss or incident commander to ensure that the fire suppression strategy selected for implementation is consistent with the land management goals and objectives for the unit. Even in countries where forest fire protection is an independent service provided by the state, frequent consultation with land managers is necessary. Forest fire management is merely one tool for more efficient land management. Forest fire management should never be allowed to become an end in itself.

Although every fire department and every forestry enterprise has its own distinctive table of organization, there are certain functions that must be undertaken on all large forest fires and certain principles of organization common to all fire management agencies. Since firefighting in many ways resembles fighting a battle, many of the organizational concepts have been borrowed directly from the military and many of the terms have military connotations.

There are five major functions that must be performed on any fire regardless of size or complexity. These are command, planning, suppression, logistics, and finance. On small fires all the functions may be performed by one or two people, whereas on very large fires any one function (except command) may require a staff of 20 or more. However, on any fire the firefighters must be equipped, led according to a definite plan, and eventually paid for their labor.

The command function serves to coordinate and direct the other four functions in a manner that ensures the most efficient use of personnel and equipment to suppress the fire within the strategic constraints established by the land manager. The command function is usually vested in a single individual called the Fire Boss or Incident Commander but, occasionally, on fires involving several jurisdictions or agencies a joint command may be established with all commanders agreeing to operate under a single fire plan. In addition to coordinating and directing, the command function is responsible for safety, public information, and interagency liaison.

The planning function is responsible for the collection and analysis of information pertinent to the fire and the development of that information into a detailed suppression plan. The essence of successful fire planning is to base the plan on current data. Forest fires are infinitely variable and subject to change, making it essential that the planner have the ability to immediately alter plans to fit a changed situation. Good communications and accurate intelligence are vital to proper planning. Nothing is more useless than a plan based on where the fire was rather than where it is and where it is expected to be throughout the planning period.

The suppression function encompasses all direct firefighting actions including fireline construction, backfiring, detecting and controlling spot fires, applying water or chemicals from ground or air, supervising all firefighting personnel, managing all suppression equipment, mop-up, patrol, and final fireline inspection. Suppression personnel have the direct responsibility for putting out the fire and ensuring that it stays out.

The service function procures, maintains, and distributes personnel and equipment to the locations at the times called for in the fire suppression plan. A strong service organization is a necessity if the suppression effort is to be successful. With increasing use of mechanized equipment and aircraft, the service function has become more difficult and challenging.

The finance function oversees the application of good business management practices and the maintenance of accurate and complete financial records in connection with the fire. Finance covers legal matters such as claims against the firefighting agency as well as handling payrolls, contracts, and similar fiscal duties.

In the United States, most organizations for suppression of large forest fires are built around one of two models. Agencies that are responsible solely for forest fire protection generally use the Large Fire Organization (LFO; see Figure 7.1). This is a traditional organization built around individual positions with rather rigid standards for training, experience, and physical fitness requirements for each position in the organization. Agencies that have multiple emergency responsibilities such as rural fire departments which handle structural fires and medical emergencies as well as forest fires often use the Incident Command System (ICS; see Figure 7.2). The ICS is designed to function on any emergency incident from earthquake to automobile accident. The ICS operates on the basis of subfunctions or *units* rather than individual positions. An example is the *Strike Team* which has a designated number of resources of the same kind and type, common communications, and a leader. The strike teams are moved about within the organization as single entities. Since an increasing number of forestry agencies are becoming involved in emergencies other than forest fire suppression, the Incident Management System is rapidly becoming the dominant method of organization in the United States. Figures 7.3 through 7.7 show the distinctions between the ICS and the LFO for each of the five organizational functions.

The Fire Boss or Incident Commander is responsible to the land manager or line officer who assigned him or her to the fire. He or she has full authority and responsibility for managing the fire control operation within the applicable laws, agency policies, and whatever constraints may be applied by the designated land manager or line officer. It is the Incident Commander's primary responsibility to organize and direct the fire operation so as to obtain speedy, efficient, and complete control of the fire.

The Safety Officer works under the direct supervision of the Incident Commander. The principal duties of the Safety Officer are to analyze the fire

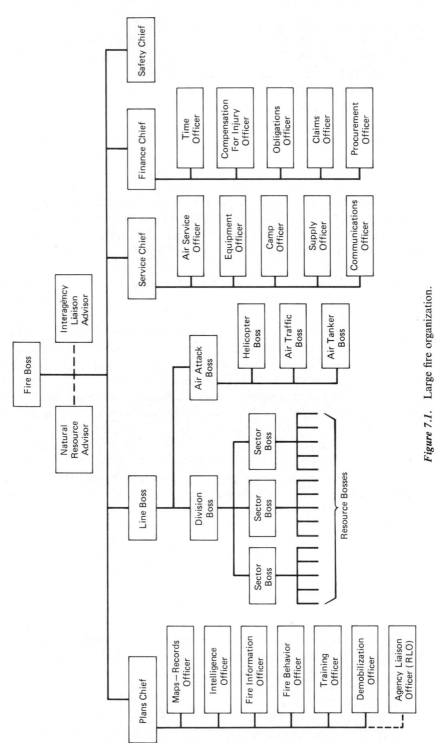

Figure 7.1. Large fire organization.

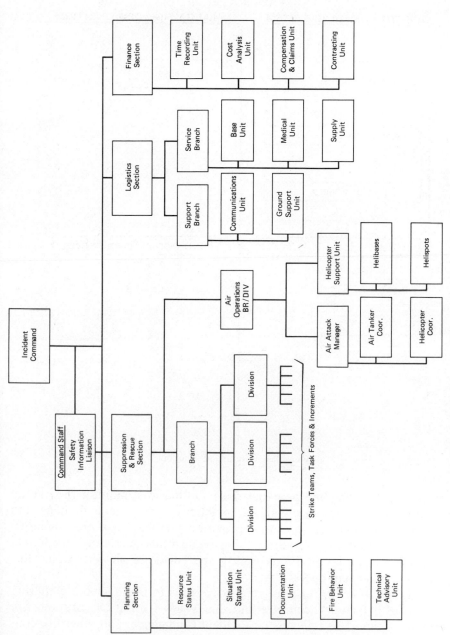

Figure 7.2. Incident command system.

177

COMMAND FUNCTION

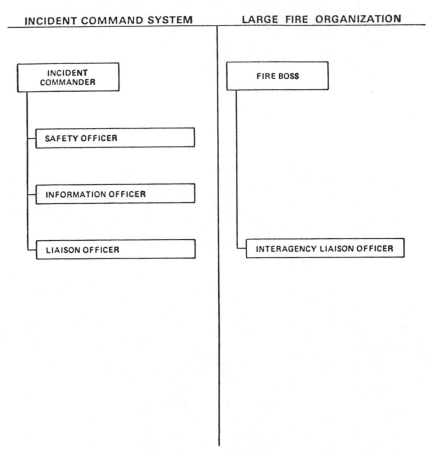

Figure 7.3. Command function.

operation for existing and potential risks and hazards, monitor the overall fire activities for compliance with safe practices, communicate findings, and recommend remedial measures to appropriate overhead positions. On large, complex fires, especially those involving extensive air operations, the Safety Officer may supervise additional safety specialists for air operations, line operations, and camp operations.

The Information Officer's primary purpose is to facilitate the gathering and release of factual, accurate, and timely news about the fire and fire control activities. This relieves the Incident Commander and other fire control personnel from pressures often imposed by the news media and the general public. When necessary, the Information Officer will establish and staff an information center to provide a focal point for news media activities. All interviews, tours, press, and television coverage of the fire are coor-

PLANNING FUNCTION

INCIDENT COMMAND SYSTEM   LARGE FIRE ORGANIZATION

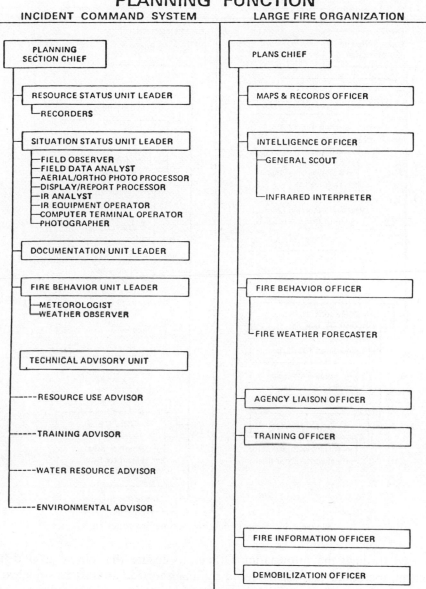

Figure 7.4. Planning function.

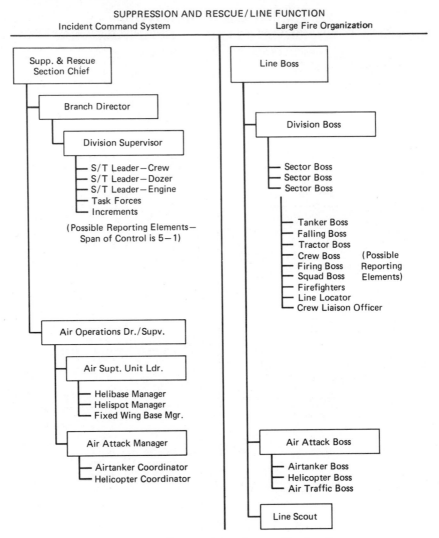

Figure 7.5. Suppression and rescue/line function.

dinated through the Information Officer to ensure that air or ground fire control operations are not hindered by unauthorized aircraft or vehicles.

The Liaison Officer position is needed on large fires where several public and private agencies may be involved in fire suppression, law enforcement, personnel welfare, medical assistance, or restoration of public works. The Liaison Officer must be familiar with the operating policies and procedures of all cooperating agencies and with the terms and restrictions of any formal agreements that may govern their activities. The Officer's principal responsibility is to keep the Incident Commander advised of cooperator's activities, plans, and problems and to assist the cooperators as necessary.

LOGISTICS/SERVICE FUNCTION

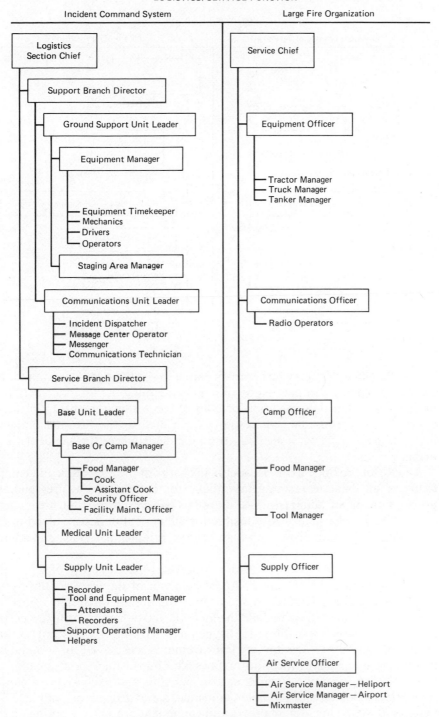

Figure 7.6. Logistics/service function.

FINANCE FUNCTION

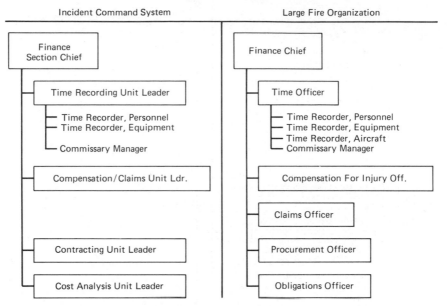

Figure 7.7.   Finance function.

The Planning Section Chief is responsible to the Incident Commander for the collection and compilation of all data concerning the fire, calculation of probabilities, and determination of control force requirements. The Chief collects and records data on resources assigned to the fire and prepares instructions for line personnel based on the decisions of the Incident Commander.

The Resource Status Unit Leader is in charge of the collection and compilation of all data on resources available for control of the fire, and the preparation of all administrative records connected with the fire control effort. The Leader is also responsible for all clerical duties involved in the preparation of action plans, unit instructions, briefing materials, and administrative reports.

The Situation Status Unit Leader supervises the gathering of all intelligence concerning the present and past behavior of the fire and all physiographic and cultural features in and around the fire area that may affect fire control operations. These include the location and behavior of the fire perimeter, including any spot fires; fuel types and hazards in, adjacent to, and ahead of the fire; location of improvements destroyed or potentially threatened by the fire; location of possible control lines, and location of infeasible line locations such as narrow canyons and excessively steep or rocky ridges; location of possible campsites, aerial drop areas, and helicopter landing spots; location of crews and equipment presently working on the fire; possible routes to the fire edge or spot fires as well as possible escape routes or safety areas for crews. The Situation Status Unit will normally include specialists in photographic analysis as well as aerial and ground observers and scouts.

The Documentation Unit Leader maintains the permanent files of all plans and records connected with the fire including financial records on fires too small to warrant establishing a finance function and helicopter time records on fires where air activity is insufficient to warrant activating an air operations unit.

The Fire Behavior Unit Leader supervises all meteorological activities on the fire and prepares written predictions of expected future fire behavior for utilization in all fire plans. The Leader also identifies any unusual fire hazards that may develop because of future combinations of weather, fuels, and topography and informs the Planning Section Chief and the Incident Commander whenever unsafe conditions are anticipated. The Leader consults with appropriate line officers on the location of planned fire lines.

The Technical Advisory Unit consists of such natural resource specialists as may be needed when a fire is burning or threatening unusually sensitive areas such as municipal watersheds, archeological areas, or endangered species habitats. The specialists are advisors to the Planning Section Chief on special measures that may be required to minimize environmental damage.

The Suppression and Rescue Section Chief is responsible for supervising all suppression and rescue operations. The Chief develops the fire control plan under the instructions of the Incident Commander and determines the need for additional resources or the presence of superfluous resources and makes appropriate recommendations to the Incident Commander. The Suppression and Rescue Section Chief assembles strike teams and task forces as needed for each work shift and designates the leader for each group.

The Branch Director is responsible for directing all ground operations connected with the suppression of the fire. The Director assigns tasks to the Division Supervisors, personally checks progress on the work assigned, reports progress relative to the fire control plan to the Suppression and Rescue Section Chief, and recommends changes in the plan as dictated by circumstances. The Branch Director coordinates all joint air–ground operations with the Air Attack Manager.

The Division Supervisor directs the ground operations on a designated section of fire perimeter. The Supervisor reviews the Division assignment with subordinate officers and makes specific task assignments to each unit. He or she coordinates operations with adjacent Divisions and personally supervises the most critical tasks assigned to the Division.

The Strike Team and Task Force Leaders are responsible for accomplishing the tasks assigned to them by the Division Supervisor efficiently and expeditiously.

The Air Operations Supervisor is responsible for the conduct of all air operations in support of the Incident Commander and for coordinating the air resources assigned to the fire with civilian and military air operations that may utilize the same airspace.

The Air Support Unit Leader is in charge of maintenance and upkeep at helibases that are equipped with helicopter maintenance materials and helispots that provide only helicopter landing services, and at any temporary air bases established by the Incident Commander to service fixed-wing aircraft.

The Air Base Managers operate the individual bases including the responsibility for mixing and supplying fire-retardant chemicals when aircraft are used in direct attack missions.

The Air Attack Manager is in charge of all direct attack missions involving helicopters or fixed-wing aircraft. The Manager establishes mission priorities and coordinates with ground operations through the Branch Director.

The Airtanker and Helicopter Coordinators manage the actual air attack operations. They notify pilots of selected targets, observe drops to evaluate pilot proficiency, and coordinate flight operations.

The Logistics Section Chief works under the direction of the Incident Commander and is responsible for furnishing all facilities and services called for in the fire control plan. This includes the establishment, maintenance, and operation of fire camps; furnishing firefighters, tools, and specialized equipment; obtaining, servicing, and operating a transportation fleet; establishing and maintaining communication systems; providing first aid facilities and access to medical assistance.

The Support Branch Director is responsible for processing firefighters and equipment into the fire organization and transporting them to and from their assigned Divisions. The Director also supervises the Communications Unit and the Equipment Service Unit.

The Ground Support Unit Leader maintains a complete inventory of all personnel and equipment assigned to the fire; provides transportation services; fuels, maintains, and repairs all ground based equipment; manages staging areas.

The Communications Unit Leader develops, installs, and services communication networks as required by the fire control plan.

The Service Branch Director is responsible for the establishment and maintenance of camp and warehouse facilities and the acquisition and disposition of all commissary supplies for the fire.

The Base Unit Leader determines the number and location of camps needed to feed and shelter the personnel anticipated in the fire control plan and plans the layout for each facility.

The Base Manager activates and manages the facilities at a fire camp.

The Medical Unit Leader provides first-aid assistance, responds to requests for medical assistance, and maintains medical records for all personnel assigned to the fire.

The Supply Unit Leader orders, receives, and stores all supplies needed on the fire. The Leader also services damaged but reusable supply items.

The Finance Section Chief works under the supervision of the Incident Commander to see that proper obligation documents are prepared for the purchase or rental of equipment, supplies, materials, and services; to adjudicate claims arising in connection with the fire; to negotiate contracts; to provide fiscal advice and assistance to the Incident Commander and other functional staff officers.

The Time Recording Unit Leader is responsible for maintaining accurate records of employee time and equipment use. The Leader also supervises the commissary where personal supplies are sold to fire personnel.

The Compensation and Claims Unit Leader processes all claims against the fire organization, either by fire personnel for injury or equipment damage, or by outsiders for damages caused by the fire or by firefighting forces.

The Contracting Unit Leader negotiates all contracts for supplies and equipment.

The Cost Analysis Unit Leader maintains a current record of all obligations incurred during the course of the fire and reports any unusual deviations to the attention of the Finance Chief.

The preceding organization charts are specific to the United States where the majority of federal wildland fire agencies follow the Large Fire Organization while many state and local departments are organized around the Incident Command System. Outside the United States, organizational patterns depend largely on which governmental or corporate entity bears the legal responsibility for forest fire protection.

The management and protection of Canada's forests, with the exception of those in the Yukon and Northwest Territories, is the responsibility of the 10 provincial governments. Each provincial and territorial government has its own forest fire management agency, the size and complexity of which depends on the scope of the fire management problem faced by the agency. Each such agency makes its own fire laws and manages fire with the type of organization best suited to its particular fire conditions. As a general rule, a province is divided into broad forest districts or regions that are further subdivided for fire management purposes. Although, in the past, fire control was managed at the smaller district level, new technologies such as computerized management systems are encouraging a more centralized organization.

In Canada the forest industries also have an important part to play in forest fire management. Large companies equip and train their woods employees to fight forest fire. Should a fire break out on land for which they are responsible, it is usual for company firefighters to take initial central action and, if needed, to work with provincial fire central forces until the fire has been contained.

In Quebec forest fire management is shared by the provincial government and special associations of forest industries, Sociétés de Conservation. These Sociétés are funded jointly by forest companies within their boundaries and by the Quebec government.

Methods of organizing for the suppression of large fires varies from one agency to another but, in general, the larger agencies follow an organization similar to that of the U.S. Forest Service described earlier.

The fire protection organization of the USSR is, in some respects, similar to that of Canada. Forestry Enterprises, which are the state-controlled corporations responsible for timber harvest and primary manufacture, have the responsibility for fire protection within their allotted five-year cutting boundaries. Each Forestry Enterprise is expected to establish a detection system, a full-time initial attack force (which usually is also trained and equipped to provide structural fire protection to the mill and workers' housing), and to train all forest workers in basic fire control techniques and organize them into squads for use on large fires when required.

For all areas outside the cutting limits of the Forestry Enterprises, forest fire protection is supplied by the Ministry of Forestry of the USSR. The 15 forest regions are divided into protection districts. Districts vary in size from two to five million hectares depending on the historical fire load. Each district is under the supervision of a *Chief Pilot-Observer* who is qualified to both command and plan fire suppression operations up to division size. The Chief Pilot-Observer has a staff of smokejumpers and rappelers who take initial attack action on all fires in their area of responsibility and are also trained to act as crew leaders and section heads on large fires. If a fire either on lands protected by the protection district or a Forestry Enterprise within the district grows beyond the capabilities of the initial attack force and the first reinforcements, the Chief Pilot-Observer assumes command of the fire and his or her staff fills the necessary planning and suppression overhead positions. By having all personnel in the district organization trained to one or two levels above their normal initial attack responsibility, the organization can expand five-fold without requiring outside assistance.

Should a fire exceed the capabilities of the district organization, the Regional Headquarters is staffed with personnel specially trained in complex suppression, planning, and logistics functions. More suppression personnel are drawn from adjacent districts and backup support is supplied from the Central Air Base in Pushkino near Moscow. Despite a relatively small protection force for an area the size of the USSR, by using centralized specialists and highly trained firefighters it is possible to adequately staff as many as five to seven large fires burning simultaneously.

In Australia, by contrast, wildland fire protection is overwhelmingly a volunteer, though highly organized, effort. The backbone of Australian fire protection is the bushfire brigade. Some 300,000 Australians are active members in one or another of Australia's 7,000 brigades. Considering that rural Australia has only slightly over 3 million inhabitants, nearly one rural resident in 10 is a trained firefighter. State, rather than federal, fire laws are operative in Australia and the relations between the brigades differ somewhat from state to state. In general, however, the brigades receive most of their financial support from insurance underwriters with a portion also coming from local and state governments. The brigades are represented at the government level by various bushfire councils, boards, and authorities whose members are selected by the brigades and represent the firefighters' interests when legislation is proposed.

Because the bushfire brigades represent a collection of independent entities, organizing for large fires that require the unification of several brigades under a single command is more difficult than it is in countries with a centralized fire protection organization. This difficulty is overcome by an elaborate system of cooperative agreements that usually specify not only which brigades will supply assistance within any part of the state, but also name the individuals to occupy particular positions in the large fire organization should one occur.

In Europe, as in Australia, forest fire control is usually a responsibility of the landowner or of volunteer fire protection groups. Unlike Australia, European volunteers are almost invariably trained and equipped for urban firefighting, and are enthusiastic but not very efficient at forest fire control. In the Mediterranean region where several countries have initiated aerial attack systems under central government control this has resulted in two separate air and ground organizations, somewhat along the Russian model, but without the clear understanding of the command structure contained in the USSR. In the Mediterranean basin where fire is a constant threat, each Provencia or Department (administrative divisions corresponding to counties in the United States) has a staff of professional fire officers for command positions. The majority of firefighters, however, are volunteers. There are very few large, unbroken tracts of wildland in Europe (the largest virgin stand is the 5000 hectare Bialowieza National Park in Poland) and major fire outbreaks usually consist of a large number of simultaneous ignitions that overwhelm the available initial attack forces rather than single large fires requiring the organization of hundreds of firefighters. Consequently, large fires in Europe are usually fought by simply assigning particular sections of fire perimeter to individual volunteer units and providing logistical support from the headquarters of whichever land management organization is responsible for the fire.

It is important to close this chapter with an emphatic restatement that the positions shown on the organization charts are not filled automatically but only sequentially as the workload on the fire increases to a point where one person can no longer carry out the function alone. Only the largest and most complex fires require a full-blown large fire organization. Most land managers spend their entire careers without ever seeing one in action, and all land managers hope that they never will.

CHAPTER EIGHT

Fire at the Urban–Forest Interface

At the turn of the last century the distinction between forest, farm, and city was generally clear cut. Transportation was slow and difficult and most people in the world lived, played, and died within a few miles of their homes. Forest fires could, and indeed often did, threaten isolated farmsteads or entire villages, but fire protection for these structures was the responsibility of the individual homeowners or of the village fire department. The city firefighter, trained in fighting structural fires, might occasionally be called upon to fight fires in the wildlands, but practically never was the forest firefighter expected to cope with a building fire.

Today, with the accelerated growth in population and the increased ease of transportation, the shape of the landscape in many countries of the world is changing. No longer is the town a central cluster of buildings surrounded by a circle of farmlands in turn surrounded by woods or forest. Now the suburbs stretch like fingers along the roads, and houses blend into the surrounding wildlands. The average forest firefighter can reasonably be expected to be confronted with a fire in a structure sometime during his or her career. Structural fires differ from forest fires in several important respects and all forest firefighters should know enough about structural fire behavior and the tactics used in suppressing building fires to be able to take effective action without undue danger to themselves or to others.

Two standards issued by the National Fire Protection Association (NFPA), headquartered in Boston, have particular relevance to the problems of fire in the urban–forest interface. Standard 224 "Standard for Homes and Camps in Forest Areas" has been prepared as a guide for officers of fire agencies for the enactment of necessary regulations. It also serves to acquaint home owners, resort owners, and others with certain good practices to prevent structural fire in forest areas and damage to valuable timberland and watershed areas. Standard 224 is aimed mainly at residents and owners of structures built in forested areas and served by rural fire departments, many of which are staffed by volunteers. It has the two-barreled objective of advising such persons on how to prevent fires in the structure that might spread to the wildlands and how to protect their structure from a wildland fire.

Standard 295 "Standard for Wildfire Control by Volunteer Fire Departments" describes the fundamentals to be considered by volunteer fire departments including the type of equipment that is necessary or useful, and some basic tactics essential for the safety of personnel and successful control of forest, grass, and brush fires.

In addition to these two standards, the NFPA issues many other publications and standards that are useful to people living in rural areas and to rural firefighters.

STRUCTURAL FIRE BEHAVIOR

There are several fundamental differences between a fire in a building and a fire in a forest:

1. Fuel loadings in buildings are typically many times those in a forest.
2. Fuel moisture inside buildings is controlled by indoor relative humidity, not directly by the external forces of sun, wind, and precipitation.
3. Most radiant heat from a fire in a building is trapped within the building; most radiant heat from a forest fire escapes into space.
4. Most convective heat from a fire in a building initially accumulates within the building; most convective heat from a forest fire is lofted high into the atmosphere.
5. Access of fresh air into buildings is severely limited; access of fresh air into forest fires is virtually unlimited.
6. Fuels in building fires include a variety of combustibles; fuels in forest fires are exclusively cellulosic.

We consider these differences in turn.

Table 8.1 shows the range of fuel loadings to be expected in typical wildland and urban fire situations. Note that the heaviest likely fuel load in the forest is less than the lighest load for a structure.

The primary effect of this difference in fuel loadings is that a fire in a building has a much longer residence time than a fire at a particular spot in a forest. This longer residence time permits much more heat absorption by

Table 8.1. Available Fuel Loading

Area	Fuel Type	Tonnes/Hectare
Forest	Grass and sward (Tasmania)	5
	Heavy brush (southern California)	100
	Maximum	26 times $\sqrt{}$age in years
Urban	Dwellings, offices, schools[a]	200–500
	Apartments	400 times no. floors
	Shops	500–1000
	Industrial and storage	300–3000 or more

[a] Excluding archives, libraries, etc.

larger structural members such as beams and wall assemblies than is the case for similar sized stems and logs in the forest. Consequently, large size fuels play a more active role in determining building fire behavior.

Cellulosic fuels inside buildings gain and lose moisture in response to changes in relative humidity just as similar fuels do in the forest. Inside a building, however, the relative humidity is determined by the heating, cooling, and air conditioning process imposed on the air within the building rather than the humidity of the air outside. In addition, wooden surfaces that are protected by paint or varnish will have much longer time lags than a similar thickness of unpainted wood. As a result, there is little fluctuation in the moisture content of interior furnishings from hour to hour; rather, they dry or moisten slowly over a period of days or weeks.

However, building fires are affected by fuel moisture just as are forest fires. Pirsko (1959) shows a strong correlation between the daily number of building fires in a large American city and the equilibrium moisture content of interior fuels (Figure 8.1). He also finds that the interior moisture content was directly related to the exterior dew point temperature rather than to exterior ambient temperature or relative humidity (Figure 8.2).

Most radiant heat from forest fires is lost directly to space. Only a small fraction is intercepted by other fuel surfaces within or ahead of the burning zone. When a fire is burning in a room, however, the only radiant energy to leave the room is that which is transmitted through the windows and opened doors. The majority is absorbed by floors, walls, ceilings, and furnishings. These will reflect some radiation and will reradiate as they become warmer. Consequently, objects at some distance from a small fire in a room will be heated more rapidly, and to higher temperatures than would the same objects at the same distance from the same fire in the open.

Once the flames from a burning object in a room get long enough to reach the ceiling, the flames will be deflected and spread beneath the ceiling. This greatly increases the view factor for all other objects in the room as shown in Figure 8.3. This results in very rapid heating of all objects in the room and is a major factor leading to the phenomenon of "flashover" which is discussed in a later section of this chapter.

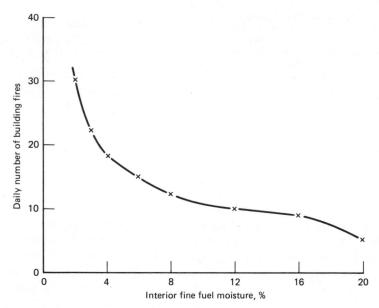

Figure 8.1. Relationship of interior moisture content to number of building fires per day in Baltimore, Maryland, 1940–1949 (from Pirsko 1959).

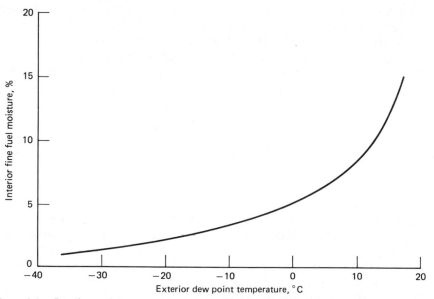

Figure 8.2. Interior moisture content vs. exterior dew point temperature (after Pirsko 1959).

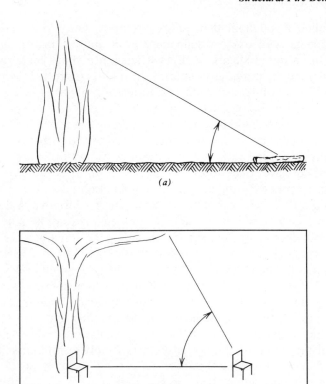

(a)

(b)

Figure 8.3.   (*a*) View factor for a log near a forest fire. (*b*) View factor for a chair in a room fire.

Similarly, convected heat is also trapped by the presence of a ceiling rather than rising until it reaches density equilibrium as it does in forest fires. The hot convected air will form a layer beneath the ceiling which grows deeper until it reaches the top of an open window or door when it then begins to flow out of the room. The convected heat does not contribute directly to heating the room or its contents, except for the ceiling and upper walls. But the heated ceiling and the hot gas beneath it, especially if very smoky, radiate heat onto the floor and furnishings which contribute toward their rise in temperature. The convected heat that moves into corridors or other rooms through open doorways serves to preheat the rest of the building and make subsequent fire spread outside the room of origin easier.

Probably the most important distinction between an enclosure fire and a fire in the open is that the air supply in a room is limited by the size and number of openings, whereas the air supply to an outdoor fire is practically unlimited. The rate of combustion of any fire is controlled either by the rate at which fuel can be heated to ignition temperature and converted to gaseous fuel (fuel control) or the rate at which oxygen can be supplied to complete the combustion reactions (ventilation control). Virtually all forest fires are fuel controlled throughout their entire lifetimes. Only very rarely, during very rapid runs, will oxygen deficiency be a limiting factor in forest fire behavior. In its initial stages, such as when a fire starts on a sofa cushion from a discarded cigarette, a room fire is also fuel controlled. What happens at floor level is uninfluenced by the accumulation of gases under the ceiling unless they become hot enough to operate a fire detector or sprinkler, or to significantly increase radiation downwards from the ceiling or upper walls. As the fire spreads across the sofa, and perhaps to the carpet or an adjoining article of furniture, the total energy output rises and more air is entrained. The layer of hot gases under the ceiling deepens until, eventually, the supply of fresh air is limited by the amount of combustion gases escaping through room openings. Since no room is airtight, there will always be some exchange of fire gases and outside air, but the combustion rate may be greatly slowed if both doors and windows are closed. Occasionally, a fire in a closed room may smolder for hours or even self-extinguish, but what more often happens is that the heated layer below the ceiling becomes sufficiently hot to break out a window. The rate of combustion then increases to a higher ventilation controlled limit; the velocity of fire gas exit and fresh air ingress being largely controlled by the height of the opening and the external wind pressure. Since the fire was burning in partially vitiated air prior to the breaking of the window, the hot gases are usually still flammable and will burst into flames on leaving the room.

This same phenomenon, room gases containing excess pyrolyzate (unburned fuel gas) and igniting spontaneously when supplied with fresh air, can occur when a door to the room is opened as well as when a window breaks. This is why firefighters should always be exceedingly cautious in opening doors if there is a possibility of smoldering fire in the room beyond. Proper tactics for ventilating structural fires are covered later in this chapter.

Pressure differences occur within the room as a result of the expansion and buoyancy of the hot fuel gases. The maximum pressure difference in a steady state, without rapid expansion such as a smoke explosion, will be approximately:

$$A = \frac{\rho h g \, (T - Ta)}{Ta}$$

where A = Pressure difference (N/m^2)
ρ = Density (kg/m^3)
h = Thickness of gas layer or height of opening, whichever is less (m)
g = Gravitational acceleration (9.81 m/sec^2)
T = Absolute fire gas temperature (°K)
Ta = Absolute ambient temperature (°K)

The total possible pressure drop is divided between a drop associated with the inlet air and a drop associated with the exiting combustion products

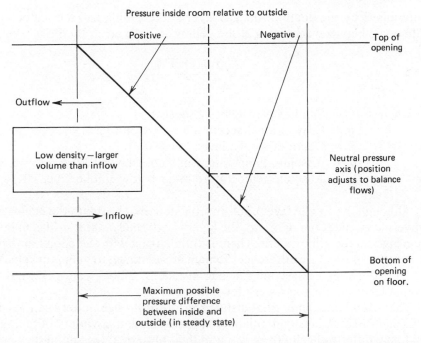

Pressure inside room relative to outside

Figure 8.4. Idealization of pressure difference determining flow into and out of opening for fully developed fire.

as shown in Figure 8.4. The total pressure drop is limited by the height across the openings and it is this which limits the flow of air and the heat release.

If the room has two openings, such as a window and a door on another wall, the effect of wind may be particularly important. Winds produce pressure drops roughly equivalent to:

$$H = \frac{V^2}{2g}$$

where H = Equivalent height of opening (m)
V = Wind velocity (m/sec)
g = Gravitational acceleration (9.81 m/sec^2)

Thus a wind of three meters per second will produce a pressure drop equivalent to that expected across a half-meter opening. This is equivalent to the outlet opening of an average house window, so with windspeeds of three meters per second or greater all air through the window would flow into the room and flames and fuel gases would flow out the doorway into the corridor or adjoining rooms.

In a building with no external openings but open doors to permit internal flow from room to room, the rate at which smoke and fire gases will spread is determined by the depth of the gas layer at the ceiling and the temperature difference between the gases at the ceiling and the air at the floor level.

$$V = \sqrt{\frac{2gh\,(T - Ta)}{Ta}}$$

where V = Smoke layer velocity (m/sec)
         g = Gravitational acceleration (9.81 m/sec^2)
         h = Depth of smoke layer (m)
         T = Absolute temperature of smoke layer (°K)
        Ta = Absolute temperature of air below smoke layer (°K)

Although the smoke layer cools by conduction of heat into the ceiling as it travels from the room of origin, the layer is extremely stable—like an inversion layer in the atmosphere. There is little mixing with the cooler air below it and the temperature differences remain great enough to maintain velocities of 1 to 10 meters per second for long distances. Smoke can travel through even a large building in a very few minutes.

The second most important distinction for the firefighter between building fires and forest fires is that buildings typically contain a variety of fuel types that may differ radically from wood in their burning rates and in their products of combustion. This poses special hazards for the untrained.

One important aspect of the flammability of any fuel is assessed by comparing the energy produced by burning the fuel in a unit mass of air with the energy required to produce a unit mass of fuel gas. This determines what Tewarson and Pion (1976) call the "Ideal" burning rate. This ideal burning rate is the rate when the energy losses from the burning surface (e.g., radiation) equals the energy supplied from other bodies (e.g., supporting external radiation). Values of some typical urban fuels are listed in Table 8.2. Note that wood is the least inherently flammable of any of the materials listed.

If one compares different materials under the same strong external heating conditions, it would be more appropriate to compare them on the basis of the fraction of energy released per gram of gaseous fuel needed to produce it from the liquid or solid. This basis tends to widen the differences between wood and many plastics.

The plastics industry points out that some natural materials including wool and wood technically (i.e., chemically) fall within the chemical definition of plastics. However, the common usage of the term "plastics" refers to synthetic polymers. Some of these increasingly to be found in buildings are shown in Table 8.3. Some can be produced in a range of densities and some can be produced in rigid and flexible form. Properties can be changed by additives. The prefix *poly* comes from the chain of repeated groups of molecules (Figure 8.5). On heating, these long molecules usually break up, some more easily than others, and the parts react with oxygen. There are many kinds of wood, differing in species, in density, and in the

Table 8.2.   *"Ideal" burning rates of common materials*[a]

Materials	"Ideal" Burning Rate g/cm^2 sec $\times$ 10^4
Benzene (liquid)	149
Styrene (liquid)	114
Heptane (liquid)	93
Methylmethacrylate (liquid)	76
Rigid Polyurethane Foam	45
Ethyl Alcohol (liquid)	40
Polystyrene (solid)	35
Flexible Polyurethane Foam	32
Methyl Alcohol (liquid)	32
Polycarbonate (solid)	25
Polymethylmethacrylate (solid)	24
Glass Fiber Reinforced Polyester	18
Polyoxymethylene (solid)	16
Polyethylene (solid)	14
Polypropylene (solid)	14
Phenolic (solid)	13[b]
Wood (Douglas fir)	13[b]

[a] From Tewarson and Pion (op. cit.).
[b] Derived from peak burning rates.

proportions of cellulose, lignin, and the like, but by comparison with the many kinds of plastics the range of behavior of wood is narrow. Many details of the properties of plastics relevant to their fire behavior are given by Hilado (1974) and the reader should also consult the National Fire Protection Association Fire Protection Handbook which is frequently revised. Many synthetics now used in buildings do not char; some may melt and may drip flaming droplets either onto the floor or onto the firefighter. If they melt, they may form pools of liquid and behave like other flammable liquids. Some plastics are used in high density form and in a low density form—a solid, sometimes flexible, foam. Many of the behavior patterns ascribed to plastic foams arise from their low density. The range of plastic behavior in fire is wider than is exhibited by wood.

Table 8.3.   **Some plastics commonly used in buildings and their more common uses**

Materials and Acronyms	Uses
Polymethylmethacrylate (PMMA)	Corregated roof lights
Polyvinyl chloride (PVC)	Floor tiles, pipes, electrical insulation
Polyethylene (PE)	Film, sheeting, plastic bottles, buckets
Polystyrene (PS)	Ceiling tiles, packaging, insulation, toys
Polyurethane	Bed mattresses, cushions, insulation, toys

Polystrene (PS)

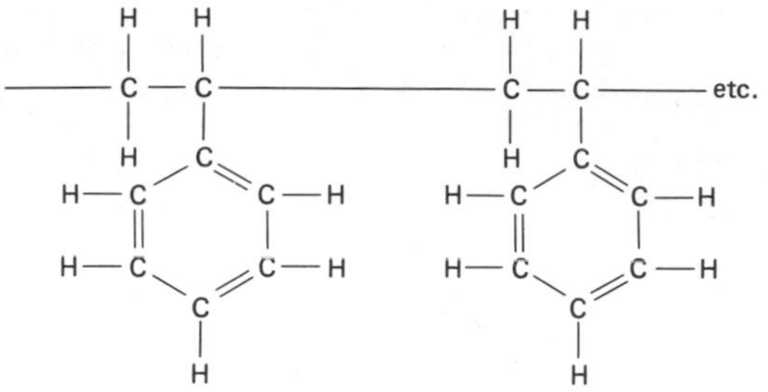

Polyvinyl Chloride (PVC)

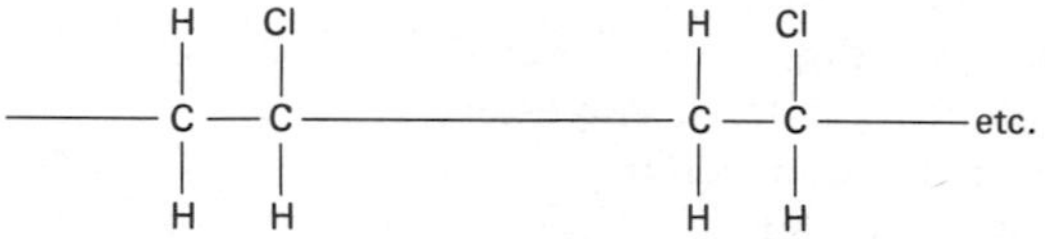

Figure 8.5.   Chain construction of polymeric materials.

The principal relationship between heating rate per unit area q and surface temperature rise θ on a thick homogeneous solid is:

$$\theta = 1.13q\sqrt{\frac{t}{K\rho C}}$$

where θ = Surface temperature rise (°C)
        q = Heating rate (cal/cm^2 sec)
        t = Heating time (sec)
        K = Thermal conductivity (cal/cm sec°C)
        ρ = Density (gm/cm^3)
        C = Specific heat (cal/gm°C)

It is this relationship and variations of it that are responsible for the widely quoted importance of the product $K\rho C$. K usually increases with ρ, whereas C varies much less. Density is thus of major importance.

It is important to emphasize that if q increases exponentially with time (i.e., as t^n), then the importance of $K\rho C$ remains although the time scale is no longer proportional to it. The time to reach a particular temperature rise will then be proportional to $(K\rho C)^{1/1+2n}$. Because the spread of flame over a surface is in a sense a sequence of ignitions, low values of $K\rho C$ tend to be associated with both rapid ignition and fast spread for materials that support flaming.

All fires produce toxic combustion products that can be life-threatening; this arises partly because the gases have reduced oxygen content, partly because they are hot, partly because they contain CO and CO_2, and partly because they produce sooty particles that absorb other toxic products of combustion. Some plastics when burned emit small but significant amounts of highly toxic gases such as hydrogen cyanide.

Wood produces small quantities of several toxic materials. Wood, silk, nylon, polyurethane foam, and other polymers that contain elemental nitrogen in their molecular structure can produce toxic hydrogen cyanide as well as carbon monoxide; although to date, the evidence indicates the latter is generally the main toxic species present. This existence of toxic materials in the combustion products is sufficient to presume a hazard can exist but if a material or a form of material such as a foam spreads fire or burns faster than another producing similar combustion products, the hazard is greater and can even be outside normal experience. Many synthetic plastics burn faster than wood under equal exposure conditions. Their smoke and toxic hazard is generally greater, so much so that their increasing presence in buildings has attracted legislation in some countries to ensure some control of fire performance.

Loss of visibility in a building is certainly no less serious than in the open especially if the building configuration is unfamiliar. The smoke from many fires (including those involving cellulosic material) can be an irritant to the eyes and the respiratory system. This is often attributed to certain aldehydes. With PVC the elemental chlorine is released as hydrogen chloride which is also a severe irritant. Some nitrogen-based plastics will contain hydrogen cyanide. Fires in industrial buildings be they manufacturing plants or storages may well contain other unfamiliar but toxic materials. Because of the variety of toxic gases now commonly produced in building fires, many urban fire departments require firefighters to wear self-contained breathing apparatus before entering a structure.

FLASHOVER

Because the phenomenon of flashover is so common in structural fires and so alien to forest fire behavior, it deserves special consideration.

Whenever an object within a room becomes ignited, the hot products of combustion are carried by convection to ceiling level where they will spread out and remain as a gradually thickening layer beneath the ceiling. Even if one window or one door is open, this pooling of hot gas will still occur until the gas layer reaches the upper sill height when gases can spill out through the opening. Only if there are two openings to the room and an adequate cross draft will the hot ceiling layer be dissipated.

Once the gas layer at the ceiling has reached a temperature of 500–650°C, the excess pyrolysis products in the convected gases are ready to be ignited by any additional source of heat or additional oxygen. If the flames from

Figure 8.6a. The transition to flashover in a simulated room fire takes only nine seconds. Crown copyright photos.

objects on the floor reach the base of the hot convective layer, or if more ventilation is supplied by breaking a window or opening a door, flames will quickly spread across the entire ceiling space (Figure 8.6a,b,c). The additional radiation from the ceiling will ignite all flammable objects in the room within a few seconds and the room becomes totally involved in fire. If the room was tightly closed at the beginning of the fire so that the smoke is rich in intermediate combustion products, the addition of air may result in an actual smoke explosion (often called a *backdraft* in urban fire terminology). In 1975 a smoking mattress caused a smoke explosion in Chatham, U.K. killing two firefighters and injuring four others. Building fires become markedly more difficult to extinguish after flashover.

Figure 8.6b.

STRUCTURAL FIRE TACTICS

In structural fire training manuals, firefighting tactics are divided into eight topics, six of which are performed sequentially and two of which may be performed at any stage in the sequence. The sequential steps are:

1. *Size-Up.* Identical to size-up in forest fire control.
2. *Rescue.* Those operations necessary to protect life.
3. *Exposure protection.* Those operations necessary to protect adjacent and contiguous property.
4. *Confinement.* Those operations that prevent the fire from spreading beyond its current involvement.

Figure 8.6c.

5. *Extinguishment*. Those operations necessary to extinguish the actively burning portion of the fire area.

6. *Mop-Up* (commonly called *overhaul* in urban fire practice). Those operations required to completely and thoroughly extinguish any residual fire or possible source of reignition.

The two nonsequential steps that may be performed any time when necessary after size-up are:

1. *Ventilation*. Those operations necessary to remove smoke, gases, or heated air from the involved structure.

2. *Salvage*. Those operations that protect the structure and its contents from fire, smoke, and damage from firefighting operations.

Note that the six sequential steps, with the exception of exposure control, are essentially identical to those in forest fire control, whereas the two nonsequential steps have no counterparts in forest fire practice. We cover the concepts that are unique to structural fire tactics later in this chapter, but since there are some differences even in the common practices, a quick step-by-step review is in order.

In size-up, two considerations that are important in structural fires but usually, though not always, absent in forest fires are life hazards and the possibility of special hazards such as toxic chemicals, stored petroleum products, heating fuels, or explosives. Although forest firefighters occasionally have to worry about civilians cut off by a fast moving head, life safety of other than firefighters is seldom a concern in a forest fire. In a structural fire, on the other hand, there is always the possibility of a trapped occupant and rescue considerations must take precedence in planning the attack on the fire. Similarly, exotic fuels can be stored anywhere within a building, though garages and basements are the most likely locations, and the size-up must include an assessment of these hazards.

Search and rescue operations in a burning building before the fire has been positively confined and control assured should only be undertaken by personnel with self-contained breathing apparatus. Since only forest fire crews with intensive training in structural fire control carry such apparatus, a discussion of search and rescue tactics here is superfluous.

The secret to confining a structural fire is to consider each building as a box containing six internal sides and six external sides having within it a nest of smaller boxes each of which also contains six internal sides and six external sides. The objective is to consider the relationship of the sides of the boxes to the path that a fire is most likely to follow and position hose streams so as to confine the fire to the box or boxes already involved. Generally, it is best to position nozzles inside the building in order to move the smoke and heat outside the box and not drive the fire from the room of origin through the rest of the building. Exterior streams should be used to protect exposures and to cool the structure above the point where interior streams are driving flames out the windows. Care should be taken not to direct exterior streams into the windows when firefighters are inside the building lest fire and steam be driven into the corridors endangering their operations.

Once the fire has been successfully contained within the room or rooms of active combustion, firefighters may proceed towards extinguishment operations.

A distinction needs to be made between extinguishing fires and extinguishing flames that consist only of gases. Flame can be extinguished by the use of sprays provided the water droplets are able to reach yet are small enough to evaporate in the flame. The rapid heat transfer can cause fine drops of water to evaporate, cool, and extinguish the flame as in open fires.

The expansion can expel gases leaving steam to inert a room space—a process of fire control without analogy for fires in the open. However, such a fire control process is not to be relied on unless the dangers of reignition are recognized and guarded against. If a spray of water enters an atmosphere of hot gases, some of the water evaporates into steam, and if enough water does this quickly enough the expelled gas can burn or scald a firefighter.

This rapid expansion may be short-lived because once the wall surfaces are cooled, the rate of heat extraction from the wall to the water falls and within seconds or minutes water is not completely vaporized.

It is easier to *knock down* a fire in an enclosure but unless the fire is very young (i.e., has not been burning a long time) and unless the fuel surfaces are easily reached by the inerting steam the advantages of knock down are soon lost. In short, the circumstances for effective knock down are rare and exploitable only by someone suitably trained.

Sprays also entrain air into the stream of droplets, which may help keep the firefighter holding the nozzle cool but if inadvertently applied to a hot underventilated fire the additional oxygen can cause a rapid burning like an explosion.

Just as in forest fighting, water is most effective when applied directly to the burning fuel at the base of the flames rather than to the flames and hot gases above. As soon as possible after knock down, firefighters should approach the burning objects directly and complete extinguishment.

Mop-up or overhaul is an identical and crucial operation in both structural and forest fires. Partially burned material is removed from the building or fireline and placed where there is no chance of fire spread should it rekindle. All partially burned materials that cannot be moved and all concealed spaces are then checked for hot spots by feeling with the bare hand. No fire is abandoned until it is absolutely dead out.

Exposure Protection

More often than having to fight fire inside a burning building, the forest firefighter can be expected to be called upon to prevent a forest fire from igniting a building or to prevent a fully involved burning building from initiating a spreading forest, brush, or grass fire. The latter operation is no different from protecting a sector of fireline against spot fires, although the firefighter should remember that many building materials, particularly, wood shingles make much more efficient firebrands than do forest materials. In extreme situations when firebrand production is larger than the prevailing work force can cope with, it may be necessary to build a fireline around the building at an appropriate distance and fire out the intervening strip.

In the case where the objective is to prevent the ignition of buildings from an approaching forest fire, the firefighter must have a basic understanding of building construction and the weak points that are threatened by a fire from outside.

The most susceptible parts of a domestic building to fire entry are open windows or doors where flames or firebrands may obtain unimpeded entry. The first action of firefighters on arriving at a threatened structure should be to close all such openings.

The roof, eaves, and gutters are usually the next points of concern. These are areas where leaves, twigs, and other debris can accumulate and supply ready tinder for any fallen spark. If it is not possible to clean out such areas, they should be hosed down periodically to ensure a moisture content that will inhibit rapid fire spread even if this will not completely preclude ignition.

Ventilators, even when protected by screens, are also likely points for fires ingress. Vents and crawl spaces at ground level should be closed by banked earth when possible, and attic vents should be protected by hose lines at the time of flame impingement.

Glass windows pose a threat because they may be broken by heat, either through expansion of the glass itself, or, in the case of metal casement windows, by the expansion of the frame. All experienced firefighters agree that flammable objects should be removed from the immediate vicinity of windows, but beyond this there is disagreement on the most effective protection measures. Some advocate covering windows with metal foil to reflect radiant heat and reduce the possibility of breakage, but others claim that the opportunity to look inside a building through uncovered windows so as to detect any interior fires in their early stages outweighs the benefit of reflective coverings.

When staffing permits, firefighters with charged hose lines should be stationed inside the threatened building to extinguish any fire that may enter the building and to ventilate on the lee side of the building so that smoke and heated gases do not accumulate.

Ventilation

Ventilation plays a vital role in the attack, containment, and extinguishment of structural fires. There is no comparable tactic in forest firefighting. Proper ventilation can eliminate the possibility of smoke explosions, reduce smoke damage to building contents, and make firefighting safer and less punishing. Improper ventilation can spread fire rapidly throughout the structure.

Ventilation should be considered whenever heat and smoke make entry into the building dangerous or impossible, or when the base of the fire cannot be located because of smoke.

Once a decision to ventilate has been made, openings should be made starting at the attic or the top floor and situated in line with the prevailing wind to provide the maximum air movement through the building. In residential construction, merely opening windows or removing attic vent covers is usually sufficient. The roof need not be opened unless the attic is actually burning.

Both the area being ventilated and the suspected area of origin should always be covered with hose streams before opening doors or windows. Ventilation will always increase the rate of fire spread and may hasten flashover. In order to take advantage of the improved visibility and clear air produced by ventilation, firefighters must be prepared to move in and suppress the seat of the fire as soon as possible.

SAFETY CONSIDERATIONS

As has been mentioned several times previously, smoke and toxic gases are the greatest hazard in fighting structural fires, whereas they are seldom a consideration in fighting forest fires. Firefighters should never enter a smoke-filled building without self-contained breathing equipment. Since this is practically never available to the forest firefighter, proper ventilation of the structure prior to entry is the only practical alternative.

Forest firefighters are conditioned to be alert to the possible collapse of fire-weakened snags, but the dangers of structural collapse in burning buildings is incomparably greater.

The fully developed fire may remain confined if the building is fully fire resistant but, if not, it endangers firefighters inside and perhaps outside the building because structural elements may lose their capacity to hold up the building. This is true not only of combustible materials but of all structural materials. For example, steel loses strength at temperatures below those usually encountered in fires. Glass can soften if heated slowly, crack or shatter if heated quickly, and concrete loses some strength. Concrete covering steel may quickly spall and slough off, exposing steel which then weakens. Masonry walls can be pushed over by expanding horizontal floors. Expansion of beams or columns and the forces induced by this process are features of fires in enclosures. Properly designed structures can withstand such damage but buildings can be altered after construction and sometimes weakened. In short, structural fire fighting is not only dangerous but danger may come from so-called "safe" materials and apparently simple alterations to "safe" buildings.

BIBLIOGRAPHY

Hilado, C. J. 1974. *Fire Technol.* 2(3):198.
Pirsko, A. R. 1959. Does weather influence urban fires? *Fire Eng.* 112(10):938–939, 1009.
Tewarson, A. and R. F. Pion. 1976. Flammability of furnishings. *Comb. and Flame* 26:85–103.

CHAPTER NINE

Managing Fire Use

USES OF PRESCRIBED FIRE

Fire is one of the oldest tools of man, and one of the most powerful. Primitive folk used fire for clearing lands for agriculture, driving game, facilitating travel, and waging war. Fire was considered important enough by the ancient Greeks to constitute one of the four basic elements of the universe and fire was worshipped as a gift of the gods or as a divinity itself by earlier and less sophisticated peoples. Today, although we have lost much of our awe toward wildland fire, we still use it for many of the same purposes and in many of the same ways as did our earliest forebears.

Land Clearing

In most of the world, fire is still the primary tool for clearing land preparatory to planting crops, developing pastures, or installing forest plantations. The advantage of fire over mechanical methods of site preparation is that the nutrients released by burning are available to the successional vegetation at the time of emergence and early growth when nutritional demands are highest. Wildland fire, when carefully prescribed and skillfully managed, can also be less destructive to site quality than mechanical clearing methods since soil disturbance is minimized and there is no soil compaction by heavy equipment. The principal disadvantage of fire in land clearing is that the effects are not uniform across the whole area treated. Depending on the distribution of fuel accumulations, some spots will be heavily burned and others barely scorched on the surface. This problem can be reduced, though not completely overcome, by scattering slashings to avoid heavy fuel loadings in any one spot. Another potential drawback to fire as a land clearing technique is that material larger than five centimeters or so in diameter is seldom completely incinerated. The residual large logs offer shade and a favorable microclimate for crops or seedlings if the area is to be hand planted, but they pose a problem of access if planting or other land treatment is to be done by machine. This problem can be avoided by windrowing all felled material, burning the windrows, and planting in the bare soil between windrows. Windrowing is only recommended when absolutely necessary since some compaction and loss of topsoil is unavoidable when preparing the site. Land clearing burns are best conducted in the fall or early winter when large diameter material is at its driest but after the soil surface and the smaller size fuels have been dampened by early rains. This results in removing a maximum volume of material with minimum heat load on the soil and a minimum chance of the fire escaping. It is essential that felled green material be given sufficient time to dry prior to burning. In most climates this requires three to four months. If the felling operation cannot be conducted prior to the dry season it may be necessary to have the land lay idle for a full year. This sometimes aids the burning operation since grasses and forbs will provide better fuel continuity, but it is seldom worth the loss of a full year's potential site productivity. Proper scheduling of the felling, burning, and planting operations will ensure optimum residue removal and plantation success with the least delay between the initial expenditures for site preparation and the first financial returns from the new crop.

Type Conversion

Fire is often the method of choice when converting from one cover type to another. If, as is often the case, the intent is to revert to an earlier stage of succession, properly prescribed fire alone may be sufficient to do the job. Examples would be converting brush fields to grasslands or removing hardwoods from mixed pine–hardwood stands. But if the intent is to control species distribution within mixed stands of species at approximately the same successional level, postfire treatments such as seeding, planting, or plowing are usually required. Examples of such type conversions are removing medusahead (*Taeniatherum asperum,* an introduced undesirable annual grass of the western United States) from perennial grasslands or to control palmetto in mixed shrub understories in Florida and Georgia. Wright and Bailey (1982) provide a thorough discussion of the use of fire for type conversion in the major vegetation types of the United States and southern Canada. The secret to successful use of fire in type conversion is a thorough understanding of the ecological requirements of each of the species involved and prescribing fires of the proper intensity at the proper time of year with the proper frequency of recurrence.

Grassland Management

Grasses are one of the earliest stages in plant succession. Only in limited areas with particular combinations of soil and climate do grasslands represent the successful climax. On the other 25 percent of the world's land surface that currently supports grassland or grass savanna, fire is a necessary component to keep the land from progressing to shrubland or forest (Kayll 1974). Under natural conditions, where herbivore numbers are determined by the carrying capacity of the site, fire return periods are short— from one to, at the most, five years. Most primitive pastoralists practice annual burning of their range, usually just prior to the beginning of the growing season. Annual burning is an acceptable practice when ranges are understocked or marginally stocked. However, overgrazing and frequent fires are a lethal combination. Overgrazing early in the growing season weakens the plants by reducing their ability to store food reserves belowground. Overgrazing also reduces the amount of plant material left to serve as fuel during dormant season fires. As a result, fires burn at reduced intensities and fail to kill invading brush and tree seedlings but burn hot enough to further weaken the grass plants. The consequence is a reduced grazing capacity the following year so that grazing pressure is increased even if no more animals are pastured. Within a very few years the site may be permanently occupied by woody vegetation which, if composed of sprouting species, may be nearly impossible to eradicate (Box 1967). Proper use of fire in grassland management requires careful regulation of grazing as well as fire. Rotational grazing and burning on a three to five-year rotation with the pasture rested for one growing season before burning and a few weeks afterwards can be quite effective in maintaining site productivity (Hilmon and Hughes 1965). Whether the loss of one-fifth to one-third of the grass crops each year is preferable to seeding, fertilizing, and other practices of intensive pasture management is an economic rather than an ecological decision.

Wildlife Management

Some of the earliest and most successful examples of modern fire management have come from the use of fire in game management. Though fire has been used by English and Scottish gamekeepers for almost two centuries in managing heathlands for grouse (Gimingham 1970), it was not until Stoddard's classic monograph, *The Bobwhite Quail* (Stoddard 1931), that the use of fire as a carefully prescribed ecological tool for habitat manipulation became a science rather than an art.

A low-intensity fire will almost always produce a net benefit to wildlife provided that it occurs outside of the nesting season. This is true because most birds and animals prefer habitat diversity or "edges," and low-intensity fires promote edge effects. Prescribed fire has been used to produce desirable habitat for a wide variety of game and nongame birds and animals. In these cases, however, the ecological requirements of the species in question must be thoroughly understood and the manager must recognize that the fire regime that favors one species will probably work against another. For

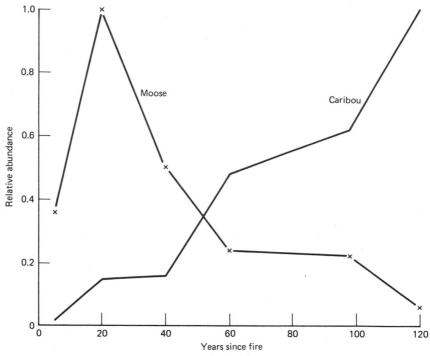

Figure 9.1.   Relative abundance of moose and caribou following fire (after Scotter 1970).

example, the relative abundance of moose and caribou following fires in the boreal forest of northern Saskatchewan are shown in Figure 9.1. The type and timing of prescribed fire to be applied is also completely dependent on the species to be benefitted. In quail management the lightest possible fire that will do an acceptable job of litter reduction is desired, whereas improving habitat for the Kirkland Warbler requires burns of crown fire intensity. An excellent review of the effects of fire on nongame as well as game species can be found in Lyon et al. (1978).

Fuels Management

The burning of slashings or of naturally occurring hazardous fuels under easy burning conditions so as to prevent conflagrations during dry or windy weather is, or has been, practiced by native peoples in every part of the world that has a recurrent fire season. Burning for hazard reduction is so universal that it was probably the first use of broadcast fire, and subsequent uses for land management purposes evolved from observations of the consequences of hazard reduction burns.

The simplest circumstance under which hazard reduction burns are contemplated is when the residual living material is undesirable or immaterial to future land management objectives. Then the objectives of a hazard reduction burn are identical to those of a prescribed fire for land clearing—dispose of the maximum amount of material possible without lasting damage to the soil and consistent with safety. The burning of slash following clearcutting is the most common instance of broadcast burning without regard for the residual stand, although roadside clearing of grass and shrublands is sometimes done to reduce the chance of fires being started by vehicle accidents or careless use of smoking materials by motorists. Grassland burning is relatively trivial, the main precaution being to burn late enough in the dry season that a second crop will not emerge to nullify the effect of the burn. Burning standing shrub cover is a tricky business, however, and is seldom justifiable for hazard reduction alone. Unless wildlife management or other ecological considerations favor the use of fire, hand or mechanical clearing is usually preferable. Green (1981), writing about prescribed burning in chaparral, lists criteria that are applicable to most Mediterranean shrub types, if not to all brushlands worldwide.

Because dead fuel carries the fire in chaparral and live fuel absorbs energy as it is dried, the ratio of dead-to-live fuel in the stand is obviously important. Chaparral less than 20 percent dead seldom burns under prescribed fire conditions, and chaparral less than 25 years old is usually less than 20 percent dead. Brush 35 to 50 years old and 30 to 45 percent dead is ready for prescribed burning. Decadent or treated brush that is 45 to 100 percent dead can be expected to burn intensely unless other factors, such as moisture content, limit the rate of combustion. Fire behavior studies indicate that fire is more intense as the amount of available fuel increases, and as the depth of the fuel bed increases. About 70 to 80 percent of small-stemmed shrubs such as chamise and *Salvia,* but only about half the volume of shrub species with stems of larger diameter, can be considered as available fuel.

The dead fuel moisture determines whether dead fuels will burn or how intensely. Brush that is 20 to 30 percent dead should be burned at about 6 to 9 percent dead fuel moisture. This moisture percentage should increase as the proportion of dead fuel increases; brush stands about 50 percent dead should be burned with dead fuel moisture of 10 to 15 percent. Live fuel moisture can also be important because considerable energy is required to drive off moisture before the live fuel will burn. For prescribed burning of mature brush, live fuel moisture should be 60 to 75 percent. As the fuel moisture drops below 60, chaparral burns more and more violently. If live fuel moisture is above 85 percent, little burning can be accomplished without some form of fuel modification.

Because a fire in standing brush is essentially identical to a crown fire in timber, it is often necessary to precede the prescribed fire with some type of mechanical or chemical treatment in order to ensure a safe burn. These techniques are discussed later in this chapter.

The burning of clearcut slash is generally simpler than burning standing brush because the area of dead, down material is surrounded by green timber and it is possible to burn when the moisture content in the slash is much lower than that of the dead fuels beneath a timber canopy. Because of the heavier fuel volumes in clearcuts, much control over the burn can be achieved by the sequence and timing of ignition. Keyhole firing, igniting the center of the block first and allowing an intense fire to develop before lighting the perimeter, can be quite successful (in flat terrain with light winds) in drawing most of the heat to the center and minimizing heat scorch to peripheral trees. Similar results can be achieved on slopes by piling concentrations of slash in locations where it is desirable to center convective activity.

Burning for hazard reduction beneath an overstory of desirable trees is, obviously, a more complex operation than burning where the overstory is undesirable or nonexistent. The burn must be intense enough to accomplish its objective of fuel reduction yet not so intense as to cause unacceptable mortality, degradation, or growth loss to the residual stand. The prescription must include some wind in order to avoid crown scorch, but wind puts an added heat load on the stem tissues by increasing combustion temperatures at the surface. Prescriptions will vary according to the fuel weights involved as well as the species, age, density, and crown characteristics of the overstory. Developing prescriptions for understory burning are covered in some detail later in this chapter, but it is well to remember that there are conditions under which successful burning is impossible and total fire protection is the only possible course of action. The FAO, for example, recommends that prescribed burning not be attempted in any plantation eucalypts grown on coppice rotations for pulpwood (FAO 1979).

Ecosystem Maintenance

In many instances the principal aim of the forest manager is simply to maintain the status quo of the ecological association. This is particularly true in park management, and we shall use park management in our examples, but it is also the preferred management direction when large isolated tracts contain potentially valuable timber where exploitation is contemplated only in the relatively distant future. In these instances fire is a potential force for maintaining the ecosystem in a state of dynamic equilibrium. In park management, ecosystem maintenance has been viewed in two quite different (indeed, nearly contradictory) contexts. In the one, the aim is to keep the property in a "natural" state of evolution. This philosophy is seen in its purest form in the United States Wilderness Act of 1964 in which areas are set aside as "areas where the earth and its community of life are untrammeled by man, where man himself is a visitor who does not remain—(and) which is protected and managed so as to preserve its natural conditions—affected primarily by the forces of nature . . ." and in the 1979 Canada Parks Policy which states "To protect for all time representative natural areas of Canadian significance—so as to leave it unimpaired for future generations"

(Van Wagner and Methven 1980). Under this philosophy the ecosystem is to be allowed to follow its natural line of succession and fire should be allowed to play its natural role in the modification of that succession. This is easier said than done, since establishing the "natural" role of fire in an area that has been subject to human influence for many decades or even centuries can be difficult, but at least the philosophy is straightforward and rigorous.

However, ecosystem maintenance has also been taken to mean preserving the landscape as it exists or existed at a particular moment in time. Freezing the landscape, as it were, so that our grandchildren may enjoy the view as we ourselves saw it as children. This is a far different management objective than maintaining a natural ecological succession and is, in the long run, impossible of attainment. When frequent surface fires were an important factor in maintaining open stands or savannas, as is the case in many parklands of Africa and the Americas, prescribed fire can, and often must, be used to preserve the essential quality of the landscape.

Proper use of fire in ecosystem maintenance, for either of the two management objectives, requires a thorough understanding of the fire history of the area and the response of the existing and previous ecosystems to fire. Developing a fire history involves more than merely determining or estimating the average return period or fire-free interval. Normal fire intensities, seasonality of fires, and the relationship of fires to weather cycles must be known in order to write appropriate prescriptions. Techniques for establishing fire histories include dendrochronology, fire scar analysis, sediment core analysis, and careful observations of species distributions and trends. Examples of these and other techniques can be found in Stokes and Dieterich (1980).

PLANNING A PRESCRIBED FIRE

Planning a prescribed fire involves a continuing dialogue between the land manager and the fire specialist. The land manager must decide the specific objectives to be accomplished and the fire specialist must determine whether these objectives can be achieved by the use of fire, and if so, how and with what consequences. This process usually takes several iterations and involves several resource specialists.

For example, management may wish to convert an old brush field into a pine plantation and is considering fire as a method of site preparation. Because the land manager wants to use planting machines, he or she specifies that the fire must be sufficiently intense to burn off all stems to within six inches of the ground. After visiting the site the fire specialist determines that a fire of that intensity will have an unacceptable risk of escaping onto the adjoining landholder's property unless the brush is chained to break off the larger stems and provide more dead fuel prior to burning. The land manager, however, calculates that the cost of chaining and machine planting will be greater than that of hand planting provided that all twigs greater than two centimeters in diameter can be removed by the fire. The fire specialist estimates that removal of live twigs up to two centimeters in diameter will require a fireline intensity of 1000–1200 kilowatts per meter, and that such a fire can be handled from a safety standpoint but will remove all litter from the site and may present an erosion hazard. A soils specialist is consulted and advises that, if the burn is conducted in early spring after the high-intensity winter storm season is over and before summer thundershowers are likely, the risk should be acceptable. However, a wildlife expert advises that if the burn is conducted too early in the spring, brush resprouts will attract rabbits and deer who will damage the newly planted trees. All parties then agree to plan to conduct a late spring site preparation burn in which all standing material less than two centimeters in diameter will be removed by the fire.

In addition to illustrating the interactions that take place in the initial stages of a prescribed fire, the preceding example makes several other pertinent points. First, it is vital to spell out the objectives in specific, measurable terms so that all parties involved clearly understand the desired and expected results. If the resource manager had simply told the fire specialist that he or she wanted a site preparation burn, without specifying the degree of stem removal expected, the fire specialist would most probably have prescribed an even less intense fire than that finally accepted as a compromise. This would have resulted in lower holding costs for the fire and a minimum probability of escape, but would have increased planting costs markedly due to the difficulty of movement through the dead brush skeletons left standing after a low intensity burn (Figure 9.2). Second, the fact that fire affects all land management objectives, not just the one for which the fire is being planned, must be recognized. By changing the vegetation, fire will affect the entire ecosystem and these changes will, in turn, have an impact on all land management considerations. Lastly, this example shows that most prescribed fires represent a compromise among competing interests—a fire that comes the closest to meeting the manager's objective while causing the least disruption to all other management considerations.

Once the specific objectives of the prescribed fire have been agreed upon, the fire specialist should again visit the site and collect the data needed to write the fire prescription and the burning plan. Several elements must be considered.

Fireline location

Just as in a wildfire, the firelines surrounding a prescribed fire should be located so as to maximize the probability of containing the fire with the least expenditure of funds on line-holding crews and equipment. It may be necessary to relocate firelines from those selected by the resource manager as the preferred burning block. The final decision on fireline location rests with the fire specialist. Resource considerations must always be subordinate to safety considerations.

Figure 9.2. (a) Too many brush skeletons make replanting difficult. (b) Fire intense enough to remove all small stems facilitates replanting. Photo by U.S. Forest Service.

Topography

In all except flat and gently rolling country topography will play a major role in determining the pattern and timing of firing. The burning plan should always include a topographic map of the area to be burned and adjacent areas that would be threatened should the fire escape.

Fuels

In most instances, fuels will not be uniform across the burning block. Estimates of available fuel loads should be made and mapped, together with measurements of litter depth. Particular attention should be given to locating areas of exceptional hazard such as unusually heavy accumulations of dead fuel or thickets that might produce spot fires. Areas where fuel continuity is lacking so that fire may not spread uniformly across the block should also be mapped.

Once this information has been obtained, the fire specialist is ready to write a fire prescription and prepare the burning plan. These are two separate documents designed for quite different purposes.

Writing a Fire Prescription

The fire prescription identifies, for particular variables, the range of conditions under which a fire is expected to meet the objectives specified by the land manager. The prescription always starts by reiterating, and sometimes refining, the objectives of the burn. In our previous example management agreed upon a late spring fire intense enough to remove all live twigs smaller than two centimeters in diameter. In the prescription, this might be further elaborated to the following:

1. Burn to be conducted between June 1 and July 7.
2. Remove at least 90 percent of all green twigs 2 centimeters in diameter.
3. Desirable, but not mandatory, to leave 1–2 centimeters of litter on at least 50 percent of the area.

Next, the prescription writer considers the range of appropriate variables individually. The variables that should be included will depend on the purpose of the fire. All of the following should at least be considered. The range should be as great as possible since the occurrence of any condition outside the specified range will result in postponement of the burn. At this stage of prescription preparation the values selected are absolutes—not to be exceeded under any circumstances.

Air temperature

Plant mortality following fire is quite sensitive to the initial temperature of the foliage and cambial tissues. In underburning for hazard reduction a maximum temperature of 5–15°C is often selected to minimize mortality and a minimum temperature representing that below which it is too uncomfortable or unsafe for work crews. On the other hand, in burning for hardwood control, a minimum temperature of 25 or 30°C may be necessary to ensure meeting the objectives, and the maximum temperature, if any, will be dictated by fire behavior considerations.

Wind

In underburning, a minimum wind velocity is usually necessary to minimize crown scorch. A maximum wind velocity is always specified for safety reasons.

Relative humidity

A minimum relative humidity is always specified because it is so directly related to spot fire potential. Usually there is a maximum relative humidity above which fine fuels will not carry fire, but in some slash burns there may be sufficient heavy fuel that fine fuel moisture is irrelevant.

Precipitation

The amount and recency of precipitation is directly related to the moisture content of both the fuels and the soil on the area to be burned. If there is a long history of burning on the area or similar areas, it may not be necessary to measure moisture contents directly; their effect may be inferred from experience on past fires. Normally, a time period and a minimum amount of precipitation are specified, for example, at least 10 millimeters of rain within the previous 10 days but none in the past 48 hours.

Moisture content

If the burn is being conducted in a cover type or during a time of year where there is little previous experience with fire, the acceptable moisture ranges for the most critical fuel elements should be specified. These might include dead fuels of several diameter classes, living foliage, duff and litter at several depths, and soil at a specified depth. Such measurements are not only valuable for the particular burn being planned, but provide the basis for assessing similar burns later on.

Time of day

It takes a finite amount of time to conduct a prescribed burn and the weather elements are constantly changing as the burning operation progresses. This is a most important consideration in preparing the burning plan, and is discussed in more detail later in this chapter. However, it is best to address it in the prescription as well. Under most circumstances it is best to start firing in the early afternoon, at the time of or shortly before peak burning conditions. In that way the risk of fire escape is minimized, or at least occurs early in the burn when the area on fire is small and the line-holding crew is fresh. Occasionally, it is desirable to burn when fire danger is increasing. One example would be a land clearing burn with a large volume of heavy fuels but with considerable fine fuel as well. In this and similar instances it is best to burn as soon as the fine fuels will carry fire so that potential spot fire-producing materials will be burned out before adjacent fuels reach maximum dryness, and so that the heavy fuels can burn as long as possible under good burning conditions. In addition, specifying both beginning and ending times for the firing operation provides positive guidance in planning the type of ignition and the size of the firing crew required.

Once the range of individual variables has been established, they must be aggregated and considered collectively. Each variable was given the widest possible latitude and if *all* the variables were to be on the high-intensity side of the scale, the fire would be unmanageable, whereas if *all* were on the low side, the fire might scarcely burn at all. If the organization is familiar with any of the more sophisticated fire danger rating systems, then calculating the range of one or more fire danger indices using the variables selected is an easy way to integrate their combined effects. The acceptable range of each index is then simply added as an additional constraint. For example, at the initiation of the burn the Rate of Spread Index must be between 7 and 15 and the Ignition Index between 15 and 35. If an appropriate danger rating system is not available, each of the ranges of each of the variables must be qualified by an appropriate constraint, for example, relative humidity 15 to 50 percent but not below 25 percent unless area has experienced 10 millimeters of rain within 4 days.

Lastly, the written prescription should include the range of acceptable fire behavior in terms that can be observed and understood by the firing crew and supervisory personnel at the time of the fire. As a minimum this should include flame heights, rates of spread, and clear instructions as to the amount of spotting or torching considered permissible.

Once the prescription has been completed it must be checked against available climatological data to determine the probability that acceptable burning conditions will occur during the planned burning season. Even the most scientifically correct prescription is useless if the conditions prescribed will never occur. If sufficient weather records are available, several computer programs have been published that allow rapid computation of the probability of occurrence of any desired set of factors (Bradshaw and Fischer 1980, Furman 1979). If good weather data are not available for the area concerned, then climatological records from a station with similar climate plus experienced judgment must suffice. The decision as to what level of probability is sufficient to justify accepting a prescription is a judgmental one and involves considerations other than the single-valued probability of occurrence. If the burn is to be a complex affair involving considerable preparation, or an expensive one requiring the reservation of aircraft or equipment, then one would like to burn under a stable weather pattern that is likely to persist for several days rather than one that may occur several times a month but last for only a day or even a few hours. If the area is isolated requiring extensive travel time in advance of burning, then one would prefer a weather pattern that can be predicted some time in advance.

If the prescription is found to be unacceptable, there are only two choices: modify the prescription or cancel the project and attempt to achieve the objectives through other means than fire. The decision, and the modification of the prescription if that is the course chosen, should be made jointly by the land manager and the fire specialist. Modifying the prescription means that the burn will probably be conducted under less than optimum conditions, and with less than optimum results. The extent to which land management objectives can be compromised rests with the land manager; the extent to which fire safety requirements can be stretched rests with the fire specialist.

Preparing a Burning Plan

Once an acceptable prescription has been written, the fire specialist prepares the burning plan. The burning plan, in essence, describes what is to be done and why, when it will be done, how it will be done, who will do it, equipment and supplies required, and cost estimates.

The first, or general section of the plan restates the objectives of the operation and the results expected. Then tasks are listed sequentially. In complex operations it is often convenient to categorize the tasks in the following groups.

Preburn preparation

Often some degree of fuel modification such as snag felling, brush desiccation, scattering of large fuel concentrations, or fuel removal around improvements and high-value residual trees is necessary prior to conducting the burning operation. Fireline construction may also be undertaken prior to burning, and often by a different crew than those chosen to light and hold the fire.

Preburn monitoring

In all but the simplest prescribed burns, some monitoring of the fuel and weather conditions must be done for at least a day or two prior to the burn. This section of the plan determines what measurements must be taken and how often. The degree of complexity depends on the variables selected and the ranges permitted in the fire prescription. Sufficient preburn monitoring should be done to determine diurnal variations. These will dictate the time available to complete the burning operation while still staying within prescription limits. Provision must also be made to continue monitoring during the progress of the burn itself so that a warning can be given if the prescription is being exceeded, and so that the results of the fire can be tested against the actual weather conditions. Only by continually documenting fire weather, fire behavior, and fire effects can prescriptions be improved for subsequent burns.

Test fire procedures

Most prescribed fire managers prefer to light a small test fire before committing themselves to burning the entire block. This enables them to judge whether the planner's expectations of fire behavior under the given conditions square well with reality. If the prescription window is narrow, the test fire often must be burned outside of prescription in order not to tie up too much burning time. The burning plan should specify the size and allowable conditions for the test fire, and also specify the results as they apply to the prescribed burn; for example, if any spot fires develop more than two meters in front of the test fire, cancel the prescribed burn and return to other duties.

Ignition procedures

The timing and sequence of ignition is the major control that the prescribed fire manager has to influence fire behavior. The ignition plan must be carefully prepared in advance, but flexible enough to accommodate on-the-spot changes as dictated by the fire itself. This means ensuring that there are adequate communications between the fire manager and the lighting crew or crews, and between crews when more than one are involved. Communications are particularly important when aircraft are used for lighting because of the speed with which aircraft can spread fire. All crews and aircraft should be provided with maps showing the expected routes and sequences of the lighting operation.

Holding procedures

This portion of the burning plan should indicate the placement of all personnel and equipment responsible for containing the fire within the burning block. It must also contain definite instructions on actions to be taken should the fire escape.

Demobilization, mop-up, and patrol

Cost-conscious management dictates that personnel and equipment be released from the burn as soon as they are no longer needed. However, a prescribed burn is no different from a wildfire in that a finite possibility for escape exists until the fire is dead out. Mop-up and patrol procedures on a prescribed burn are identical to those on a wildfire and must be provided for in the burning plans.

Postburn evaluation

Prescribed burning costs money, and it is important for management to know what it bought with its expenditure of funds. The prescribed fire planner also needs to know to what extent the prescription accomplished the objectives for which it was intended. Careful monitoring and documentation of the results of each prescribed burn is necessary if management is to learn from experience (Figure 9.3). In some cases, as in our brush-burning example, the results are obvious immediately after the fire and the evaluation can be completed before mop-up is over. However, in many instances, particularly in underburning, results are not apparent for days, weeks, or months after the burn. Even in a light underburn for hazard reduction, the net postburn fuel loading is not known until fire-killed vegetation has dried and fallen. In burns aimed at vegetative manipulation it may be necessary to monitor the site periodically for several years following the fire.

Appendices

In long or complicated burning plans it may be necessary to summarize the financial and logistical requirements rather than leaving them scattered in the individual sections of the plan.

For most prescribed fires the burning plan need not be a long and complex document. Often the plan can be condensed to a single page. Excellent descriptions of burning plan development for different purposes as well as sample plans can be found in Fischer (1978), Martin and Dell (1978), and Mobley et al. (1973).

CONDUCTING A PRESCRIBED FIRE

Conducting a prescribed burn governed by a comprehensive burning plan within the limits of a sound prescription can be almost routine, whereas the conduct of a burn with an ill-prepared plan can resemble a slapstick comedy. On even the best planned burn, however, there will be some unexpected variations and the prescribed burn manager should be mentally prepared to deal with the unexpected.

Immediately upon arrival at the burn site the holding crew foreman should check and correct deficiencies on all firelines around the entire perimeter of the burning block. This is particularly important if the lines were prepared some weeks previous to the burn date. At the same the burn manager should test all communications equipment and ensure that all suppression equipment is in good operating order.

Before igniting the test fire, weather observations should be made and checked against the forecast. The test fire need not be conducted within the prescription limits, but before lighting any fire the manager should be reasonably certain that the prescribed conditions will occur as forecast. If measured weather elements differ significantly from those anticipated, the manager should report to headquarters and obtain an updated forecast.

Immediately before lighting the test fire the manager should alert the fire dispatcher and request that the dispatcher, in turn, notify adjacent landowners. It may also be necessary at this time to post signs on public roads and prepare for traffic control if the wind is such that visibility may be impaired.

The test fire allows the manager to check actual fire behavior against that predicted by the prescription and provided for in the burning plan. The test fire need not be within prescription nor need it be ignited in the same pattern as the prescribed burn itself, as long as the manager has the experience to extrapolate the test fire behavior to that of the prescribed fire. Often the best test fire is a single spot, allowed to spread long enough to establish fire intensity and rate of spread on the head, flanks, and rear and also to determine the rate of acceleration of the head. This information will enable the manager to make the final decisions on the spacing of strips or spots to be used in firing the burning block. It also gives the manager an early warning of smoke production and dispersal problems that may occur later.

After the test fire has been observed, the manager conducts a final briefing with the firing and holding crews ensuring that everyone understands the assignments. If lighting will be done by aircraft, the briefing should be conducted by radio with the aircraft in orbit overhead.

Before initiating the prescribed burn, the weather must be rechecked to be sure that the burn will be conducted under prescription. Once the actual lighting operation has begun it should proceed positively and according to plan unless spot fires or breakovers become so serious that the holding crews are unable to cope with them. Delaying the firing operations, or acting

(a)

Figure 9.3. (*a, b, c*) Underburning for hazard reduction and hardwood suppression when done by prescription and following a burning plan can achieve management objectives without damaging either the overstory or the soil. Photos by U.S. Forest Service.

(b)

(c)

tentatively when confronted with expected breakovers usually results in loss of control over fire behavior and more serious problems later in the burn. If breakovers are more serious than contemplated in the burning plan, the entire prescribed burning operation should be shut down and the fire treated as a wildfire.

Since variations in firing techniques are the managers' greatest and sometimes sole control over fire behavior and smoke production, we review the various options and their pros and cons.

A backing fire is produced by igniting a line of fire along the upwind side of the prepared baseline such as a road, stream, or fireline running at right angles to the wind and allowing the fire to burn into the wind. There are several advantages to backing fires: they produce the least smoke; they do the least damage to overstory foliage; they have the fewest safety problems since the rate of spread is nearly independent of wind velocity and burning embers are blown into the area previously burned. However, backing fires have one overwhelming disadvantage. They move very slowly, typically less than one meter per minute, and thus the area that can be burned within a reasonable prescription period is limited unless baselines are quite closely spaced. Inasmuch as preparing fireline is usually the single most expensive action on a prescribed fire, backing fires are usually not used as the principal firing technique except on small research plots or when underburning in exceptionally heavy ground fuels where no other technique is feasible.

Flank firing is accomplished by spreading lines of fire directly into the wind, usually starting from a baseline that has been widened by a backing fire. Flank fires have the advantage of being faster than backing fires but less intense and erratic than headfires. However, flanking fires require absolutely steady wind conditions and exceptional firing crew coordination (Figure 9.4). It is easy for a crew member to become trapped if the wind shifts slightly and one firing crew member has lagged behind the others. Flank firing is often used to secure the sides between strips of head or backing fires, and to straighten ragged edges of fireline, but it is seldom used as primary technique on an entire burning block.

The head fire is the most rapid, and most often used manual technique for prescribed burning. It is also the smokiest and the most difficult to control. In practice, head firing is almost invariably conducted as a series of strips where an initial line of fire is set as a backing fire, a flank fire is set at one end of the baseline and successive head fires are ignited at right angles to the flank fire (see Figure 9.5). The distance between strips is adjusted so that the head fire cannot achieve maximum acceleration before burning into the next downwind strip. Since there is always some turbulence, a chance of spot fires, and increased foliage damage at the junction zone where two strips meet, the optimum spacing between strips is the maximum that will just assure safe control of the fire. Because of the increased flame heights, underburning with strip headfires requires cooler teperatures than do other firing techniques. One advantage, however, is that headfires can be effective at higher humidities and fuel moistures than is possible otherwise.

Figure 9.4. Flank firing requires that all the firing crew maintain a parallel line. Photo by Jay Bentley.

Spot firing is the preferred technique for aerial ignition but can be used by ground crews as well. In spot firing, individual fires are started in a grid pattern. The spots are spaced at such a distance that the individual fires will merge at a predetermined time. In underburning the timing is such that flame merging occurs in the evening when burning conditions have eased and crown scorch is minimized. In land clearing burns with heavy fuels, on the other hand, the objective is to obtain maximum fire intensity. Maximum fire intensity of two or more interacting fires is achieved when the fires are about three flame heights apart at the time each fire reaches maximum normal

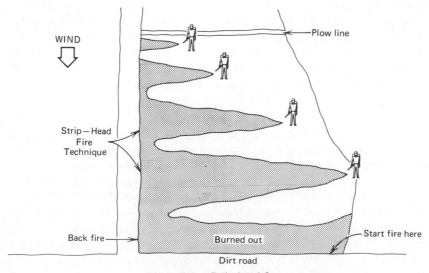

Figure 9.5. Strip head fire.

flame height. When perfectly executed, this results in the entire burning block aflame at the same time. The spacing required is a function of wind, fuel moisture, fuel loading, and the size of the area to be ignited. Since area ignition is too dangerous to undertake under windy conditions because of the possibility of massive long-distance spotting, wind is ignored in the equation.

$$S = 0.0012 \, (17.5 - 1.1M) W^{1.67} A^{0.25}$$

where S = Optimum spacing of ignitions (meters)
        M = Fuel moisture content (percent dry weight)
        W = Available fuel loading (t/ha)
        A = Burning block area (ha)

Ignition at optimum spacing will result in fire intensities approximately five times those of a fire developing from a single ignition. It is seldom possible to achieve optimun spacing of ignitions because of inherent variations in fuel loading across the burning block as well as logistical considerations: a 10-meter optimum spacing requires 100 simultaneous ignitions per hectare. Intensities drop off rapidly as ignition spacing exceeds the optimal.

$$I = 1 + R + R^2 + R^3 + R^4$$

where I = Intensity compared to that of a single line fire
        R = Ratio of optimal spacing to actual spacing

However, it is still possible to achieve useful increases in fire intensity by using area ignition techniques. Returning to our brush burning example: if the size of the burning block is 30 hectares, the fuel loading 40 tonnes per hectare, and we plan to burn with a fuel moisture content of 6 percent, the optimal spacing for area ignition would be 14.5 meters. If we plan to burn the block by aerial spot firing using 100 ignitors for the entire block, our actual spacing will be 55 meters, a ratio of 0.26. Even at this spacing our fire will be 35 percent more intense than if it were line-fired and the probability of removing standing twigs will be that much enhanced.

Perimeter firing, as its name implies, is a technique of firing the exterior boundaries of the burning block and letting fire sweep over the entire area. It is often augmented by lighting one or more spot fires near the center of the block to assist in pulling fire toward the center. Perimeter firing is not recommended except in very light fuels or in special situations such as clearcut slash blocks in the spring when the surrounding timber still retains snow cover. Perimeter firing involves the loss of any control over fire behavior once the circle has been closed, and intense convective activity can occur when the fires merge with the consequent danger of spot fires. The advantage of perimeter firing is that it is the least expensive technique available— provided that the fire stays under control.

Center firing is the exact opposite of perimeter firing, yet seeks to gain the same end, an intense fire with its center of convection approximately in the middle of the burning block. In center firing a number of spots are set in the middle of the burning block. After they have developed to the point where a strong convection column has been formed, additional spots are set sufficiently close to the original ignitions that they are drawn into the main column. This process is repeated until the whole block has been burned. Center firing is well adapted to large concentrations of heavy fuel such as land clearing burns or clearcut slash in stands with a high cull factor. Center firing can be dangerous in light fuels since if the center burns out before the entire block has been ignited, the focus of convective activity will shift to the site of most intense burning which may be an unpredictable and highly undesirable location. Center burning is best accomplished by aerial ignition. This gives the manager some flexibility in setting new spots to try to control the focus of convection if it fails to hold in the center. Because of the difficulty of moving crews on foot through heavy fuels, such control is impossible if manual ignition is used.

Chevron burning is a technique used in hilly topography to bring fire down from the ends of ridges. One crew member strings fire down the center of the ridge while others ignite lines of fire at 45 and 90° angles to the course. This results in a star-shaped burning area with junction zones confined to the apex of the unburned wedges between the lines of fire (see Figure 9.6).

Besides choosing an appropriate firing technique, the prescribed burn manager can exert some control over fire behavior by manipulating the fuel in advance of the burn. Fuel manipulation is expensive, however, often more expensive than the burning operation itself. Most managers try to avoid the necessity for fuel manipulation, or at least to integrate it into their normal land management activities such as logging or timber stand improvement. Fuel manipulation and firing techniques are interdependent. Fuel concentrations are highly undesirable, for example, if strip headfiring is to be used. In spot firing fuel concentrations are of less consequence, whereas for center firing they are indispensable.

Fuels can be manipulated by changing fuel volumes (scattering or removing material), by changing compaction (piling, crushing, or lopping), or by changing fuel moisture (cutting, girdling, or poisoning). Under some circumstances herbicides may be the cheapest and most effective method of lowering fuel moistures since they may be rapidly applied by air and can be utilized to desiccate virtually any size class of material from foliage alone to the entire plant. Considerations in the use of herbicides prior to prescribed burning are well covered in a monograph by Green (1977), whereas various methods of hand and mechanical fuel manipulation are covered by Roby and Green (1976).

Fire retardants can be useful in prescribed burning. Retardants can be used to reinforce conventional control lines, either along their full length as with narrow roadsides, or at spots where fuel accumulations are unusually heavy. When burning in light fuels, retardant can be used to prepare a wet

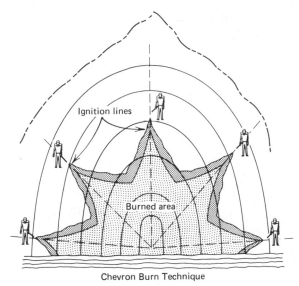

Chevron Burn Technique

Figure 9.6.   Chevron burn.

line for backfiring, thus avoiding the necessity of clearing a line to mineral soil. The wet line technique is particularly suitable for preparing baselines for flank firing or strip headfiring.

In reinforcing firelines or preparing wet lines retardants are usually mixed at the same concentration as they would be for aerial application on the same fuel type. Retardant can also be used in dilute concentrations to minimize the possibility of spot fires by treating areas of flash fuels downwind of the control line and to minimize differences in fire intensity by treating concentrations of heavy fuels inside the area to be burned. Areas treated with dilute retardant will burn out completely, thus achieving the objectives of the burn but at a slower rate and with much lower intensity than untreated fuels. Proper application of retardant can overcome many of the problems associated with burning in discontinuous fuels such as underburning in partially cut stands where slash concentrations are intermingled with natural fuels. One chemical company has prepared a field manual on the use of fire retardant in prescribed burning (Monsanto n.d.).

A sprinkler system consisting of a series of agricultural-type heads spaced along a hose line may also be used to provide a wet area around or downwind of the area to be burned. A prerequisite of this type of protection is, of cource, a readily available water source and a pumping system capable of providing the volume of water necessary to sustain a large number (10 to 40) of sprinkler heads.

Fire can accomplish many desirable land management objectives when it is carefully and wisely used. The term *prescribed fire* to categorize the fire used for such purposes is particularly apt since the value of the fire prescription as well as the medical prescription lies not in its ingredients, but in the training, knowledge, and diagnostic skill of the one who prescribes it and supervises its execution.

BIBLIOGRAPHY

Box, T. W. 1967. *Brush, fire, and west Texas rangeland*. Proc. 6th Ann. Tall Timbers Fire Ecol. Conf., pp. 7–19.

Bradshaw, L. S. and W. C. Fischer. 1980. *Computers, climatology, and fire use*. Proc. 6th Conf. on Fire and Forest Met., Soc. Amer. Foresters, pp. 78–82.

FAO. 1979. *Eucalypts for planting*. FAO Forestry Series No. 11, 677 pp.

Fischer, W. C. 1978. *Planning and evaluating prescribed fires—a standard procedure*. U.S. For. Serv. Gen. Tech. Report INT-43, 19 pp.

Furman, R. W. 1979. *Using fire weather data in prescribed fire planning*. U.S. For. Serv. Gen. Tech. Report RM-19, 8 pp.

Gimingham, C. H. 1970. *British Heathland ecosystems: the outcome of many years of management by fire*. Proc. 10th Ann. Tall Timbers Fire Ecol. Conf., pp. 293–321.

Green, L. R. 1977. *Fuelbreaks and other fuel modification for wildland fire control*. U.S.D.A. Agric. Handbook No. 499, 79 pp., illus.

Green, L. R. 1981. *Burning by prescription in chaparral*. U.S. For. Serv. Gen. Tech. Report PSW-51, 36 pp.

Hilmon, J. B. and R. H. Hughes. 1965. *Forest Service research on the use of fire in livestock management in the south*. Proc. 4th Ann. Tall Timbers Fire Ecol. Conf., pp. 261–275.

Kayll, A. J. 1974. Use of fire in land management. In T. T. Kozlowski and C. E. Ahlgren, Eds., *Fire and Ecosystems*, Academic, New York, pp. 483–511.

Lyon, L. F. and others. 1978. *Effects of fire on fauna: a state-of-knowledge review*. U.S. For. Serv. Gen. Tech. Report WO-6, 41 pp.

Martin, R. E. and J. D. Dell. 1978. *Planning for prescribed burning in the inland northwest*. U.S. For. Serv. Gen. Tech. Report PNW-76, 67 pp.

Mobley, H. E. and others. 1973. *A guide for prescribed fire in southern forests*. U.S. For. Serv. Unnumbered Pub., 40 pp., illus.

Monsanto Corp. n.d. *Phos-chek fire retardant in prescribed burning*. 19 pp., illus.

Roby, G. A. and L. R. Green. 1976. *Mechanical methods of chaparral modification*. U.S.D.A. Agric. Handbook No. 487, 46 pp., illus.

Scotter, G. W. 1970. *Wildfires and barren-ground caribou*. Proc. 10th Ann. Tall Timbers Fire Ecol. Conf., pp. 85–105.

Stoddard, H. L. 1931. *The bobwhite quail, its habits, preservation, and increase*, Scribner, New York.

Stokes, M. A. and J. H. Dieterich. 1980. *Proceedings of the fire history workshop*. U.S. For. Serv. Gen. Tech. Report RM-81, 141 pp., illus.

Van Wagner, C. E. and I. R. Methven. 1980. *Fire in the management of Canada's National Parks: philosophy and strategy*. Parks Canada, Unnumbered Occ. Paper, 18 pp.

Wright, H. A. and A. W. Bailey. 1982. *Fire ecology*, Wiley, New York, 501 pp.

CHAPTER TEN

Fireline Safety

Forest firefighting is an inherently dangerous occupation. In the United States, the accident fatality rate for forest firefighters is 51 per 100,000 man-years, nearly ten times the average for all work-related fatalities but significantly less than the 84 per 100,000 experienced by the urban fire services (NFPA 1976). The lost time accident rate, however, is 6150 per 100,000, six times the average for all occupations and more than three times that for urban firefighters. Because fighting fire in the forest involves strenuous labor in a high-temperature environment, often in steep or broken terrain far from surface transportation, it will always have more than its share of hazards. But constant attention to safe working practices can keep the toll of death and injury to an absolute minimum. Safety is a prime responsibility of every person on the fire—from the incident commander to the cook's helper.

CLOTHING

It is more important to arrive at a fire properly attired than it is at any social function. Going to the opera without a top hat might result in a few scornful looks, whereas going to a forest fire without a hard hat might result in losing the top of your head.

Starting from the skin side and working out, underwear should be made of cotton, both for adequate water vapor passage and to avoid the danger of skin burns from melting acrylics should embers burn unnoticed through the outer clothing. An undershirt should always be worn to provide an extra layer of insulation against radiant heat from the fire.

The shirt should be long-sleeved and worn with the sleeves down and buttoned. Many firefighters prefer, and some fire organizations require, shirts to be fabricated from Nomex (trademark registered by E. I. du Pont de Nemours and Co., Inc., Wilmington, Delaware). Nomex is a synthetic aromatic polyamide fiber that can be subjected to continuous operating temperatures of 250°C while still retaining strength, flexibility, and abrasion resistance. The USSR manufactures a similar aromatic polyamide fiber known as *Sulfon T*. Upon continuous exposure to flame such fibers char rather than melting or burning to ash. Cotton or wool are also acceptable as shirt materials. Most synthetics and blends containing more than 15 percent nylon or polyester should be strictly avoided since they can melt and produce serious burns when exposed to embers or direct flame contact.

The choice of pants fabrics and weights depends largely on the cover and weather conditions expected. Canvas pants are often worn when working in heavy brush or thorn scrub, whereas lightweight cotton is more comfortable when working in light fuels. Nomex pants are also available, but since the instances of burns below the waist but above the boot tops are much less frequent than burns on the arms or back, they are seldom mandatory. Firefighter's pants should always be loose fitting, especially around the thighs. The ubiquitous American "blue jeans" have no place on the fireline since radiant heat is conducted through the material directly to the skin.

A firefighter's feet are the most used, and often the most neglected part of the body. Footwear should be high-topped (preferably 20 to 25 centimeters) lace-type hiking boots, of high quality leather with nonslip tread soles. Two pair of socks should be worn; an outer pair of wool and an inner pair of light cotton. This combination keeps the foot dry by passing moisture through to the wool sock and reduces friction by adding a second interface between the boot and the feet and ankles. Socks should be changed daily and if washing facilities are not available, the firefighter should pack enough socks to last for the duration of the assignment.

Work gloves are a necessity for hand tool workers except those who use hand tools daily year-long. Light supple leather gloves are preferable, but canvas gloves with leather palm reinforcement are acceptable.

A light jacket is recommended, particularly in climates with large variations in diurnal temperature and a wool watch cap or stocking cap that can be stowed in a jacket pocket can be a comfort on cold nights.

PROTECTIVE DEVICES

A myriad of protective devices have been developed for specialized firefighting positions such as smokejumpers and tractor operators. In this book we discuss only those devices that should be considered by anyone anticipating fireline duty.

The hard hat is the single most important protective device and should be required of every firefighter regardless of the cover type in which the fire is burning. Even in a grass fire, where the risk of falling objects can be considered minimal, the head can fly off a tool and brain an adjacent worker. Hard hats are usually made of metal (mostly aluminum), fiberglass, or plastic compositions. Aluminum has the advantage of light weight but the disadvantage of being electrically conductive. Fiberglass or plastic hats offer protection from arcing if firefighting activities are conducted near live electric lines or equipment. Hard hats should always be equipped with chin straps if they are to be worn in or around aircraft.

In the early 1960s the Commonwealth Scientific and Industrial Research Organization of Australia conducted an intensive series of studies on thermal hazards facing forest firefighters and investigated a number of possible protective devices. Their findings and some of the lesser known devices are discussed later in this chapter. One device that has stood the test of time and has been modified and adopted by fire management agencies in several parts of the world is the aluminized survival shelter (King 1965). Basically, the shelter consists of highly reflective aluminum foil bonded by heat-resistant nontoxic glue to a glass cloth backing. When trapped, the victim (by permitting oneself to be trapped by fire, a person has ceased to be a firefighter and has become a victim) lies prone on the ground, feet facing the oncoming flames and envelops himself or herself in the shelter with the reflective side out. The extent to which the shelter is tenable depends on the air space between the shelter walls and the victim. Most of the differences in design between the fire shelters used in various countries have to do with the devices used to maintain a separation between the walls and the victim and yet keep the shelter from tearing or blowing away in the turbulence when the fire passes over.

Survival shelters have saved several lives over the years, but they should be regarded as absolute last resort equipment and never as a substitute for sound firemanship. The use of fire shelters is equivalent to abandoning a ship at sea—someone, somewhere, made a serious error in judgment.

Safety boots, with metal plates in the toe and instep, have been recommended for workers using cutting tools since 75 percent of cutting tool injuries are to those portions of the foot. Safety shoes have their drawbacks, however. They are somewhat heavier and less flexible than regular boots and hence less comfortable for long hikes, particularly going down steep hills. In addition, the metal is an excellent conductor of heat and can cause burns to the foot when the wearer stands in hot ashes, as often inadvertently happens during mop-up operations.

Most injuries to chain saw operators occur within six inches of the kneecap. These injuries can be greatly minimized by wearing a protective chap covering the outer leg from waist to midshin as shown in Figure 10.1. The chaps are made of canvas with a quilted synthetic fiber filling. If the chain contacts the leg, bunches of filling are pulled into the saw, stalling the motor before the saw teeth reach the skin.

Chainsaw operators, pumptenders, helicopter spotters, and other fire personnel regularly exposed to noise levels above 100 decibels should be provided with hearing protection (Ramsey et al. 1973). Various types of earmuffs and ear plugs are available. Pliable plugs of silicone, rubber, or expandable foam are relatively inexpensive and mold themselves to fit any ear.

Protective goggles are a must item for heliport workers and any other

Figure 10.1. Special chaps prevent chainsaw injuries. Photo by U.S. Forest Service.

personnel who are routinely exposed to blowing dust or dirt. They also offer some protection against eye irritation from smoke for fireline crews, but many firefighters believe that the nuisance of trying to keep the lenses clean outweighs the benefits

Several items have been developed to protect fireline workers from smoke and heat. These include reflective creams to cut down radiant heat transfer to exposed skin, wire mesh face masks to reduce radiation on the face, and various filtered face masks to cut down the irritants in smoke. Although these devices contribute to comfort in firefighting, they have some inherent dangers of their own. Filters can remove the particulates, tars, and acids that make smoke so irritating, but not the carbon monoxide that makes it so dangerous. Radiant heat reflectors can keep skin temperatures to a level where clothing will ignite before the exposed hands or face give a pain warning to stand back from the fire. By muffling the body's normal danger signals, some protective devices can lead to situations where the firefighter is effectively dead before he or she is uncomfortable. Protective devices should be used to alleviate the discomforts of unavoidable working conditions; they should never be used to permit working in an environment that would otherwise be intolerable.

HAZARDS OFF THE FIRELINE

Many firefighters deaths and injuries are not directly related to the fire itself, but to the hazards of moving through and living in rough and often unfamiliar country and working long hours under a high degree of stress.

When starting for a fire by auto or truck, firefighters should never ride in the same space with loose tools. If separate storage compartments or attached tool boxes are not available, all tools should be wrapped in canvas and tied securely to the vehicle. Drivers should not exceed legal speed limits even on emergency fire calls. Experience has shown that, in the aggregate, delays due to occasional accidents while speeding will outweigh the time saved on the successful trips. All firegoing vehicles should carry at least the minimum forest firefighting equipment (shovel, axe, and bucket) and also a fire extinguisher in case the vehicle itself should catch fire. Firegoing vehicles have been known to start new fires when exhaust systems contact dry grass, and it is highly embarrassing to be caught in such a situation without proper equipment.

Quite often, the last stretch of travel to a forest fire is by foot. Here, again, a deliberate pace rather than a frantic dash is most productive in the long run. There is little gained if a crew arrives at the fire 15 minutes earlier than they might have otherwise, but are too exhausted to work after they arrive. While walking, firefighters should be spaced about two meters apart carrying their tools by their sides, never over the shoulder. If the status of the fire is unknown, the route should be chosen to intercept the fire on its flanks or from below. It is always dangerous to come downhill to the top of a fire, even if the fire is being driven by a downslope wind. The wind may change but the slope will not and the rear of the fire can become the head quite suddenly, and with disastrous consequences.

Insect stings and snake bites are common hazards in many forests of the world and firefighters should be provided with appropriate repellents and medication. At least one person in each crew should carry a first-aid kit and be knowledgeable in its use.

Should your crew be lucky enough to travel to the fire by helicopter, there are several rules that every firefighter should know and obey at heliports or helispots. Always approach and leave a helicopter from the forward quadrant where you are visible to the pilot. Hats, unless firmly secured by chin straps, should be carried rather than worn when approaching or leaving helicopters. On sloping ground, always maintain a position lower than the helispot. Never stand or loiter on higher ground. Follow the pilot's directions at all times.

If the fire is a prolonged one necessitating a fire camp, rigorous sanitary rules must be enforced. Nothing plays havoc with a good fire plan like an epidemic of dysentery. Sleeping areas should be designated in locations away from traffic, helicopter landing routes, and livestock. There should always be an emergency plan showing escape routes and safety zones should it be necessary to evacuate the camp.

FIREFIGHTING HAZARDS

Heat

As a result of an extensive survey of firefighter disabilities in Australia, Alan King (1962) determined that heat stress was the most common problem on the fireline. During strenuous activity a firefighter will lose 0.5 grams per second or 1.5 liters per hour of body fluids from the lungs and as perspiration. This amounts to a maximum cooling rate of 290 calories per second. If the heat absorbed by the body, including heat produced by muscular activity, exceeds this value, the body temperature will rise at a rate of approximately 1°C per 63,000 calories of excess heat. Since vigorous exercise produces about 150 calories per second within the body and exposure to full sunlight contributes another 50, any absorbed radiation or convected heat from the fire above 90 calories per second will eventually be evidenced by increased body temperature and heat sickness. The first symptoms are usually a mild headache, dizziness, and profuse perspiration. These can be alleviated by increasing fluid intake. Fireline workers should drink deeply and often. The normal sweating rate for firefighters is something over $\frac{1}{2}$ liters per hour and can exceed 2 liters per hour under extreme heat loads. Dehydration up to five percent of body weight can be tolerated but losses beyond this will accelerate and aggravate heat stress symptoms. If too much salt is lost in perspiration, severe cramps in the legs and abdomen will result. Normal salt intake (20–30 grams per day) is sufficient to prevent heat cramps under normal fireline conditions and salt tablets are not necessary unless the noon meal is skipped or consists solely of fruit, candy, or other salt-free substances. If body fluids are not replenished following the onset of heavy perspiration, or if heat loads accumulate sufficient to raise the body temperature by 2°C, heat stroke is likely to occur. During heat stroke perspiration ceases, the skin becomes hot, dry, and reddish, breathing is rapid and shallow, body temperature rises rapidly, and the victim is quickly unconscious or delirious. Heat stroke is extremely dangerous, often resulting in death or permanent brain damage. The victim should be kept as cool as possible with the skin moistened frequently, and evacuation to a hospital should be initiated promptly.

Carbon Monoxide

Carbon monoxide is a product of incomplete combustion. It is formed when there is too little oxygen in the fire environment to allow complete oxidation of carbon to carbon dioxide, or when the oxidizing gases are cooled quickly below their reaction temperatures. Carbon monoxide yields from forest fires range from 10 to 250 grams of CO per kilogram of fuel burned with the higher amounts found in high-intensity, rapidly spreading fires where oxygen supply is limiting, and in fires with a high proportion of smoldering material. Carbon monoxide production in smoldering combustion is about 10 times that in flaming combustion. Normal carbon monoxide levels at a fire front are 100 to 200 parts per million at the fire edge and 10 to 20 parts per million 30 meters downwind.

Carbon monoxide reacts with hemoglobin in the blood much more readily than does oxygen or carbon dioxide. Thus carbon monoxide interferes with the normal transport of oxygen and CO_2 between the tissues and the lungs. A carboxyhemoglobin level of 40 percent will cause unconsciousness and 60 percent is fatal. Carbon monoxide even at very low levels also reacts directly with some nerve cells (Grunnet 1974), particularly those of the central nervous system. Thus the early symptoms of carbon monoxide poisoning, and the only symptoms if only low levels of CO are involved, are impairment to alertness, judgment, vision, and psychomotor ability. These are succeeded by cardiac and pulmonary changes that are also difficult to detect and only when carboxyhemoglobin levels reach 20 percent, or halfway to the level sufficient to cause unconsciousness, do headaches and nausea occur that can warn a victim that all is not well.

It takes from one to two hours for blood levels to reach equilibrium with the 100 to 200 parts per million ambient CO levels associated with *hot line* work on forest fires, and it takes at least three times as long for CO to be removed from the blood once the victim has been returned to a clean air environment. Consequently, workers doing direct attack at the fire front should be rotated every couple of hours and limited to one hot line assignment per day whenever possible. The greatest danger of carbon monoxide to forest firefighters is its insidiousness. Firefighters may feel that they are functioning perfectly long after their mental acuity has deteriorated to a point where they are a danger to others as well as themselves.

Burns

When laymen, or even many less experienced firefighters, think of someone being burned to death in a forest fire their mental picture is usually one of a conflagration with a wall of flame consuming everything before it. This is not true. Conflagrations often trap and burn civilians, particularly when forest fires sweep into suburbs on a wide front, but nearly all firefighters have a sufficient understanding of fire behavior and enough training to stay out of the way of a conflagration. Studies in the United States and Canada show that most firefighters have been burned in deceptively light fuels on small fires or relatively quiet sectors of large fires (NWCG 1980, Wilson 1977). This occurs because the small or quiet fire gives a false sense of security and fire can move through fine fuels with a speed that gives little time to recover from errors in judgment. Nor is unusual fire behavior a prevalent cause of fire fatalities. An analysis of 125 tragedy fires showed that 33 percent of the fire behavior-related fatalities were caused by fires running upslope, 24 percent by a sudden wind shift, 15 percent by head fires accelerating when moving into a new fuel type, 11 percent by heavy spot fire activity, and only 17 percent by such "unusual" occurrences as fires running downslope or thunderstorm downdrafts (NWCG op. cit.). The only thing unusual about the fire behavior that caused the vast majority of firefighter fatalities was the victim's failure to anticipate it. Simply heeding the fire behavior maxim that "the wind may change but the slope won't" might have helped avoid the one fatality out of three that occurred when firefighters got caught above a fire and had no escape route.

The principal cause of incapacitation and death in flame burns typical of those suffered by forest firefighter fatalities is thermal overload, similar to heat stroke but occurring in a much shorter time frame. Studies of the effect of flame weapons on fully clothed soldiers have shown that, for exposures lasting less than 30 seconds, 100 percent of the subjects are totally incapacitated by total thermal loads (radiation plus convection) of 18,000°C-sec (1000°C for 18 sec, 18,000°C for 1 sec or any similar combination), 50 percent are totally incapacitated at 15,000°C-sec, and no instances of total incapacitation can be expected at 9500°C-sec or less (Ingram and McHugh 1975). To put these figures in a more familiar context, consider a line fire in light fuels with a flame temperature of 1000°C and a flame height of 3 meters. A firefighter running toward, through and away from such a fire at 5 meters per second would receive the equivalent of 2000°C-sec while approaching and leaving the flames. Thus survival could be expected to be certain if travel through the flames took less than 7.5 seconds. At 5 meters per second, a firefighter could pass through a 37-meter flame depth and still live. Few fires in light fuels have flame depths this large.

In most firefighter fatalities, however, the unsuccessful strategy has been to try to run away from the fire and to continue running until exhaustion or the radiant heat load from the fire front fells the victim and allows the flame front to pass over him or her. Under these conditions both the radiant heat load and the residence time of the victims in the flame front exceed the maximum survival time.

Of course the best way to avoid such draconian measures as running through walls of flame is to stay out of situations where such measures become necessary. In North America such mnemonic devices as the Eight Firefighting Commandments, the Ten Standard Firefighting Orders, and the

Thirteen Situations that Shout Watch Out have been used to instill the principles of safe firefighting practices. In the long run, however, only a firm understanding of fire behavior together with experienced leadership and good crew discipline can prevent fire tragedies.

THE EIGHT FIREFIGHTING COMMANDMENTS

It is easy to get behind the "8" Ball if you don't obey the EIGHT FIRE-FIGHTING COMMANDMENTS

WEATHER	dominates fire behavior so keep informed.
ACTION	must be based on current and expected fire behavior.
TRY OUT	at least two safe escape routes.
COMMUNICATIONS	maintain them with your crew, your boss, and adjoining forces.
HAZARDS	to watch for are flashy fuels, steep slopes, and chimneys.
OBSERVE	changes in wind direction or velocity, humidity, clouds.
UNDERSTAND	your instructions and make sure yours are understood.
THINK	clearly, be as alert, and act decisively before your situation becomes critical.

Remember to *WATCH OUT* on the fireline.

THE TEN STANDARD FIREFIGHTING ORDERS

1. Keep informed on FIRE WEATHER conditions and forecasts.
2. Know what your FIRE is DOING at all times—observe personally, use scouts.
3. Base all actions on current and expected BEHAVIOR of FIRE.
4. Have ESCAPE ROUTES for everyone and make them known.
5. Post LOOKOUTS when there is possible danger.
6. Be ALERT, keep CALM, THINK clearly, ACT decisively.
7. Maintain prompt COMMUNICATION with your men, your boss, and adjoining forces.
8. Give clear INSTRUCTIONS and be sure they are understood.
9. Maintain CONTROL of your men at all times.
10. Fight fire aggressively but provide for SAFETY first.

THE 13 SITUATIONS THAT SHOUT WATCH OUT!

1. YOU—in heavy cover with unburned fuel between YOU and FIRE.
2. YOU—in country you have not seen in daylight.
3. YOU—feel weather getting hotter and drier.
4. YOU—feel like taking a nap near fireline.
5. YOU—cannot see main fire and YOU are not in communication with anyone who can.
6. YOU—notice the wind change.
7. YOU—in an area where terrain and/or cover make travel slow.
8. YOU—are getting frequent spot fires over your line.
9. YOU—are building a line downhill toward a fire.
10. YOU—have been given assignment and instructions not clear to you.
11. YOU—are attempting to make a frontal assault on a fire with tankers.
12. YOU—on a hillside and rolling fire can ignite fuel below you.
13. YOU—are in an area were YOU are unfamiliar with local factors influencing fire behavior.

Airtankers and Helicopters

In the early days of the airtanker program in the United States it was popular for firefighters to maneuver themselves so as to be on the edge of a retardant drop. The resulting speckles of retardant on their hard hats and clothing showed that "they had been where the action was." This practice ceased abruptly after several injuries and at least one fatality showed that, although most loads of retardant break up and lose momentum within a second or two of their release from the aircraft, occasionally part of the load will maintain coherence and hit the ground at nearly the same speed as the aircraft was flying at the time of release (Figure 10.2). When several gallons of liquid hit the ground with a forward speed of 50 meters per second or so, they will uproot bushes and dislodge rocks as well as any firefighters in their path. Today's safety practices call for all firefighters to be removed from the target area. If unable to retreat, the firefighter should lie face down with hard hat in place, and head towards the approaching aircraft. Handtools should be placed to the downhill side and slightly behind the body. If possible, the firefighter should grasp something firm to prevent being dislodged and rolled about.

Airtankers pose another safety hazard which is more difficult to guard against because it is invisible. Every aircraft generates a wake while in flight. The pressure differential over the wing or rotor surfaces that give the aircraft its lift also generates a pair of counter-rotating vortices that lie parallel to the

Figure 10.2.   Retardant drops occasionally maintain cohesiveness. Photo by Canadian Forestry Service.

line of flight and rotate downward along the center line and upwards on each side. Each vortex is about one wingspan in diameter. Vortex strength, or windspeed, is governed by the size of the wing, the speed of the aircraft, and the wing loading. The greatest vortex windspeeds (about 80 meters per second) occur when the generating aircraft is large, loaded, and flying at minimum cruising speed. The vortices sink at a rate of 100 to 150 meters per minute, losing strength over time, and are usually dissipated within two minutes—less if the air is unstable and winds gusty. Consequently, aircraft flying higher than 300 meters above the ground pose no problem but lower flying aircraft may. If the vortices have not dissipated by the time they reach the surface, they will separate and move away from the flight center line at about 150 meters per minute. Vortex velocities will typically have been reduced to 40 meters per second by the time the vortices reach the surface. To the firefighter on the ground, vortex turbulence is felt as a wind gust lasting from 15 to 30 seconds. In patchy fuels where timber or brush are mixed with open grassy areas, flames and embers may be lofted into the crowns and initiate crown fires and spotting (Davis and Chandler 1965).

Helicopters in level flight produce wake vortices as do fixed-wing aircraft. Since helicopters are smaller and lighter than airtankers, their vortices are much weaker and have never been associated with adverse fire behavior. However, helicopters also create an induced flow or *downwash* that can have very serious effects indeed (Shields 1969). Downwash velocity depends on the loading at the rotor disc and can be calculated from the formula:

$$V = 5.0 \frac{\sqrt{W}}{AD}$$

where   V = Downwash velocity (m/sec)
         W = Gross aircraft weight (kg)
         A = Rotor disc area (m²)
         D = Air density (kg/m³)

Typical values of downwash velocities immediately beneath hovering helicopters range from 15 meters per second for small (2 to 3 passenger) helicopter through 25 meters per second for larger passenger ships to 65 meters per second or more for large, multirotor heavy-lift freight carriers.

In forward flight the downward component of induced flow drops off rapidly as shown in Figure 10.3, reaching a value of one-half the hovering downwash when the helicopter reaches a forward speed of 15 meters per second.

Downwash is damped out in still air at a rate of 1 meter per second

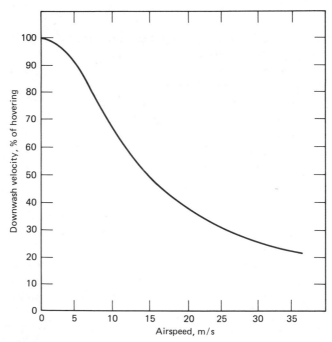

Figure 10.3.   Downward velocity in forward flight (approximate).

decrease in downward velocity for every 3.5 meters below the ship. Thus a heavy cargo helicopter flying across a fire at 15 meters per second will have a noticeable effect on the ground (4 meters per second wind) even if flying at a height of 100 meters. Were the ship to hover for a closer look, the resulting 36 meters per second downwash at the ground could have drastic consequences.

The hazards of downwash can be avoided if pilots are instructed to conduct all reconnaissance and firefighter ferrying operations at altitudes of at least 100 meters and to avoid hovering in the vicinity of the fire, particularly near the fire's perimeter. Heavy cargo ferrying should avoid the fire area as much as possible even if this means rerouting flights from the shortest routes.

Some downwash effects are unavoidable during water or retardant dropping operations and when lowering rappelers. Rappeling can, and should, be conducted at a safe distance from the fire edge. However, direct attack with water or chemicals, by necessity, involves some risk of adverse downwash effects on fire behavior. Ground crews should be directed to remain at least 100 meters away from helitanker targets and pilots should make their drops at the maximum altitude and airspeed consistent with accuracy.

Motorized Equipment

Although the advent of motorized equipment such as tractors and fire engines has contributed greatly to our ability to suppress forest fires, the misuse of such equipment has been the cause of a number of fire fatalities. The basic problem with virtually all the equipment-related firefighter deaths studied to date has been that the operators felt such a sense of power and security by being in the equipment that they moved into positions where they never would have gone on foot. Then when the equipment failed or became immobilized, they had no means of escape. An enclosed vehicle offers a fairly high degree of safety from fire, as we discuss in more detail in a later section, and even an open bulldozer can afford some protection. However, a tried and true principle of firefighting is "never drive into a situation where you can't walk out." A similar truism for bulldozers and other off-road vehicles working in steep country is "never operate on a grade too steep to back up" (Anon. 1976). On large fires, many fire agencies require that vehicles be operated in pairs so that the second machine is available for rescue of all occupants should one machine break down.

Since fire equipment is often used on poor roads or off-road under conditions of poor visibility and often when the operator is under an unusual degree of stress, it is important to have operators who are thoroughly familiar with the equipment and its limitations. It is preferable to leave an expensive machine standing idle in fire camp than to entrust it to an untrained operator.

Backfiring

The greatest tragedy in forest firefighting occurs when firefighters are killed or injured because of backfires set by their coworkers. The key to avoiding such a tragedy is communication. A backfire should never be initiated until the supervisor is certain of the location of all personnel who may be affected by the action. This includes not only the members of the firing and holding crews, but of adjacent crews and any line scouts, weather observers, or other individuals who may have assignments away from prepared firelines. When a lighting crew must be split, as when firing a saddle or sending a small group ahead to cut off a rapidly spreading finger of fire, it is essential to maintain either visual or radio contact so that each group can be constantly aware of the progress and any difficulties encountered by the other. Any person ahead of the lighting crew faces the possibility of being confronted by three fires simultaneously—the main fire, the backfire, and the escaped backfire—only experienced and competent people should be allowed to be exposed to such a potential hazard.

Electrical Hazards

Forest firefighters are occasionally exposed to fires burning beneath high-tension powerlines. Activities adjacent to powerlines should be undertaken with the utmost caution unless it is certain that the lines have been deactivated and will not be recharged. Not only are fallen lines an obvious danger, but powerlines in place can arc to the ground along hose streams, retardant drops (as illustrated rather vividly in Figure 10.4), or even along ionized pathways in flames and dense smoke. Powerline rights of way should never be used as firebreaks or backfiring lines unless positive arrangements have been made with the utility company to deenergize the lines.

Night Firefighting

Night is often the best time for effective firefighting. Humidities are usually the highest, winds the lowest, and temperatures most conducive to hard physical labor. However, darkness brings its own particular hazards to the fireline. Smoke is generally invisible at night and spot fires can only be located when the flames or glowing embers are directly visible. Minor accidents, particularly sprains, falls, and injuries from rolling rocks are more prevalent at night. Fire-weakened snags and dead limbs are difficult to identify, and night operations should be curtailed during periods of high winds in cover types where falling snags or limbs may be present.

Effective firefighting at night requires adequate lighting and motivated fire crews. Supervision is difficult at night and it is easy to slip off into the darkness for a short unauthorized rest break.

Figure 10.4.   Fire retardants are good electrical conductors. Photo by San Bernardino, California *Sun Telegram.*

Reflective paint and ribbon can be very helpful in marking hazards, fireline locations, and escape routes, and generally extending the effective range of firefighters' head lamps. Reflective markings are particularly necessary on those personnel who work around tractors, plows, or other fireline building equipment.

With proper safety precautions the night firefighter can accomplish more with greater comfort than his or her daytime counterpart.

PROTECTING CIVILIANS

The primary responsibility of the forest firefighter, or any firefighter, is to safeguard the lives of humans threatened by the fire. All other responsibilities are secondary to life safety. For recreationists or other forest visitors, this usually involves no more than advice on safe routes for leaving the fire area or establishing a convoy service if exit requires travel through

Figure 10.5.   When the fire threat to a residence is unmistakable, it may be safer to stay than to leave. Mack Lake, Michigan, May 5, 1980. Photo by Michigan Department of Natural Resources.

the fire itself. Working with forest residents, however, is often not so easy. Residents are reluctant to leave their homes until the fire threat is unmistakable, by which time it may be safer to stay than to leave (Figure 10.5). The rate at which a structure transmits flames and smoke to the interior after being ignited on the outside is relatively slow compared to the time for passage of a forest fire front and occupants can usually remain inside the house long enough for life-threatening conditions outside to abate to tolerable levels. Last-minute evacuees face the prospect of driving along smoke-covered roads with uncertain knowledge of the exact fire location and the probability of panic greater than it would have been in familiar surroundings at home. In most cases, except where dwellings are clearly untenable such as those in ravines surrounded by heavy fuels, it is safer to remain and spend whatever time is available taking remedial measures such as wetting down roofs, removing shrubbery adjacent to the house, closing all openings, and covering windows that may be exposed to intense radiation with aluminum foil.

Residents who remain with their houses and cannot be protected by trained firefighters should be cautioned against premature backfiring around their properties. Backfires set by local property owners can create havoc with the overall strategy for control of the fire and endanger firefighters as well as adjacent property.

Just as shelter in a building is usually preferable to trying to escape a fast-running fire by vehicle, so staying in a vehicle is preferable to trying to escape on foot. A hard-topped vehicle with the windows rolled up offers fair protection against both radiant heat and excess smoke. Though there have been some fatalities, both firefighter and civilian, to people trapped in vehicles, none have been attributed to either smoke inhalation or carbon monoxide poisoning. Clothing burns or excessive heat loads from long exposure to fires in heavy fuels have been the cause of death in these cases. Numerous tests on vehicle fires have shown that undamaged gasoline tanks will not explode or contribute to the fire load until the tires nearest the tank have become fully involved and been burning for several minutes. Except in the case of crashed or overturned vehicles, there should be plenty of time for the fire outside to cool to tolerable limits before evacuation of a vehicle becomes necessary.

Those electing to escape by vehicle should be instructed that the safest procedure, if it becomes obvious that an encounter with a fire front is inevitable, is to find the widest or most sheltered spot in the road where adjacent fuels are least, park the vehicle on the side of the road away from the approaching flames, turn on headlights, and wait for the fire to pass over. This is preferable to attempting to minimize the time surrounded by flames by driving into unknown fuel loads where pain from radiation on the hands or face may make control of the vehicle impossible.

Whenever possible evacuees should be convoyed out of the fire area with a firefighter's vehicle at the head and rear of the convoy. This not only allows a professional assessment of the hazards ahead, but provides a psychological sense of security to the evacuees and prevents excessive speed and reckless driving.

Forest firefighting is a dangerous job. The hazards can be minimized only if all fire management personnel recognize their responsibility for ensuring the safety of themselves, their coworkers, and the public in their charge.

BIBLIOGRAPHY

Anon. 1976. *Handbook on use of bulldozers in forest fire control.* British Columbia For. Serv., For. Prot. Handbook No. 8, 14 pp.

Davis, J. B. and C. C. Chandler. 1965. Vortex turbulence—its effects on fire behavior. *Fire Contr. Notes* **26**(1):4–6, 16.

Grunnet, M. L. 1974. Long-term nervous system effects resulting from carbon monoxide exposure. In *Physiological and Toxicological Aspects of Combustion Products,* Nat. Acad. Sci. (U.S.), pp. 119–129.

Ingram, R. R. and R. F. McHugh. 1975. *Handbook of human vulnerability criteria. Biomedical evaluation of thermal effects.* Edgewood Arsenal Special Pub. EB-SP-76011-7, pp. 37–46.

King, A. R. 1962. *The efficiency of rural firefighters.* CSIRO Chem. Res. Lab. Tech. Paper No. 4, 12 pp.

King, A. R. 1965. *A prototype survival tent for forest firefighters.* CSIRO Unnumbered Pub., 11 pp., illus.

NWCG. 1980. *Report of the U.S.–Canadian task force on study of fatal/near-fatal wildland fire accidents.* Unnumbered Report, 76 pp.

NFPA. 1976. *Fire protection handbook,* 19th ed., Nat. Fire Prot. Assoc., Boston, 1263 pp.

Ramsey, G. S., D. M. Townsend, and J. S. Bland. 1973. *Noise and the portable forest fire pump.* Canadian For. Serv. Info. Report FF-X-37.

Shields, H. J. 1969. *Helicopter rotor downwash effects.* U.S. For. Serv. Special Report ED&T 1818, 13 pp.

Wilson, C. C. 1977. Fatal and near-fatal forest fires, the common denominator. *Intl. Fire Chief* **43**(9):9–15.

CHAPTER ELEVEN

Forest Fire Terminology and Conversion Factors

In this book we have used the metric units most commonly found in forest fire practice. Because these may differ from the units common in engineering practice and because some countries still use English standards of measurement, the following conversion factors may be helpful. They are not numerically exact but are sufficient for practical purposes.

Length

1 centimeter (cm) = 0.39 inches (in.)
1 meter (m) = 3.3 feet (ft)
1 kilometer (km) = 3300 ft
= 0.62 miles (mi)
= 50 chains (ch)

Area

1 square centimeter (cm^2) = 0.16 in.^{2}
1 square meter (m^2) = 10.8 ft^2
1 hectare (ha) = 10,000 m^2
= 2.5 acres (ac)
1 square kilometer (km^2) = 0.39 mi^2
= 250 ac

Volume

> 1 cubic centimeter (cm^3) = 0.06 in.^{3}
> 1 liter (l) = 0.26 gallons (gal)
>   = 0.035 ft^3

Weight

> 1 gram (gm) = 0.035 ounces (oz)
> 1 kilogram (kg) = 2.2 pounds (lb)

Heat (Energy)

> 1 calorie (cal) = 0.004 British Thermal Units (BTU)
>   = 4.2 Joules (J)
> 1 cal/cm^2 = 3.7 BTU/ft^2

Temperature

> degrees Celsius (°C) = degrees Kelvin (°K) − 273
>   = [degrees Fahrenheit (°F) − 32] × $\frac{5}{9}$

Velocity

> 1 meter/second (m/sec)   = 3.3 ft/sec
>   = 2.2 mi/hr
>   = 3.6 km/hr
> 1 meter/minute (m/min)   = 0.055 ft/sec
>   = 3 ch/hr

Power

> 1 Watt (W) = 1 J/sec
>   = 0.24 cal/sec
>   = 3.4 BTU/hr

Pressure

> 1 kilopascal (kP) = 0.15 pounds/square inch (PSI)
>   = 10 millibars (mb)
>   = 7.5 millimeters of mercury (mm Hg)
>   = 0.1 meters of head (m water)

Fuel Loading

  1 tonne/hectare (t/ha) $=$ 0.1 kg/m^2
                           $=$ 0.45 tons/acre (t/a)
                           $=$ 0.021 lb/ft^2

Heat Content

  1 cal/gm $=$ 1.8 BTU/lb

Irradiance

  1 kW/m^2 $=$ 0.024 cal/cm^{2}sec
             $=$ 5.3 BTU/ft^{2}min

Fireline Intensity

  1 kW/m $=$ 2.4 cal/cm sec
          $=$ 0.29 BTU/ft sec

Thermal Conductivity

  1 cal/cm^{2}sec(°C/cm) $=$ 240 BTU/ft^{2}hr(°F/ft)

Glossary of Terms

Fire terminology is not adequately standardized, even within the English-speaking countries of the world. The terminology used in this book follows the standards set by the Food and Agricultural Organization of the United Nations wherever possible. Terms in this glossary are taken from the following references in order of priority:

FAO Wildland Fire Management Terminology
Edited by C. Bentley Lyon. 1982.

FAO Terminology of Forest Science, Technology, Practice and Products
Edited by F. C. Ford-Robertson. 1971.

Amer. Met. Soc. Glossary of Meteorology
Edited by R. E. Huschke. 1959.

ABORT: To jettison a load of water or retardant from an aircraft.

ACCELERANT: Any substance (such as oil, gasoline, etc.) that is applied to a fuelbed to expedite the burning process.

ACCEPTABLE DAMAGE: Damages that do not seriously impair the flow of economic and social benefits from the wildlands.

ACCEPTABLE FIRE RISK: The potential fire loss that a community is willing to accept rather than provide resources to reduce such a loss.

ACCESSIBILITY BURN: Burning off understory prior to the sale of forest products to improve the efficiency of timber marking and harvesting.

ACTIONABLE FIRE:
(1)   Generally, any fire that requires suppression.
(2)   More particularly, a fire started or allowed to spread in violation of law, ordinance, or regulation.

ACTIVITY FUELS: Fuels resulting from or altered by forestry practices such as timber harvest and thinning, as opposed to naturally created fuels.

ADAPTER: A device for coupling hoses of the same size but which have nonmatching hose threads or for connecting a threaded coupling to a quick-connect coupling.

ADIABATIC: Without gain or loss of heat.

ADVANCING A LINE: Moving the hose line toward a given area from the point where the hose-carrying apparatus has stopped.

AERIAL DETECTION: A system for or the act of discovering, locating, and reporting fires from aircraft.

AERIAL FUELS: The standing and supported forest combustibles not in direct contact with the ground and consisting mainly of foliage, twigs, branches, stems, bark, and vines.

AERIAL IGNITION: The igniting of wildland fuels by dropping incendiary devices or materials from aircraft.

AERIAL OBSERVER: A person specifically assigned to discover, locate, and report fires from aircraft and to observe and describe conditions at the fire scene.

AERIAL RECONNAISSANCE: Use of aircraft for observing fire behavior, values threatened, control activity, and other critical factors to facilitate command decisions on tactics needed for suppression.

AIR ATTACK: The direct use of aircraft in the suppression of wildfires.

AIR ATTACK BASE: A permanent facility at which aircraft are stationed for use in air attack operations.

AIR–GROUND DETECTION: Any fire-detection system combining fixed point coverage of key areas by ground detectors with aerial detection that is varied according to needs.

AIR NET (AIRCRAFT NETWORK):   Applies to radio frequencies primarily used for air operations.

AIR OFFICER: The term used by some agencies to identify the staff person responsible for either of the following:
   (1)   Establishing and operating aerial services within an administrative unit.
   (2)   Establishing and operating aerial services on a going fire.

AIR OPERATIONS OFFICER: The person responsible for all air operations (air attack, aerial detection, cargo dropping, transport, etc.) within an administrative unit or from an operating base.

AIRTANKER: A fixed-wing aircraft fitted with tanks and equipment for releasing water or fire-retardant chemicals on fires.

ALLOWABLE BURNED AREA: The maximum average acreage burned over a given period of years that is considered an acceptable loss for a given area under organized fire control.

ANCHOR POINT: An advantageous location, generally a fire barrier, from which to start constructing a fireline. Used to minimize the chance of being outflanked by the fire while the line is being constructed.

AREA IGNITION = SIMULTANEOUS IGNITION = FORCED BURNING: Igniting, throughout an area to be broadcast burned or backfired, a number of individual fires either simultaneously or in quick succession, and so spaced that they soon influence and support each other to produce fast spread of fire throughout the area.

ASPECT: The direction toward which a slope faces.

ATMOSPHERIC STABILITY: The degree to which the atmosphere resists turbulence and vertical motion.

ATTACK TIME = RESPONSE TIME: Elapsed time from the end of report time to the first organized attack; includes both get-away time and travel time.

ATTACK UNIT: A single vehicle or aircraft and its associated personnel and material provided for the purpose of responding to and abating a fire or other emergency.

AVAILABLE FUEL: The portion of the total fuel that would actually burn under various specified conditions.

AVERAGE WORST DAY: The average fire danger of the highest 15 percent of the days occurring in the average worst year.

AVERAGE WORST FIRE YEAR: The third worst established fire season in the last 10, as determined by the sum of the daily fire danger or burning indices during the regularly financed fire season.

AZIMUTH: The horizontal angle or bearing of a point, measured clockwise from the true (astronomic) north. NOTE: the azimuth plus 180° is termed the *back azimuth*.

BACKBURN: Any prescribed fire burning against the wind. (In Australia, synonymous with BACKING FIRE.)

BACKFIRE: A fire set along the inner edge of a control line to consume the fuel in the path of a forest fire and/or change the direction of force of the fire's convection column. (In Australia, synonymous with BACKING FIRE.)

BACKPACK PUMP = KNAPSACK PUMP: A portable sprayer with hand pump fed from a liquid container fitted with shoulder straps.

BACKING FIRE: A prescribed fire or wildfire burning into or against the wind or down the slope without the aid of wind.

BAFFLE: A partitioned wall placed in vehicular or aircraft water tanks to reduce shifting of the water load when starting, stopping, or turning.

BARRIER: Any obstruction to the spread of fire—typically, an area or strip devoid of combustible material.

BASE AREA: An area representative of the major fire problems on a protection unit. From the base area, the base fuel model and slope class are chosen.

BASELINE: In prescribed burning, the initial line of fire, usually set as a backing fire along a road, stream, or firebreak, that serves to contain subsequent burning operations.

BASE STATION: A fixed central radio dispatching station controlling movements of one or more mobile units on the same radio frequency.

BAYS (OF A FIRE):   Marked indentations in the fire perimeter.

BERM: In fire suppression, a ridge of soil and debris along the edge of a fireline, resulting from line construction. May be created on the downhill side to stop rolling material.

BIRD DOG: Aircraft and experienced fire officer used in assessing and carrying out air operations and target selections.

BLACKLINE: Preburning of fuels adjacent to a control line before igniting a prescribed burn. Blacklining is usually done in heavy fuels adjacent to a control line during periods of low fire danger to reduce heat on holding crews and lessen chances for spotting across control line. In fire suppression, blackline denotes a condition where there is no unburned material between the line and the fire edge.

BLIND AREA: The ground or the vegetation growing thereon, (1) that is not visible to a lookout and lies more than a specified depth below its line of sight, and (2) that lies at the limit of visibility of the lookout and lacks a good background.

BLOCK PLAN: A detailed prescription for treating a given burning block with fire.

BLOW DOWN: An area of (previously) standing timber that has been blown over by strong winds or storms.

BLOWUP: A sudden increase in fire intensity and rate of spread, sufficient to preclude immediate control or to upset existing suppression plans; often accompanied by violent convection.

BOARD OF REVIEW: A committee selected to review results of fire control action on a given unit, the specific action taken on a given unit, or the specific action taken on a given fire in order to identify reasons for both good and poor action, and to recomnmend or prescribe ways and means of doing a more efficient job.

BONE YARD:
   (1)   A mop-up term. To systematically work an entire area inside of fire, scraping embers and charcoal off logs and branches, feeling with hands, and piling in a portion of the burned area that has been cleared of all burning material.
   (2)   The cleared area described.

BOOSTER PUMP: An intermediary pump for supplying additional lift in pumping water uphill past the first pump capacity.

BOX CANYON: A steep-sided, dead-end canyon.

BREAKOVER = SLOPOVER = BREAKAWAY = BREAKOVER FIRE:
(1)   A fire edge that crosses a control line intended to confine the fire.
(2)   The resultant fire.

BROADCAST BURNING:
(1)   Allowing a prescribed fire to burn over a designated area within well-defined boundaries for reduction of fuel hazard or as a silvicultural treatment, or both.
(2)   Burning over an entire area.
(3)   A prescribed fire set to burn slash left in situ (Australia).

BROWN AND BURN: Application of an herbicide in order to desiccate living vegetation prior to burning.

BRUSH = SCRUB: A growth of shrubs or small trees usually of a type undesirable to livestock or timber management. A collective term that refers to stands of vegetation dominated by shrubby woody plants or low-growing trees regardless of whether some of the components are cropped.

BURN: An area over which fire has run.

BURNING BLOCK: In prescribed burning, an area having sufficiently uniform conditions of stand and fuel to be treated uniformly under a given burning prescription. The size ranges from the smallest that allows an economically acceptable cost per acre, up to the largest that can conveniently be treated in one burning period.

BURNING OFF: Generally, setting fire—with more or less regulation—to areas carrying unwanted vegetation such as rough grass, slash, and other fuels.

BURNING OUT: Setting fire so as to consume islands of unburned fuel inside the fire perimeter.

BURNING PERIOD: That part of each 24-hour period when fires spread most rapidly, typically from 10 AM to sundown.

BURNING TORCH: Any flame-generating device used to ignite forest fuels.

CAMPAIGN FIRE = PROJECT FIRE: A fire normally of a size and/or complexity that requires a large organization and possibly several days or weeks to suppress.

CANDLE (CANDLING) = TORCH (TORCHING):   A tree (or small clump of trees) is said to candle when its foliage ignites and flares up, usually from bottom to top.

CANDLE BARK = RIBBON BARK (AUST.):   Long streamers of bark decorticated from some eucalypt species that form firebrands conducive to very long distance spotting.

CARDINAL DIRECTIONS: North, south, east, west; to always be used in giving directions and information from the ground or air in describing the fire (e.g., the west flank or east flank, not right or left flank).

CARGO DROPPING: The dropping of equipment or supplies, with or without a parachute, from an aircraft in flight.

CARGO HOOK: A mechanically and electrically operated hook attached to the bottom of a helicopter to which are attached sling loads.

CARGO RACK: An externally mounted rack for transporting supplies or cargo aboard a helicopter.

CAT: Any tractor with treads instead of wheels.

CAT LINE: A fireline constructed by a tractor with a bulldozer or scraper.

CENTER FIRING: A method of broadcast burning in which fires are set in the center of the area to create a strong draft; additional fires are then set progressively nearer the outer control lines as indraft builds up so as to draw them in toward the center.

CENTRIFUGAL PUMP: A pump that expels water by centrifugal force through the ports of a circular impeller, rotating at high speeds. With this type of pump, the discharge line may be shut off while the pump is running.

CHARGED LINE: A line of fire hose filled with water under pressure and ready to use.

CHECK LINE: A temporary fireline constructed at right angles to the control line, and used to interrupt the spread of a backfire as a means of regulating the heat or intensity of the backfire.

CHECK VALVE: A valve that permits flow in one direction but prevents a return flow.

CHEVRON BURN: A prescribed burning technique used in hilly areas to fire ridge points or ridge ends. Lines of fire are started simultaneously from the apex of a ridge point and progress downhill.

CLEAN BURN = CLEAR BURN: Any fire, whether deliberately set or accidental, that destroys all aboveground vegetation and litter along with the lighter slash thus exposing the mineral soil.

COLD TRAILING: A method of controlling a partly dead fire edge by careful inspection and feeling with the hand so as to detect any fire, and then extinguishing it by digging out every live spot and trenching any live edge.

COMBUSTION: Consumption of fuels by oxidation, evolving heat, and generally flame (neither necessarily sensible) and/or incandescence.

COMMAND: The act of directing, ordering, and/or controlling firefighting forces by virtue of explicit legal, administrative, or delegated authority.

COMMAND POST (CP) = FIRE HEADQUARTERS: The location from which all fire operations are directed. There is normally only one command post for each fire situation or other incident.

COMMERCIAL FOREST LAND: Land that is producing, or is capable of producing, crops of industrial wood and that is not withdrawn from timber use by statute or regulation.

COMMISSARY: A supply of items such as candy, tobacco products, toilet items, and work clothes that are made available for sale to firefighters working on a forest fire.

CONDITION OF VEGETATION: State of growth or degree of flammability of vegetation that forms part of a fuel complex. The term herbaceous stage is at times used when referring to herbaceous vegetation alone. In grass areas minimum qualitative distinctions for stages of annual growth are usually green, curing, and dry or cured.

CONFINE A FIRE: To restrict the fire within determined boundaries established either prior to or during the fire.

CONFLAGRATION: A raging, destructive fire. Often used to connote such a fire with a moving front as distinguished from a fire storm.

CONFLAGRATION THREAT = CONFLAGRATION POTENTIAL: The likelihood that wildfire capable of causing high damage will occur.

CONTAIN A FIRE: To take suppression action as needed, which can reasonably be expected to check the fire's spread under prevailing conditions.

CONTROL A FIRE: To complete control line around a fire, any spot fires therefrom, and any interior islands to be saved; burn out any unburned area adjacent to the fire side of the control lines; cool down all hot spots that are immediate threats to the control line until the line can reasonably be expected to hold under foreseeable conditions.

CONTROL FORCE: Personnel and equipment used to control a fire.

CONTROL LINE: A comprehensive term for all the constructed or natural fire barriers and treated fire edges used to control a fire.

CONTROLLED BURNING—See PRESCRIBED BURNING:

COOPERATOR: A local person or agency who has agreed in advance to perform specified fire control services and has been properly instructed to give such service.

COUNTER FIRE: Fire set between main fire and backfire to hasten spread of backfire. Also called draft fire. The act of setting counter fires is sometimes called front firing or strip firing (In European forestry, synonymous with BACKFIRE.

COUPLING: A device to connect the ends of adjacent hoses or other components of a hose-lay.

COVER TYPE: The designation of a vegetation complex described by dominant species, age, and form.

COVERING RESPONSE—See MOVE-UP:

CREEPING FIRE: A fire spreading slowly over the ground, generally with a low flame.

CREW BOSS: A person in supervisory charge of usually 5 to 30 firefighters and responsible for their performance, safety, and welfare.

CROWN: The upper part of a tree or other woody plant carrying the main branch system and foliage.

CROWN COVER: The ground area covered by a crown as delimited by the vertical projection of its outermost perimeter.

CROWN FIRE: A fire that advances from top to top of trees or shrubs more or less independently of the surface fire. Sometimes crown fires are classed as either running or dependent, to distinguish the degree of independence from the surface fire.

CROWN OUT: With reference to a forest fire, to rise from ground level and begin advancing from tree top to tree top. To intermittently ignite tree crowns as a surface fire advances.

CROWN SCORCH: Browning of the needles or leaves in the crown of a tree or shrub caused by heat from a fire.

DEAD FUELS: Fuels having no living tissue and in which the moisture content is governed almost entirely by atmospheric moisture (relative humidity and precipitation), air temperature, and solar radiation.

DEAD OUT: The status of a fire when all phases of suppression, including the patrol phase, are completed.

DEEP-SEATED FIRE: A fire burning far below the surface in deep duff, mulch, peat, or other combustibles as contrasted with a surface fire. A fire that has gained headway and built up heat in a structure so as to require greater cooling for extinguishment; deep charring of structural members, a stubborn fire.

DEMOBILIZATION CENTER—See MOBILIZATION CENTER:

DENSITY ALTITUDE: The pressure altitude corrected for temperature deviations from the standard atmosphere. Density altitude bears the same relation to pressure altitude as true altitude does to indicated altitude.

DESICCANT: A chemical that, when applied to a living plant, causes or accelerates the drying out of its aerial parts.

DIFFICULTY OF CONTROL—See RESISTANCE TO CONTROL:

DIRECT FIRE SUPPRESSION = DIRECT ATTACK = DIRECT METHOD: Any treatment of burning fuel, for example, by wetting, smothering, or chemically quenching the fire, or by physically separating the burning from unburned fuel.

DISPATCH:
  (1)   The act of ordering attack units and/or support units to respond to an emergency.
  (2)   The implementation of a command decision to move a resource or resources from one place to another.

DISPATCHER: A person employed to receive reports of discovery and status of fires, confirm their location, take action promptly to provide the firefighters and equipment likely to be needed for control in first attack, send them to the proper place, and support them as needed.

DOWNLOADING: A calculated reduction in payload to provide a margin of safety.

DRAFT FIRE—See COUNTER FIRE:

DRIFT: The effect of wind on smoke or on a retardant drop.

DRY RUN: A trial pass over the target area by an airtanker.

DUFF: Forest floor material composed of the L (litter), F (fermentation), and H (humus) layers in different stages of decomposition.

EARLY BURNING: Prescribed burning early in the dry season before the leaves and undergrowth are completely dry or before the leaves are shed, as an insurance against more severe fire damage later on.

ECOTYPE:
(1) A subdivision of a biological group that maintains its identity through isolation and/or environmental selection.
(2) A locally adapted population of a species that has a distinctive limit of tolerance to environmental factors.

EDDY: Any circulation drawing its energy from a flow of much larger scale, and brought about by pressure irregularities as in the lee of a solid obstacle.

EDGE FIRING: A method of broadcast burning in which fires are set along the edges of an area and allowed to spread inward.

EDUCTOR = EJECTOR—See SUCTION BOOSTER:

ELAPSED TIME: The total time taken to complete any step(s) in fire suppression. NOTE: Generally divided chronologically into discovery time, report time, get-away time, travel time, attack time, control time, mop-up time, and patrol time.

ELAPSED TIME STANDARDS: The maximum amounts of time allowed by administrative rule for given steps of fire suppression.

ELEVATION LOSS: In hydraulics, the loss of pressure caused by raising water through hose or pipe to a higher elevation. The loss is equal to 9.8 kP per meter of increase in elevation above the pump.

ENGINE—See GROUND TANKER:

ESCAPE ROUTE: A route away from danger spots on a fire; should be pre-planned.

ESCAPED FIRE: A fire that has exceeded initial attack capabilities.

EXPOSURE:
(1) Property that may be endangered by a fire burning in another structure or by a wildfire. In general, property within 12 meters of a fire may be considered to involve exposure hazard, although in very large fires, danger may exist at much greater distances.
(2) Direction in which a slope faces, usually with respect to cardinal directions.

(3)   The general surroundings of a site, with special reference to its openness to winds and sunshine.

EXPOSURE FIRE: Fires in buildings classified as exposure fires are those originating in other than buildings, but that ignite buildings. A fire originating in one building and spreading to another is classified under the original cause of fire.

EXTERNAL LOAD: A load that is carried or extends outside of the aircraft fuselage.

EXTINGUISHING AGENT: A substance used to put out a fire by cooling the burning material, blocking the supply of oxygen, or chemically inhibiting combustion.

EXTRA BURNING PERIOD: For any particular fire that is neither contained nor controlled, any 24-hour period following the termination of the first burning period.

EXTRA FIREFIGHTER—See PICKUP FIREFIGHTER:

EXTRA PERIOD FIRE: A fire not controlled within a prescribed time limit.

EXTREME FIRE BEHAVIOR: Extreme implies a level of wildfire behavior characteristics that ordinarily precludes methods of direct control action. One or more of the following is usually involved: high rates of spread, prolific crowning and/or spotting, presence of fire whirls, a strong convection column. Predictability is difficult because such fires often exercise some degree of influence on their environment and behave erratically, sometimes dangerously.

EXTREME FIRE DANGER: The highest fire danger class.

FALSE SMOKE: Any phenomenon likely to be mistaken for smoke from a wildfire, such as fog or dust from cattle-driving or road traffic.

FEELING FOR FIRE: Examining burned material after the fire is apparently out and feeling with the bare hands to find any live embers.

FINAL = FINAL RUN: An air tanker is said to be "on final" when it is on line with the target and intends to make the drop on that pass. Applies also to cargo dropping.

FINE FUELS = FLASH FUELS: Fuels such as grass, leaves, dropped pine needles, fern tree moss, and some kinds of slash that ignite rapidly and are consumed rapidly when dry.

FINGERS OF A FIRE: The long narrow extensions of a fire projecting from the main body.

FIRE AGENCY: An official group or organization compelled and authorized under statutes of law, the responsibility for control of fire within a designated area or upon certain designated lands.

FIRE ATLAS: An ordered collection of fire maps, charts, and statistics used as a basis for the fire control plan.

FIRE BEHAVIOR: The manner in which a fire reacts to the variables of fuel, weather, and topography.

FIRE BELT: A strip, cleared or planted with trees, maintained as a firebreak.

FIRE BOMBER—See AIRTANKER:

FIRE BOSS = INCIDENT COMMANDER: The person responsible for all fire suppression and service activities on a fire.

FIREBREAK: Any natural or constructed discontinuity in a fuelbed utilized to segregate, stop, and control the spread of fire or to provide a control line from which to suppress a fire.

FIRE CACHE: A supply of fire tools and equipment assembled in planned quantities or standard units at a strategic point for exclusive use in fire suppression.

FIRE CAMP: A location equipped to provide service and support for firefighters and equipment being used to suppress a fire.

FIRE CONCENTRATION:
(1) Generally, a situation in which numerous fires are burning in a locality.
(2) More specifically, the number of fires per unit area or locality for a given period, generally a year.

FIRE CONTROL—See FIRE SUPPRESSION:

FIRE CREW: A general term for two or more firefighters organized to work as a unit.

FIRE DANGER RATING: A fire management system that integrates the effects of selected fire danger factors into one or more qualitative or numerical indices of current protection needs.

FIRE DAY: A standard 24-hour period beginning at 1000 hours. During this period most wildfires undergo a predictable speeding up and slowing down of intensity, depending primarily upon the influence of weather and fuel factors.

FIRE DEATH: A fire casualty that is fatal or becomes fatal within one year of the fire.

FIRE DISTRICT:
(1) A geographic subdivision under organized protection from forest fires.
(2) An area covered by one jurisdiction for fire control purposes, as defined in working plans.
(3) A rural or suburban fire organization, usually tax supported, that maintains fire companies and apparatus.

FIRE DUTY: Actual physical engagement in firefighting service as distinguished from staff work at headquarters; work at an individual fire done by an individual firefighter or unit.

FIRE EDGE: Any part of the boundary of a fire at a given moment. NOTE: the *entire* boundary is termed the fire perimeter.

FIRE EFFECTS: The physical, biological, and ecological impact of fire on the environment.

FIREFIGHTER: A person whose principal function is fire suppression.

FIREFIGHTING FORCES: Qualified firefighters, together with their equipment and material, used to suppress wildland fires.

FIREFINDER: A device or instrument used by lookouts to determine the horizontal bearing and sometimes the vertical angle of a fire from a lookout.

FIRE GUARD:
  (1)   A general term for a firefighter, lookout, patrol, prevention guard, or other person directly employed for prevention and/or detection and suppression of fires.
  (2)   An artificial barrier constructed for the purpose of protecting a high-value area from fires and to provide a control line from which to carry out fire suppression.

FIRE HAZARD:
  (1)   A fuel complex, defined by volume, type condition, arrangement, and location, that determines the degree both of ease of ignition and of fire suppression difficulty.
  (2)   A measure of that part of the fire danger contributed by the fuels available for burning.

FIRE HAZARDOUS AREAS: Those wildland areas where the combination of vegetation, topography, weather, and the threat of fire to life and property create difficult and dangerous problems.

FIRE HEADQUARTERS—See COMMAND POST:

FIRE INJURY: A fire injury is one suffered as the result of a fire that requires (or should require) treatment by a practitioner of medicine within one year of the fire, regardless of whether treatment was actually received.

FIRE LANE: A cleared way, broad enough to permit single-lane vehicular access in a remote area.

FIRELINE:
  (1)   A loose term for any cleared strip used in control of a fire.
  (2)   A cleared, permanent firebreak, generally of considerable width.
  (3)   That portion of a control line from which flammable materials have been removed by scraping or digging down to the mineral soil.
  (4)   A line cleared around an actionable fire, generally following its edge to prevent further spread of the fire and effectively control it.

FIRELINE INTENSITY (BYRAM'S INTENSITY):   The product of the available heat of combustion per unit area of ground and the rate of spread of the fire. The primary unit is kiloWatts per meter of fire front.

FIRE LOAD: The number and size of fires historically experienced on a given unit over a given period (usually one day) at a given index of fire danger.

FIRE MANAGEMENT: All activities required for the protection of burnable forest values from fire and the use of fire to meet land management goals and objectives.

FIRE MANAGEMENT AREA: One or more parcels of land having a common set of fire management objectives.

FIRE MANAGEMENT PLAN: A statement, for a specific area, of fire policy and prescribed action. NOTE: May include maps, charts, tables, and statistical data.

FIRE PLANNING: The systematic technological and administrative management process of designing organization, facilities, and procedures to protect wildland from fire.

FIRE PRESUPPRESSION: Activities undertaken in advance of fire occurrence to help ensure more effective fire suppression. Includes over-all planning, recruitment and training of fire control personnel, procurement and maintenance of firefighting equipment and supplies, fuel treatment, and creating, maintaining, and improving a system of fuelbreaks, roads, water sources, and control lines.

FIRE PREVENTION: All activities concerned with minimizing the incidence of destructive fires.

FIRE PROGRESS MAP: A map maintained on a large fire to show at given times the location of the fire perimeter, deployment of suppression forces, and progress of suppression.

FIRE-PROOFING: Treating fuels, timber, and so on with fire retardants so as to reduce the danger of fires starting or spreading, for example, fireproofing roadsides, campsites, or structural timber. NOTE: As the definition implies, the protection afforded is not absolute but relative.

FIRE PROTECTION: All activities to protect wildland from fire.

FIRE PROTECTION DISTRICT—See FIRE DISTRICT:

FIRE PUMP: An engine-driven pump, usually gasoline-powered, specifically designed for use in fire suppression, that may be carried by a person or transported on skids or a trailer.

FIRE REPORT: An official record of a fire, generally including information on cause, location, action taken, damage, costs, and so on, from start of the fire until completion of suppression action. These reports vary in form and detail from agency to agency.

FIRE RETARDANT: Any substance (except water) that by chemical or physical action reduces flammability of fuels or slows their rate of combustion, for example, a liquid or slurry applied aerially or from the ground during a fire control operation.

FIRE RISK:
(1) The chance of fire starting, as affected by the nature and incidence of causative agencies.
(2) Any causative agency.

FIRE RUN: A rapid advance of a fire front characterized by a marked transition in intensity and rate of spread with respect to that noted before and following the advance.

FIRE SCAR:
    (1) A healing or healed-over injury caused or aggravated by fire on a woody plant.
    (2) The destructive mark left on a landscape by fire.

FIRE SEASON: The period(s) of the year during which fires are likely to occur, spread, and do damage to forest values sufficient to warrant organized fire control.

FIRE STORM: Violent convection caused by a large continuous area of intense fire; often characterized by destructively violent surface indrafts, a towering convection column, long-distance spotting, and sometimes by tornadolike vortices.

FIRE SUPPRESSION = FIRE CONTROL: All the work and activities connected with fire-extinguishing operations, beginning with discovery and continuing until the fire is completely extinguished.

FIRE SUPPRESSION ORGANIZATION:
    (1) The management structure, usually shown in the form of an organization chart, of the personnel collectively assigned to the suppression of a going fire.
    (2) The supervisory and facilitating personnel so assigned.

FIRE TRACE: A temporary, cleared (often burned), narrow strip from which to counterfire or do prescribed burning.

FIRE TRAP:
    (1) An accumulation of highly combustible material, rendering fire fighting dangerous.
    (2) Any situation in which it is highly dangerous to fight fire.

FIRE TRIANGLE: An instructional aid in which the sides of a triangle are used to represent the three factors (oxygen, heat, and fuel) necessary for combustion and flame production. When any one of these factors is removed, flame production ceases.

FIRE TRUCK—See GROUND TANKER:

FIRE WHIRL: A spinning, vortex column of ascending hot air and gases rising from a fire and carrying aloft smoke, debris, and flame. Fire whirls range from a foot or two in diameter to small tornadoes in size and intensity. They may involve the entire fire area or only a hot spot within the area.

FIRING = FIRING OUT: The intentional setting of fires to fuels between the control line and the main body of fire in either a backfiring or burning out operation.

FIRING TECHNIQUE: A method of igniting a wildland area to consume the fuel in a prescribed pattern, for example, heading or backing fire, spot fire, strip-head fire, and ring fire.

FIRST ATTACK—See INITIAL ATTACK:

FIX: A geographical position determined by visual reference to the surface, by reference to one or more radio navigation aids, by celestial plotting, or by any other navigational device.

FIXED POINT DETECTION: Detection of fires from lookout towers or other semipermanent locations, as distinguished from roving ground patrols or aerial detection.

FLANK FIRE:

(1)   A fire set along a control line parallel to the wind and allowed to spread at right angles to it toward the main fire.

(2)   A firing technique consisting of treating an area with lines of fire set into the wind that burn outward at right angles to the wind.

(3)   That part of the fire perimeter aligned parallel with the prevailing wind direction. See FLANKS OF A FIRE.

FLANKING = FLANKING A FIRE = FLANKING FIRE SUPPRESSION: Working along the flanks, whether simultaneously or successively, from a less active or anchor point toward the head of a fire in order to contain the latter.

FLANKS OF A FIRE: Those parts of a fire's perimeter that are roughly parallel to the main direction of spread.

FLAREUP: Any sudden acceleration of fire spread or intensification of the fire or a part of the fire. Unlike blowup, a flareup is of relatively short duration and does not radically change existing control plans.

FLASH FUEL—See FINE FUELS:

FLASHOVER:

(1)   Rapid combustion and/or explosion of trapped, unburned gases. Usually occurs only in poorly ventilated areas. Can occur on wildland fires when gases are trapped in topographic pockets or accumulate over a broad area when there is a temporary lull in air movement.

(2)   In structural fire terminology flashover occurs when radiation and convection from burning objects within an enclosure heat the walls and other objects within the enclosure to their ignition temperature and all flammable interior surfaces begin to flame. Flashover in a room is marked by a large increase in flame volume and a sudden, marked rise in gas temperature.

FLIGHT PLAN: Specified information relating to the intended flight of an aircraft that is filed orally or in writing with an air traffic control facility.

FLY CAMP—See SPIKE CAMP:

FOLLOW-UP = REINFORCEMENT: The action of augmenting the first person or persons who go to a fire by sending additional personnel or equipment to facilitate suppression.

FOOTPRINT—See PATTERN:

FORB: Any herbaceous plant that is neither a grass nor at all like one, for example, such weeds as geranium, buttercup, or sunflower.

FORCED BURNING—See AREA IGNITION:

FOREST:

(1)   Generally, an ecosystem characterized by a more or less dense and extensive tree cover.

(2)   More particularly, a plant community predominantly of trees and other woody vegetation growing more or less closely together.

FOREST FIRE—See WILDFIRE:

FOREST PROTECTION: That branch of forestry concerned with the prevention and control of damage to forests arising mainly from human action (particularly unauthorized fire, grazing and browsing, felling, fumes, and smoke) and of pests and pathogens, but also from storm, frost, and other climatic agencies.

FOREST RESIDUE: The accumulation in the forest of living or dead, mostly woody material that is added to and rearranged by human activities such as forest harvest, cultural operations, and land clearing.

FRICTION: The resistance to relative motion between two bodies in contact.

FUEL: Combustible material.

FUELBREAK: Generally wide (20 to 300 meters) strips of land on which the native vegetation has been permanently modified so that fires burning into them can be more readily controlled.

FUEL MANAGEMENT: The act or practice of controlling the flammability and reducing the resistance to control of forest fuels through mechanical, chemical, or biological means, or by fire.

FUEL MOISTURE CONTENT = FUEL MOISTURE = FM: The water content of a fuel particle expressed as a percent of the over dry weight of the fuel particle.

FUEL TREATMENT = HAZARD REDUCTION: Any manipulation (e.g., lopping, chipping, crushing, piling, and burning) of fuels for the purpose of reducing their flammability.

FUEL TYPE: An identifiable association of fuel elements of distinctive species, form, size, arrangement, or other characteristics that will cause a predictable rate of fire spread or difficulty of control under specified weather conditions.

GEAR PUMP: A positive displacement pump using closely meshed gears to propel water when high pressures and low volumes are desired. Can only be used safely with clear water.

GOING FIRE: Any forest fire on which suppression action has not reached an extensive mop-up stage.

GRASSLAND: Any land on which grasses dominate the vegetation.

GREEN FUELS—See LIVING FUELS:

GRID IGNITION: A method of lighting prescribed fires where ignition points are set individually at a predetermined spacing through an area. If close enough, synonymous with AREA IGNITION.

GROUND CREW—See HAND CREW:

GROUND EFFECT: Reaction of a helicopter rotor downwash against the ground surface forming a "ground cushion" that increases lifting capability of that section of air.

GROUND FIRE: Fire that burns the organic material in the soil layer (e.g., a "peat fire") and often also the surface litter and small vegetation.

GROUND FUEL: All combustible materials below the surface litter, including duff, tree or shrub, roots, punky wood, peat, and sawdust that normally support a glowing combustion without flame.

GROUND TANKER = ENGINE = FIRETRUCK = PUMPER: A vehicle equipped with tank, pump, and necessary tools and equipment for spraying water and/or chemicals on grass, brush, and timber fires.

GROUND TRUTH: Verification at the site of what has been observed and/or measured from an aircraft, satellite, or other platform.

HAND CREW = GROUND CREW: A fire crew, trained and equipped to fight fire with hand tools.

HAND LINE: A control line constructed with hand tools. Normally, it is a narrow line constructed through country too rough for the use of tractors.

HANGOVER FIRE = HOLDOVER FIRE = SLEEPER FIRE:
(1) A fire that remains dormant for a considerable time after it starts.
(2) A fire that starts up again after appearing to be extinguished.

HANGUP: A situation in which a tree is lodged in another and prevented from falling to the ground.

HAZARD—See FIRE HAZARD:

HAZARD REDUCTION—See FUEL TREATMENT:

HEAD (HYDRAULICS): The height to which an incompressible fluid will be lifted by the application of a specified force.

HEAD = (FIRE) FRONT: That portion of a fire edge showing the greatest rate of spread (i.e., generally to leeward or upslope).

HEAD FIRE = HEADING FIRE: A fire spreading or set to spread with the wind or uphill. If set, synonymous with LINE IGNITION.

HEAT TRANSFER: The process by which heat is imparted from one body to another, through conduction, convection, or radiation.

HEAVY FUELS: Fuels of large diameter, such as snags, logs, and large branchwood, or of a peaty nature, that ignite and burn more slowly than flash fuels.

HELD LINE: All the prepared control line that contains the fire until mopping up is completed. Excludes lost line, natural barriers not counterfired, and unused secondary lines.

HELIPORT: A permanent or semipermanent landing spot for one or more helicopters, accessible by road, where fuel, service, and supply can be made available.

HELISPOT: A temporary landing spot for helicopters normally constructed on or near fireline for access of personnel and supplies, generally without auxiliary facilities and often without road access.

HELITACK: The use of helicopters and accessories in direct fire suppression actions.

HELITACK CREW: A crew of firefighters specially trained in the tactical and logistical use of helicopters for fire suppression.

HELITANK: A specially designed tank, generally of fabric or metal, fitted closely to the bottom of a helicopter and used for transporting and dropping suppressants or retardants.

HIGH DROP: An air tanker drop made from a higher than normal altitude above the vegetative canopy. A high drop may be ordered for either tactical or safety reasons.

HOLDING FORCES: Forces assigned to do all required suppression work following line construction but generally not including extensive mop-up.

HOLDOVER FIRE—See HANGOVER FIRE:

HOSE-LAY: The arrangement of connected lengths of fire hose and accessories on the ground, beginning at the first pumping unit and ending at the point of water delivery.

HOSE STRANGLER: A crimping device for stopping the flow of water in a hose.

HOT SPOT: A particularly active part of a fire.

HOT-SPOTTING: Checking the spread of fire at points of particularly rapid spread or special threat.

INCENDIARY FIRE: A wildfire set by anyone to burn, or spread to, vegetation or property not owned or controlled by that person, and without consent of the owner or the owner's agent.

INCIDENT COMMANDER—See FIRE BOSS:

INCREMENTAL DROP: An air tanker drop in which the tank doors are opened in sequence so that retardant cascades somewhat continuously, as opposed to a SALVO drop.

INDIRECT ATTACK = INDIRECT METHOD = INDIRECT FIRE SUPPRESSION: A method of suppression in which the control line is located some considerable distance away from the fire's active edge.

INITIAL ACTION:
    (1) The steps taken after report of a fire and before actual firefighting begins.
    (2) Resources initially committed to an incident.

INITIAL ATTACK = FIRST ATTACK:
    (1) The first action taken to suppress a fire, whether it be by ground or air.
    (2) Resources initially committed to an incident.

INSTABILITY—See ATMOSPHERIC STABILITY:

INTERMITTENT SMOKE: Smoke that becomes visible only at intervals.

INTOLERABLE LOSS: The level of damage or loss greater than that which may be sustained by a given resource and still achieve specified management production goals.

ISLAND: An unburned area within a fire perimeter.

JUMPING FIRE—See SPOTTING FIRE:

JURISDICTION: The geographical area for which a single agency or an administrative unit of an agency is responsible for providing fire protection.

KNAPSACK PUMP—See BACKPACK PUMP:

KNOCK DOWN: To reduce the flame or heat on the more vigorously burning parts of a fire edge.

LADDER FUELS: Fuels that provide vertical continuity between strata. Fire is able to carry from surface fuels into the crowns with relative ease.

LARGE FIRE:
    (1) For statistical purposes, a fire burning more than a specified land area, for example, 100 hectares or 300 acres.
    (2) A fire burning with a size and intensity such that its behavior is determined by interactions between its own convection column and weather conditions above the surface.

LEAD PLANE: Aircraft used to make trial runs over the target area to check wind and smoke conditions and topography, and to lead air tankers to specific targets and supervise their drops.

LEGITIMATE SMOKE: Smoke from any authorized use of fire, as in locomotives, industrial operations, or permitted debris burning.

LIFT: Distance in meters of elevation between a static source of water and the suction chamber of a pumper.

LIGHT BURN: Degree of burn that leaves the soil covered with partially charred organic material; large fuels are not deeply charred.

LIGHTNING FIRE: A wildfire caused directly or indirectly by lightning.

LIMBING: Removing the branches from a felled tree.

LINE CAMP—See SPIKE CAMP:

LINE FIRING: Setting fire to only the border fuel immediately adjacent to the control line. (See STRIP BURNING).

LINE HOLDING: Making sure that the established fireline has completely stopped the progress of the fire.

LINE IGNITION = LINE FIRE (AUST.):   Setting fire in a continuous line; usually at right angles to the wind direction.

LINE LOCATER: The person responsible for on-the-ground location of fireline to be constructed.

LINED FIRE HOSE: Fire hose with a smooth inner coating of rubber or plastic to reduce friction loss.

LITTER: The top layer of the forest floor composed of loose debris of dead sticks, branches, twigs, and recently fallen leaves or needles, little altered in structure by decomposition. (The L layer of the forest floor.)

LIVE BURNING: The burning of green slash progressively as it is cut.

LIVE LINE = LIVE REEL: A hose line or reel on a fire engine carried preconnected to the pump, ready for use without making connections to pump or attaching nozzle; a charged line containing water under pressure.

LIVING FUELS: Naturally occurring fuels in which the moisture content is physiologically controlled within the living plant.

LONG-TERM RETARDANT: A chemical that has the ability to inhibit spread of flame through reactions between products of combustion and the applied chemical even after its water component has evaporated.

LOOKOUT:
(1)   A person designated to detect and report fires from a fixed vantage point.
(2)   A location and associated structures from which fires can be detected and reported.
(3)   A member of a fire crew designated to observe the fire and warn the crew when there is danger of becoming trapped.

LOOKOUT POINT: A vantage point selected for fire detection or observation.

LOPPING: Cutting branches, tops, and small trees after felling into lengths such that resultant slash will eventually lie close to the ground.

LOPPING AND SCATTERING: Lopping the slash created by primary conversion and spreading it more or less evenly over the ground.

LOST LINE: Any part of a fireline rendered useless by a breakaway of the fire.

MANICURED LINE: A fireline built exactly to standards.

MAN-PASSING-MAN: A method of managing personnel on fire suppression whereby eachworker is assigned a specific task, for example, clearing or digging on a specific section of the control line, and, having completed that task, passes other workers in moving to a new assignment.

MASS FIRE: A fire resulting from many simultaneous ignitions that generates a high level of energy output.

McLeod Tool: A short-handled combination hoe and rake, with or without removable blades.

Mineral Soil: Soil layers below the predominantly organic horizons; a soil that has little combustible material.

Mixmaster: The person in charge of fire retardant mixing operations, with responsibility for quality of the slurry and for the loading of aircraft in land-based air tanker operations.

Mobilization: Action required to expand or create a fire organization with capability of handling a project-size or a disaster fire.

Mobilization Center: An off-incident location at which emergency service personnel and equipment are temporarily located pending assignment, release, or reassignment.

Moderate Burn: Degree of burn in which all organic material is burned away from the surface of the soil that is not discolored by heat. Any remaining fuel is deeply charged. Organic matter remains in the soil immediately below the surface.

Mopping Up = Mop-up: Making a fire safe after it has been controlled, by extinguishing or removing burning material along or near the control line, felling snags, trenching logs to prevent rolling, and the like.

Mother Tanker—See Nurse Tanker:

Move-Up: A system of redistributing the remaining personnel and equipment following a dispatch of other forces among a network of fire stations so as to provide the optimum response in the event of additional calls for emergency assistance.

Mutual Aid: Any form of direct assistance from one fire service to another during time of emergency, based upon a prearrangement of the agencies involved and generally made upon the request of the receiving agency. (See OUTSIDE AID.)

Natural Barrier: Any area where lack of flammable material obstructs the spread of forest fires.

Natural Fire: Any fire of natural origin, for example, caused by lightning, spontaneous combustion, or volcanic activity.

Natural Fuels: Fuels resulting from natural processes and not directly generated or altered by forestry practices.

Noncommercial Forest Land: Land incapable of yielding crops of industrial wood because of adverse site conditions, or productive forest land withdrawn from commercial timber use through statute or administrative regulation.

Nonstatistical Fire: Any fire not posing a threat to the resources or property of the jurisdictional agency, whether or not action was taken by the agency.

NORMAL FIRE SEASON:
  (1) A season in which weather, fire danger, and number or distribution of fires are about average.
  (2) The period of the year that normally comprises the fire season.

NURSE TANKER = MOTHER TANKER: Water tank truck used to supply one or more ground tankers stationed at a fire.

ONE LICK METHOD: A progressive system of building fireline without changing relative positions in the line. Each worker does one to several "licks," or strokes, with a given tool and then moves forward a specified distance to make room for the worker behind.

OPEN BURNING: Uncontrolled burning of wastes in the open or in an open dump.

ORBIT: The circular holding pattern of an airtanker in the vicinity of a fire waiting for orders to make a drop.

OUTSIDE AID: Firefighting assistance given to adjacent areas and nearby communities by contract or other agreement that covers conditions and payment for assistance rendered and services performed. Contrasted to MUTUAL AID, in which neighboring firefighting organizations assist each other without charge.

OVERHEAD: Supervisory or specialist personnel working in some capacity related to the control of a going fire (or fires) but not including leaders of regularly organized crews and equipment operators while engaged in their regularly assigned duties.

OVERWINTERING FIRE: A fire that persists through the winter months until the beginning of a fire season.

PARACARGO: Anything intentionally dropped, or intended for dropping, from any aircraft by parachute, by other retarding devices, or by free fall.

PARALLEL ATTACK = PARALLEL METHOD = PARALLEL FIRE SUPPRESSION: A method of suppression in which fireline is constructed approximately parallel to, and just far enough from the fire edge to enable workers and equipment to work effectively, though the line may be shortened by cutting across unburned fingers. The intervening strip of unburned fuel is normally burned out as the control line proceeds, but may be allowed to burn out unassisted where this occurs without undue delay or threat to the line.

PARALLEL BURNING—See STRIP BURNING:

PARALLEL PUMPING: A procedure whereby the flow from two fire pumps is combined into one hose line.

PARTIAL SLASH DISPOSAL: Slash disposal by any method or combination of methods, resulting in the destruction of only a portion of the slash on a given area.

PARTS OF A FIRE: On typical free-burning fires the spread is uneven, with the main spread moving with the wind or upslope. The most rapidly moving portion is designated the HEAD of the fire, the adjoining portions of the perimeter at right angles to the head are known as the FLANKS, and the slowest moving portion is known as the REAR, the BASE, or the BACK.

PATCH BURNING:
(1)   Burning felling debris, grass, and the like in patches for the purpose of preparing sites for group planting or sowing.
(2)   Prescribed burning for the purpose of forming a barrier to subsequent burning.

PATROL:
(1)   Generally, to travel over a given route to prevent, detect, and suppress fires.
(2)   More specifically, to go back and forth vigilantly over a length of control line during and/or after construction, to prevent breakaways, control spot fires, and extinguish overlooked hot spots.
(3)   A person or group of persons who carry out patrol actions.

PATTERN: The distribution of an aerially delivered retardant drop on the target areas in terms of its length, width, and momentum (velocity × mass) as it approaches the ground. The latter determines the relative coverage levels of retardant within the pattern.

PAYLOAD: The weight of passengers and/or cargo being carried.

PEAK FIRE SEASON: That period of the fire season during which fires are expected to ignite most readily, to burn with greater than average intensity, and to create damages at an unacceptable level.

PERIMETER: The exterior boundary of a fire area.

PICKUP FIREFIGHTER: A nonagency individual hired locally to assist in firefighting actions on one specific fire.

PILING AND BURNING: Piling slash resulting from logging and subsequently burning the individual piles.

PLAN OF ATTACK: The selected course of action and organization of personnel and equipment in fire suppression, as applied to a particular fire or to all fires of a specific type.

POCKETS: Unburned indentations in the fire edge formed by fingers or slower burning areas.

POINT OF ATTACK: That part of the fire on which work is started when suppression forces arrive.

POISE: Unit of viscosity, defined as tangential force per unit area required to maintain unit difference in velocity between two parallel planes separated by one centimeter of fluid.

POSITIVE DISPLACEMENT PUMP: Rotary, gear, or piston type of pump that moves a given quantity of water through pump chamber with each stroke or cycle. A positive displacement pump is capable of pumping air and thereby is self-priming. Must have pressure relief provisions if plumbing or hoses have shutoff valves or nozzles.

PREATTACK PLANNING: Within designated blocks of land, planning the locations of firelines, base camps, water supply sources, helispots, and so on; planning transportation systems, probable rates of travel, and constraints of travel on various types of attack units; determining what types of attack units likely would be needed to construct particular firelines, their probable rate of line construction, topographic constraints on line construction, and the like.

PREMARKING BURN: Burning off underbrush prior to the sale of forest products to improve the efficiency of timber marking and harvesting.

PREPAREDNESS = READINESS:

(1)   Condition or degree of being completely ready to cope with a potential fire situation.

(2)   Mental readiness to recognize changes in fire danger and act promptly when action is appropriate.

PRESCRIBED BURNING = PRESCRIBED FIRE: Controlled application of fire to wildland fuels in either their natural or modified state, under specified environmental conditions that allow the fire to be confined to a predetermined area and at the same time to produce the intensity of heat and rate of spread required to attain planned resource management objectives.

PRESCRIPTION: A written statement defining the objectives to be attained, as well as the condition of temperature, humidity, wind direction and speed, fuel moisture, and soil moisture under which the fire will be allowed to burn, generally expressed as acceptable ranges of the various indices, and the limit of the geographic area to be covered.

PRESUPPRESSION—See FIRE PRESUPPRESSION.

PREVENTION—See FIRE PREVENTION.

PRIMARY LOOKOUT: A lookout point that must be operated to meet planned minimum visible area coverage in a given locality. For that reason, continuous service is necessary during the normal fire season and the lookout (person) is not sent to fires.

PRIMING: Filling pump with water when pump is taking water not under a pressure head. Necessary for centrifugal pumps.

PROGRESSIVE HOSE-LAY: A hose-lay in which double shutoff (gated) wyes (Y's) are inserted in the main line at intervals and lateral lines are run from the wyes to the fire edge, thus permitting continuous application of water during extension of the lay.

PROGRESSIVE METHOD OF LINE CONSTRUCTION: A system of organizing workers to build fireline in which they advance without changing relative positions in line. There are two principal methods of applying the system: the STEP-UP, method and the ONE LICK method.

PROJECT FIRE—See CAMPAIGN FIRE:

PROTECTION—See FIRE PROTECTION.

PROTECTION BOUNDARY: The exterior perimeter of an area within which a given agency has assumed a degree of responsibility for forest fire control.

PROTECTION FOREST = PROTECTED FOREST: An area, wholly or partly covered with woody growth, managed primarily to regulate stream flow, maintain water quality, minimize erosion, stabilize drifting sand, or exert any other beneficial forest influences.

PROTECTION UNIT: A geographical area that is administratively defined and is the smallest area for which organized fire suppression activities are formally planned.

PROVINCIAL FOREST—See STATE FOREST:

PUMPER—See GROUND TANKER:

PUNK: Partly decayed material such as old wood in which fire can smolder unless it is carefully mopped up and extinguished.

PYROLYSIS: The thermal or chemical decomposition of fuel at an elevated temperature.

RADIATION:
  (1) The propagation of energy in free space by virtue of joint undulatory variations in the electric or magnetic fields in space, that is, by electromagnetic waves.
  (2) Transfer of heat through a gas or a vacuum, other than by heating of the intervening space.

RAPPELING: A technique of landing firefighters from hovering helicopters that involves sliding down ropes with the aid of friction-producing devices.

RATE OF SPREAD: The relative activity of a fire in extending its horizontal dimensions. NOTE: Is expressed either as rate of increase of the fire perimeter, as a rate of increase in area, or as a rate of advance of its head, depending on the intended use of the information.

READINESS—See PREPAREDNESS:

REAR = BACK (AUST.)
  (1) That portion of a fire spreading directly into the wind.
  (2) That portion of a fire edge opposite the head.
  (3) The slowest spreading portion of a fire edge.

REBURN:
  (1) Repeat burning of an area over which a fire has previously passed but has left fuel subsequently ignitable.
  (2) Also the area so reburned.

RECONNAISSANCE = RECON: To examine a fire area for the purpose of obtaining information about current and probable fire behavior and other related fire suppression information.

RELATIVE HUMIDITY: The dimensionless ratio of the actual vapor pressure of the atmosphere to its saturation vapor pressure.

REPORT TIME: Elapsed time from discovery of a fire until the first of the personnel charged with initiating action for fire suppression is notified of its existence and location.

REPORTABLE FIRE: Any wildfire that requires suppression action to protect natural resources or values associated with natural resources, or is destructive to natural resources.

RESERVE: Personnel or apparatus not in first line duty, but available in abnormal emergency conditions.

RESISTANCE TO CONTROL = DIFFICULTY OF CONTROL: The relative difficulty of constructing and holding a control line, as affected by fire behavior and difficulty of line construction.

RESOURCES:
  (1)   The personnel and equipment available for suppression of a wildfire.
  (2)   The natural resources of an area such as timber, grass, watershed values, recreation values, and wildlife habitat.

RESPONSE: The movement of an individual piece of fire protection equipment together with its operating crew from its assigned standby location to another location, or to an emergency incident in reaction either to dispatch orders or to a reported alarm. (One response per incident regardless of the number of return trips.)

RESPONSE TIME—See ATTACK TIME:

RETARDANT—See FIRE RETARDANT:

RETARDANT BASE: The ground facilities for mixing, storing, and loading fire retardant.

RETARDANT COVERAGE: The area of fuel covered and degree of coverage on the fuel by a retardant.

RETARDANT DROP: Retardant cascaded from either an airtanker or a helitanker.

RHEOLOGY: The science dealing with the deformation and flow of matter.

RIBBON BARK—See CANDLE BARK:

RISK:
  (1)   The chance of fire starting as determined by the presence and activity of causative agents.
  (2)   A causative agent.
  (3)   A number related to the potential number of firebrands to which a given area will be exposed during the rating day.

ROTARY GEAR PUMP: A positive displacement pump employing closely fitting rotors or gears to force water through the pump chamber.

ROTOR BLAST: The air turbulence occurring under and around the main rotor system(s) of an operating helicopter.

ROUGH: The accumulation of living and dead ground and understory vegetation, especially grasses, forest litter, and draped dead needles, sometimes with addition of underbrush. Most often used in the southern United States.

ROUNDWOOD: Boles, stems, or limbs of woody material; that portion of the dead wildland fuels that are roughly cylindrical in shape.

RUN—See FIRE RUN:

RUNNING FIRE: A fire spreading rapidly with a well-defined head.

RURAL–URBAN INTERFACE—See URBAN/WILDLAND INTERFACE:

SAFETY ISLAND: An area (usually a recently burned area) used for escape in the event the line is outflanked or in case a spot fire causes fuels outside the control line to render the line unsafe. In firing operations, crews progress so as to maintain a safety island close at hand, allowing the fuels inside the control line to be consumed before going ahead.

SALVO: The dropping by an airtanker of its entire retardant load at one time.

SCORCH LINE = SCORCH HEIGHT: The level up to which foliage has been browned by fire.

SCOUT: A staff worker in a fire suppression organization assigned duties of gathering and reporting timely information such as existing location and behavior of a fire, progress in control, and the physical conditions that affect the planning and execution of the suppression job.

SCRATCH LINE: An unfinished preliminary control line hastily established or constructed as an emergency measure to check the spread of fire.

SCRUB—See BRUSH:

SEASONAL MONTHLY AVERAGE: Historically, the average number of human-caused fires occurring on a protection unit per month during the established fire season.

SECONDARY LINE: Any fireline constructed at a distance from the fire perimeter concurrently or after a primary control line has already been constructed on or near to the perimeter of the fire.

SECONDARY LOOKOUT:
(1) A lookout point intermittently used to supplement the visible area coverage of the primary lookout system when required by fire danger, poor visibility, or other factors.
(2) The person who occupies such a station.

SECTOR: A designated segment of fire perimeter or control line comprising the suppression work unit for two or more crews under one leader.

SEEN AREA: The ground, or vegetation growing thereon, that is directly visible under specified atmospheric conditions from an established or proposed lookout point or aerial detection flight route.

SEVERE BURN: Degree of burn in which all organic material is burned from the soil surface discolored by heat, usually to red. Organic material below the surface is consumed or charred.

SHADED FUELBREAK: Fuelbreaks built in timbered areas where the trees on the break are thinned and pruned to reduce the fire potential yet retain enough crown canopy to make a less favorable microclimate for surface fires.

SHORT-TERM RETARDANT: A chemical that has no inherent fire-retarding property, but alters the viscosity or retards the evaporation of water.

SHRUB: A woody perennial plant differing from a perennial herb in its persistent and woody stem(s), and less definitely from a tree in its lower stature and the general absence of a well-defined main stem.

SHUT-OFF NOZZLE: A common type of fire hose nozzle permitting flow of the stream to be controlled by the firefighter at the nozzle rather than only at the source of supply; a controlling nozzle.

SIAMESE: A hose fitting (preferably gated) for combining the flow from two or more lines of hose into a single stream; one male coupling to two female couplings.

SIMPLE HOSE-LAY: A hose-lay consisting of consecutively coupled lengths of hose without laterals. The lay is extended by inserting additional lengths of hose in the line between pump and nozzle.

SIMULTANEOUS IGNITION—See AREA IGNITION:

SIZE-UP: The elevation of a fire by the officer in charge to determine a course of action for suppression.

SKID TRAIL: Any road or trail formed by the process of skidding logs from stump to landing.

SLASH: Unusual concentrations of fuel resulting from such natural events as wind, fire, or snow breakage, or such human activities as logging or road construction.

SLASH DISPOSAL: Treatment of slash to reduce the fire hazard or for other purposes.

SLEEPER FIRE—See HANGOVER FIRE:

SLING: A net attached by a lanyard to a helicopter cargo hook and used to haul supplies.

SLING LOAD: Any cargo carried beneath a helicopter and attached by a lead line and swivel.

SLIP-ON TANKER: A tank, a live hose reel or tray, an auxiliary pump, and an engine combined into a single one-piece assembly that can be slipped onto a truck bed or trailer.

SLOPOVER—See BREAKOVER:

SLURRY: A suspension of insoluble matter in water. In fire suppression, it is a general term applied to any long or short-term retardant after the mixing process has been completed.

SMOKE: A term used when reporting a fire or probable fire in its initial stages. In fire control the following types of smokes are recognized: legitimate smoke, false smoke, drift smoke, intermittent smoke, smoke haze, and smoke column.

SMOKE CANDLE = SMOKE GENERATOR: A pyrotechnical product that emits smoke of a uniform color, like that of a small fire, and at a standard rate. NOTE: Used to check the visibility of a simulated small fire and to test the alertness of lookouts.

SMOKE COLUMN: Smoke that is definable in vertical form.

SMOKEJUMPER: A firefighter who travels to fires by aircraft and parachute.

SMOLDERING FIRE: A fire burning without flame and barely spreading.

SMUDGE: A spot in a fire or along a fire's edge that has not yet been extinguished, and is producing smoke; a term commonly used during the mop-up stage of a fire.

SNAG: A standing dead tree or standing portion from which at least the leaves and smaller branches have fallen. Often called a *stub* if less than six meters tall.

SOLID STREAM—See STRAIGHT STREAM:

SORTIE: A single round trip made by an airtanker from air attack base to a fire and return.

SPAN OF CONTROL: The maximum number of subordinates who can be directly supervised by one person without loss of efficiency. In fire suppression the number varies by activity, but is in the general range of three to eight.

SPANNER: A metal wrench used to tighten and free hose connections.

SPEED OF ATTACK:
   (1)   The elapsed time from origin of fire to arrival of the first suppression force.
   (2)   With STRENGTH OF ATTACK specified, the elapsed time from origin of a fire to arrival of forces necessary to hold the burned area to an acceptable or predetermined limit within a specified fuel type.

SPIKE CAMP = FLY CAMP: A camp with minimum facilities, established along a fireline for the subsistence and equipping of firefighters assigned to that portion of the fire perimeter.

SPLIT DROP: A single drop made from one compartment at a time from an aircraft with a multicompartment tank.

SPOT BURNING: A modified form of broadcast burning in which only the larger accumulations of slash are fired and fire is confined to these spots.

SPOT FIRE: Fire set outside the perimeter of the main fire by flying sparks or embers.

SPOTTING: Behavior of a fire producing sparks or embers that are carried by the wind and start new fires beyond the zone of direct ignition by the main fire.

SPOTTING FIRE = JUMPING FIRE: A fire that spreads by spot fires, the process being termed SPOTTING.

STAGING AREA:
 (1)   An area within a fire camp where personnel and equipment are assembled for transportation to the line.
 (2)   A location where incident personnel and equipment are assigned for immediate availability.

STAND-BY CREW: A group of trained firefighters stationed at a dispatch point for rapid deployment.

STATE FOREST:
 (1)   Forest owned and administered by the state, that is, by the national government.
 (2)   PROVINCIAL FOREST. Forests owned and administered by a state or province and not by the Federal government.

STATIC PRESSURE: Water pressure head available at a specific location when no fire flow is being used so that no pressure losses due to friction are being encountered. The static pressure is that pressure observed on the pumper inlet gauge before any water is taken from the hydrant.

STATIC WATER SUPPLY: A supply of water at rest that does not provide a pressure head for firefighting, but that may be employed as a suction source for fire pumps such as water in a reservoir, pond, or cistern.

STEP-UP METHOD: A progressive method of building fireline without changing relative positions on the line. Work is begun with a space of five meters or so between workers. Whenever one worker overtakes another, all those ahead move one space forward and resume work.

STRATEGY: An overall plan of action for fighting a fire that gives regard to the most cost-efficient use of personnel and equipment in consideration of values threatened, fire behavior, legal constraints, and objectives established for research management. Leaves decisions on the tactical use of personnel and equipment to line commanders in the suppression function.

STRAIGHT STREAM = SOLID STREAM: Water or retardant projected directly from the nozzle as contracted with a fog or spray cone.

STRENGTH OF ATTACK: The number of firefighters and/or machines with which a fire is attacked.

STRIKE TEAM: Specified combination of suppression and rescue resources and a leader.

STRING DROP = TRAIL DROP: To drop retardant from separate compartments in rapid succession to give an extended drop pattern on the ground.

STRINGER: A narrow finger or band of fuel that connects two or more patches or areas of wildland fuel.

STRIP BURNING:
(1) Setting fire to a narrow strip of fuel adjacent to a control line and then burning successively wider adjacent strips as the preceding strip burns out.
(2) Burning only a relatively narrow strip or strips through an area of slash, leaving the remainder.
(3) Burning the slash on strips generally 30 to 90 meters wide along roads or barriers so as to subdivide the slash area into blocks.

STRIP HEAD FIRING: Setting a line or series of lines of fire near and upwind of a firebreak so they burn with the wind into the firebreak. A technique used to quickly burn out an area.

STRUCTURE FIRE: A fire originating in and burning any part or all of any building, shelter, or other structure inhabited, worked in, or used by people to house or store equipment, livestock, feed, or other items, or used for amusement, recreational, business, or educational purposes.

SUCTION BOOSTER = EDUCTOR = EJECTOR: A type of jet syphon device usually supplied from the tank on fire apparatus and used to bring water to a pumper from greater distances and to higher elevations than is possible with suction depending upon atmospheric pressure.

SUCTION HOSE: A hose, reinforced to prevent collapse due to atmospheric pressure, used to draft water into a fire pump.

SUCTION LIFT: In fire service, the number of meters of vertical lift from the surface of the water to the center of the pump impeller.

SUPPLIES: Minor items of equipment and all expendable items assigned to fire.

SUPPRESS A FIRE: Extinguish a fire or confine the area it burns within fixed boundaries.

SUPPRESSANT: An agent used to extinguish the flaming and glowing phases of combustion by direct application to burning fuels.

SUPPRESSION—See FIRE SUPPRESSION.

SUPPRESSION CREW: Two or more firefighters stationed at a strategic location, either regularly or in emergency, for initial action on fires.

SUPPRESSION FIRING: The various applications or uses of fire to speed up or strengthen control action on wildfires. Many terms are used for various types of suppression firing: burning out, backfire, line firing, counter firing, burned strip, and so on.

SURFACE FIRE: Fire that burns only surface litter, other loose debris of the forest floor, and small vegetation.

SURFACE FUEL: The loose surface litter on the forest floor, normally consisting of fallen leaves or needles, twigs, bark, cones, and small branches that have not yet decayed sufficiently to lose their identity. Also grasses, shrubs, and tree reproduction less than one meter in height, heavier branchwood, down logs, stumps, seedlings, and forbs interspersed with or partially replacing the litter.

SURFACTANT (FROM "SURFACE-ACTIVE AGENT")—See WETTING AGENT:

SURGE: A rapid increase in flow that may result in an attendant pressure rise.

SWAMPER:
   (1)   A worker with an axe who cuts and clears away brush, and limbs small trees and down timber.
   (2)   A worker on a cat crew who pulls winch line, helps maintain equipment, and so on to speed suppression work on a fire.

SWAMPOUT: To clean out brush and other material around the base of trees and where trees are to be bucked prior to falling or bucking as protection against saw kickback, and to provide safe footing.

SWIVEL: An accessory used between the helicopter cargo hook and sling load to allow free turning of the load.

TACTICS: Determining exactly where and how to build a control line and what other suppression measures are necessary to extinguish the fire.

TANDEM: Two or more units of any one type working one in front of the other to accomplish a specific fire suppression job; the term can be used in connection with crews of firefighters, power pumps, bulldozers, and so on.

TANK AND GATING SYSTEM: Tanks, doors, and release mechanism installed in aircraft for cascading fire retardants.

TANKER—See AIRTANKER AND GROUND TANKER:

TASK FORCE: A group of fire control resources informally assembled for a specific mission.

TAYLOR INSTABILITY: Wavelike deformation induced on the front surface of a liquid mass (e.g., retardant) that ultimately results in large particles or globs.

TEST FIRE: A controlled fire set to evaluate such things as fire behavior, efficiency in detection, or control measures.

THERMAL IMAGERY: The display or printout from an infrared scanning device.

THICKENED SOLUTION: A solution that has a viscosity exceeding 200 centipoise.

TORCH (TORCHING)—See CANDLE (CANDLING).

TRIAL DROP—See STRING DROP:

TRANSLATIONAL LIFT (HELICOPTER):   Lift that is gained when translating from a hover into forward flight. This additional lift increases with increasing airspeed, and is derived by the rotor system moving into undisturbed air.

TRAVEL TIME: Elapsed time from the departure of the initial attack crew until they arrive at and begin work on the fire.

TRENCH: A ditch dug on a slope below a fire, generally as a part of the fireline, designed to catch rolling burning material.

TURN THE CORNER: To contain a fire along a flank, and begin containing it across the head.

UNDERBURNING: Prescribed burning with a low-intensity fire in activity-created or natural fuels under a timber canopy.

UNDERCUT LINE = UNDERSLUNG LINE: A fireline below a fire on a slope. Should be trenched to catch rolling material.

UNLINED FIRE HOSE: Hose commonly of cotton or synthetic fiber construction without rubber tube or lining. Such hose is provided attached to first-aid stand pipes in buildings. Similar hose is often used for wildfire fighting because of its light weight. At a given flow, pressure loss due to friction in unlined hose of a stated diameter is approximately twice that of lined fire hose.

UNTHICKENED SOLUTION: A solution whose viscosity is less than 200 centipoise.

URBAN/WILDLAND INTERFACE = RURAL–WILDLAND INTERFACE: That line, area, or zone where structures and other human development meets or intermingles with undeveloped wildland or vegetative fuels.

VALUES-AT-RISK: Any or all of the natural resources or improvements that may be jeopardized if a fire occurs.

VISCOUS WATER: Water that contains a thickening agent to reduce surface runoff.

VISIBILITY: The greatest distance at which selected objects can be seen and identified or its equivalent derived from instrumental measurements.

VISIBILITY DISTANCE: The maximum distance at which a smoke column of specified size and density can be seen and recognized as smoke by the unaided eye.

VISIBLE AREA—See SEEN AREA:

VORTEX TURBULENCE: Miniature whirlwinds trailing from the wingtips of any aircraft in flight. Vortex will be in the form of a horizontal whirlwind with velocities up to 25 miles (40 kilometers) per hour or more. Also created by the action of helicopter rotor blades.

WATER BAR: A shallow channel, or raised barrier, for example, a ridge of packed earth or a thin pole laid diagonally across the surface of a road or trail so as to lead off water, particularly storm water. (Frequently installed in firelines on steep slopes to prevent erosion.)

WATER BOMBER—See AIRTANKER:

WATER HAMMER: Impact energy due to sudden shutting of fire nozzles, proportional to the mass multiplied by the square of the velocity.

WATER SOURCE: Any strategically located supply of water that is readily available for pumps, tanks, trucks, helicopters, or camp use.

WATER THIEF: A type of bleeder valve designed for installation at convenient points in hose lines to permit drawing off water for filling backpack pumps or other use without interfering with pump or nozzle operation.

WEATHERING: The action of natural atmospheric conditions on any material exposed to them. Weathering includes both physical and chemical changes.

WET LINE: A fire edge being contained by water and/or retardants, but *not* by fireline.

WET STORAGE: Fire retardants mixed with water and stored in tanks at air attack bases for immediate use by airtankers.

WETTING AGENT = SURFACTANT: An additive that reduces the surface tension of water or other liquid causing it to spread and penetrate more effectively.

WET WATER: Water containing a wetting agent.

WIDOW-MAKER: A loose limp or top, or piece of bark lodged in a tree that may fall on anyone working beneath it.

WILDFIRE = WILDLAND FIRE: Any fire occurring on wildland except a fire under prescription.

WILDLAND: An area in which development is essentially nonexistent, except for roads, railroads, powerlines, and similar transportation facilities. Structures, if any, are widely scattered and are primarily for recreation purposes.

WILDLAND FIRE—See WILDFIRE:

WINDFALL: A tree that has been uprooted or broken off by the wind.

WOODLAND: Plant communities in which trees, often small and characteristically short-boled relative to their depth of crown, are present but form only an open canopy, the intervening areas being occupied by a lower vegetation, commonly grass.

WYE: A hose connection with two outlets, preferably gated, permitting two connections of the same coupling diameter to be taken from a single supply line.

ZONE (FIRE):   A geographical portion of a very large fire, usually handled more or less as a separate major fire with its own command staff and fire camps.

AUTHOR INDEX

SUBJECT INDEX